ROLES
of
AUTHORITY

⚜

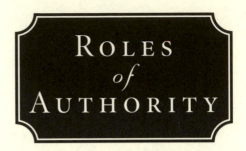

ROLES
of
AUTHORITY

*Thespian Biography and
Celebrity in
Eighteenth-Century
Britain*

✌

CHERYL WANKO

TEXAS TECH
UNIVERSITY
PRESS

✌

This book is typeset in Adobe Minion. The paper used in this book meets the minimum requirements of ANSI/NISO Z39.48-1992 (R1997). ∞

Designed by Barbara Werden

Printed in the United States of America

LIBRARY OF CONGRESS CATALOGING-IN-PUBLICATION DATA

Wanko, Cheryl.
    Roles of authority : thespian biography and celebrity in
eighteenth-century Britain / Cheryl Wanko.
        p.   cm.
Includes bibliographical references and index.
    ISBN 0-89672-499-9 (cloth : alk. paper)
    1. Theater—Great Britain—History—18th century. 2. Actors—Great
Britain—Biography—History and criticism. 3. Actors—Great
Britain—Biography. I. Title.

PN2593 .W36 2003
792'.092'241—dc21

                                    2002153522

03 04 05 06 07 08 09 10 11 / 9 8 7 6 5 4 3 2 1

Texas Tech University Press
Box 41037
Lubbock, Texas 79409-1037 USA
1.800.832.4042
ttup@ttu.edu
www.ttup.ttu.edu

✁

ACKNOWLEDGMENTS

I COMPOSE these acknowledgments with both relief and enjoyment, since they conclude a project that has spanned many years, and they allow me to recognize those without whom I could never have reached the point of writing acknowledgments. This book began as a Penn State dissertation in 1990, and over the intervening years it has been thrown down and taken up again; it has bedeviled not only me but the people kind enough to help me with it; and, like both actors and mercury, it has assumed many shapes. During its transformations, I have accumulated many debts that I now have the pleasure of acknowledging.

My primary debt is to my dissertation advisor, Robert D. Hume, under whose direction I completed the original manuscript. Since then, he has been constantly willing to read and reread my revisions and re-revisions

and always ready to offer encouragement. His example as a scholar and guide is continually present, reminding me of the high standards to which I should aspire. I can only hope that I have approached such standards as he sets and, if I do not, I readily admit that the problem lies with the aspirant and not the standards. The rest of my dissertation committee—John Harwood, Charles Mann, James L. West III, and J. Philip Jenkins—read my work thoroughly and sensitively.

My other main debt is to the staff of the Pennsylvania State University Special Collections Library. As well as serving on my committee, the late curator, Dr. Charles Mann, supported my work by purchasing copies of many of the biographies I needed. The curator of rare books and manuscripts, Ms. Sandra Stelts, helped immeasurably as I tried to track them down. (The famous silver bag that housed the voluminous notes and correspondence relating to my project lives on in Penn State Rare Books Room lore.) Without their support, I could not have even begun this project.

Since the project's inception, I have received funding from the Pennsylvania State University in the form of fellowships. Pennsylvania State System of Higher Education faculty development grants and West Chester University's local grants also aided me in my work. This funding not only allowed me to travel to archives, it enabled me to purchase essential materials and services for completion of this book.

The staff of the archives at which I worked responded promptly to all of my requests. Thank you to the staff at the Harvard Theatre Collection, the Houghton Library, the British Library, the Bodleian, the University of Pennsylvania Annenberg Rare Book and Manuscript Library, the Folger Shakespeare Library, and the Rosenbach Museum and Library in Philadelphia. I am grateful to these and many other libraries that supplied microforms and photocopies, and I am sorry that I cannot record all of their individual contributions here. Judith Keeling, Virginia Downs, and the production staff at Texas Tech UP edited and produced this beautiful book, and I am grateful for their faith in my project and their hard work.

Finally, any project needs friends to help sustain its struggling author. I would like to thank those who read sections or who simply offered moral support: Amy Elizabeth Smith, Jody Harman, John Walker, and my family, who, even as I type this, are accepting "the book project" once again as an excuse for sequestering myself from them.

CONTENTS

❧

❧

CONTENTS

❧

✂

ILLUSTRATIONS

‰

‰

Roles
of
Authority

�֍

INTRODUCTION

⤸

CELE'BRITY. n. s. [*celebritas,* Lat.]
Celebration, fame.

SAMUEL JOHNSON,
Dictionary (1755)

I N 1771 the theater historian and thespian biographer Benjamin Victor exclaims ruefully: "The *Painter's* Art lives on the Canvas—but the Actor's must die with him!"[1] Nearly all of those who write about the stage are similarly disconcerted by the ephemerality of their subject. All that is left of past performances are written records. Yet the types of records available signal to us the ways in which performance and the theater were positioned within a culture and the ways in which they in turn helped form the culture. From the late seventeenth century we have some diaries, such as Pepys's; manuscript records of

the Lord Chamberlain; attacks and defenses of the stage; and a few dramatic playlists. But around the beginning of the eighteenth century, a completely new source of information emerges: biographies and autobiographies of actors and actresses.[2] These texts pursue more than ephemeral performance; they record the ephemeral life, attempting to capture in lasting fame these performers whose evanescence Victor mourns. Why did this type of text appear at this particular time? This study poses answers to this question by examining the first hundred years of these new works and considering their importance to the meaning of the theater in eighteenth-century Britain.

The vast number of these publications is surprising—nearly two hundred alone in this period—as is the fact that they have been so infrequently discussed by scholars, though they have often been mined for their theatrical data.[3] The lack of attention to these publications, however, is not difficult to explain. Individual copies are fairly rare and widely dispersed. In addition, they do not match our present expectations of serious biography. They are short and scrappy, comprising all kinds of materials little connected to their ostensible biographical subjects, from scenes of plays to last wills and testaments. Often lively, witty, and bawdy, many brazenly attempt to capitalize on the popularity of the latest performer.

The print market's ability to respond and contribute to popularity is a primary determinant of these new types of print records. The expanding print market after the lapse of the Printing Act in 1695 has been noted by many. The work of Dustin Griffin, Julie Stone Peters, and Alvin Kernan, among others, shows that conceptions of drama and authorship depend in part on their transmitting media.[4] The market influenced the terms of the biographies' production—their timely appearances, their links to theatrical events, their borrowings from other genres, and their proliferation as the eighteenth century wore on—as well as their changing contents, a fluctuating mélange of professional, managerial, critical, literary, and personal detail, resulting in new views of performers and their art. The appearance of these biographies was facilitated by the growing demand for all biographies, by the decreasing cost of printing, and by the increasing participation of print in all leisure activities, as noted by J. H. Plumb.[5] These biographies, in turn, contributed to the expanding market.

The large number of biographies printed at the end of the seventeenth century thrust into public observation classes of people who had previous-

ly been beneath the notice of the educated and literate. Francesco Alberoni notes: "The media of mass communication begin to present to the public persons who belong to the extended community and who become an object of interest, identification and collective evaluation."[6] Stage performers had always experienced public exposure through their nightly performances, and print increased their availability for consumption as commodities. They gained publicity simply for being public or, as Daniel Boorstin has remarked of twentieth-century figures, they become "known for [their] well-knownness."[7] Pierre Bourdieu's summary of the cultural market process can describe the interaction between taste or public fascination with players and the medium for satisfying those tastes: "Thus the tastes actually realized depend on the state of the system of goods offered; every change in the system of goods induces a change in tastes. But conversely, every change in tastes resulting from a transformation of the conditions of existence and of the corresponding dispositions will tend to induce, directly or indirectly, a transformation of the field of production, by favouring the success, within the struggle constituting the field, of the producers best able to produce the needs corresponding to the new dispositions."[8] Early players' biographies and theatrical criticism stimulate interest in players that, in conjunction with other events in the theater and print worlds, transforms the "field of production." More printed information is generated as a kind of "cultural feedback" occurs, which Tyler Cowen has identified as the "snowball effect": more print exposure incites more curiosity and thus causes demand for more print.[9] One need only note the numerous responses to and imitators of Colley Cibber's *Apology for the Life of Colley Cibber* (1740) to find an example of this process, and it is not confined to the theatrical world.

Plus, as Bourdieu has hinted, this continuing accumulation of print cultural artifacts also helps educate its audience, helps give readers the codes they need to understand the cultural event not only of the theatrical production but also of the larger "performance" of the theater within the struggles over high and low culture that occurred throughout the eighteenth century. To whom does the theater belong, the educated elite in the boxes or the apprentices and servants who could purchase gallery tickets? While the assumptions of an aristocratic "coterie" audience during Charles II's time have been significantly modified to show the presence of many social segments in the Restoration audience, and while we cannot

know for certain who read these cheap performer biographies, the appearance of this genre at the end of the seventeenth century can be interpreted as one method of educating those from classes that may have found the glittering world of the theater culturally intimidating. If they could afford (or borrow) one of these biographies—usually priced at about one shilling at the end of the century—they had an opportunity to acquire cultural competence in the privacy of their own homes. They could align themselves with the attractive world of the stage through their knowledge and thus display the trappings of valuable cultural capital, participating in the quest for upward mobility through "aping" the habits of their "betters," an occurrence so many political and social writers of the time decried. In this way, people not born to the cultural cognoscenti can train themselves in aesthetic and cultural appreciation: they can access some of the specialized knowledge or familiarity that upper classes claim as "genteel," deriving naturally from their more refined status, thus unmasking the "unnatural" naturalizing process. When, in speaking as the tragedian Thomas Betterton in *The Life of Mr. Thomas Betterton, the Late Eminent Tragedian* (1710), Charles Gildon gives extended lessons on the proper gestures and intonations for good acting, his words may be read by the educated person as a review of oratorical suggestions he (or, less likely, she) might already have encountered in his classical or French reading but, for those who do not have this inherited hoard of information or the leisure and money to attend the theater frequently, Gildon's lessons are a "guide to the art."

The increasing levels of publicity in which these biographies and their various readers participate begin creating a prototypical figure with whom our century is very familiar: the celebrity. What exactly are celebrities? We are so accustomed to thinking of them as products of our own time that locating their nascent presence in the eighteenth century might at first seem like an ahistorical attempt to force a modern cultural construct onto the early modern period. Certainly, I cannot claim that the type of celebrity I discern in eighteenth-century England occurs on the same scale or through the same media as twentieth-century American or British celebrity culture or, increasingly, global models. Yet Richard Schickel's statement that "there was no such thing as celebrity prior to the beginning of the twentieth century" seems unnecessarily sweeping.[10] The eighteenth century's similar obsession with performers, their changing social presence, the increase in popular visual imagery, and the growth of cheaper,

more widely distributed print all contribute to a culture that began to esteem different public figures than it had previously, figures who are similar to those commanding people's attention today. Alexandra Halasz has examined Richard Tarleton's "celebrity image" in Elizabethan England; Peter M. Briggs has argued for Laurence Sterne's literary celebrity in 1760; and Judith Milhous has proposed celebrity status for the dancer Auguste Vestris in 1780–1.[11] I hope this book provides a model of eighteenth-century celebrity that includes and expands a larger cultural context for their case studies.

Celebrity is a form of large-scale public attention, customarily labeled "fame" in previous times.[12] But celebrity is a new market- and media-driven form of attention that differs greatly from a traditional, neoclassical ideal of fame. In *The Frenzy of Renown,* Leo Braudy convincingly shows how early figures such as Alexander the Great could not have achieved lasting fame without such media manipulations as court historiographers and personalized currency; however, he overlooks the advances in publicity gained by performers in the eighteenth century—an odd omission, considering that such people are the majority of modern celebrities.[13] Celebrities differ from the traditionally "famous" in that they have rarely executed any heroic actions, nor have they been born into a noble or royal class in which such regard naturally accompanies station. Players receive notice through their performances of important roles, the appeal of their art, their physical attractiveness, or their proximity to figures of high status: the wealthy, the wellborn, the royal. While their fame may be provoked by some singular act such as an impressive performance, their continued presence in the public eye depends on the media and on their ability to present themselves (or have others present them) as fascinating people. In a "consumer culture, becoming a celebrity is based on personality rather than character: 'The characteristic demanded of celebrities is to have a personality, to possess the actor's skills of presenting a colourful self. . . . These are seen to replace the more traditional views of character which emphasized moral consistency.'"[14]

As Cowen correctly points out, however, since celebrities are derived from a commercial system that thrives on proliferation rather than consolidation of market power, they differ from traditional heroes not only in their ability to project personality rather than moral consistency but also in the relative harmlessness that that emphasis on personality encourages.

5

They do not start wars, slaughter legions of enemies, or burn foreign king-doms; they merely pretend to do so onstage, while their public personae garner acclaim. He states: "Fame and merit have never been tightly con-nected, no matter what era we examine or whether we define merit in terms of fan preferences or some alternative moral standard. Commercial-ized fame, while taking relative recognition away from moral leaders, also has taken renown away from tyrants and violent rulers." [15] Though Cowen reasons here from an assumed position of moral certainty—conditioned by his historical moment, his view of morality does not include the vio-lence that earlier periods would have found normal—the relative levels of violence associated with performers and war heroes is indisputable. Charles Churchill, the duke of Marlborough, may gain fame, wealth, and royal approval for his victories in continental wars, but he is subject as well to the increasing public scrutiny, criticism, and the redefinition of those actions as something other than "victories" that mass print allows. He shares admiring attention with a wider cast of public figures, including players; print serves to dilute the fame of traditional war heroes like Marl-borough while concurrently boosting that of others.

Celebrity also differs from classical fame in its impermanence—celebri-ties are fashions of the season rather than enduring cultural heroes. This is perhaps due to the fact that celebrities do not engage in empire-building and other large-scale activities. Yet as allowing performers presence in the public sphere becomes more acceptable, celebrities can achieve a certain amount of staying power, if only as historical relics, since the actual achievements of their art, as Victor laments, is gone. Sarah Siddons is remembered today (if remembered at all) more as the subject of glorious late-eighteenth-century portraits than as a living actress. The celebrity's relative impermanence is a function of his or her primary status as a com-modity and thus subject to the same market forces that control other com-modities, dictating use and then disposal. Their value to their society is variable and constantly under examination as they vie for the attention that will increase their value as performers, and as readers and spectators judge their merit in relation to other performers and public servants. Actors are less valued as mouthpieces in plays of morality and heroic forti-tude as the didactic function of drama as a whole decreases, but then soci-ety is left with the puzzling question of exactly what kind of utility these widely acclaimed performers satisfy, and how they should be recompensed

for this utility. Questions about the social value of acting and actors come up continually over the course of the century—fueled in part by the attention and increasing compensation they receive.

In its development, celebrity refigures fame and heroism for a more commercial society. As different types of people become celebrated throughout the eighteenth century—thresher and washerwoman poets, boxers, clergymen, female soldiers, opera singers, and performers—writers such as Pope and Edward Young will decry love of fame, "the universal passion," which encourages these fops, hacks, and dunces. According to these writers, such upstarts have little to recommend them but their persevering drive for attention, and they will be forgotten after the next Grub Street sensation arrives. The underlying fear seems to be that celebrities will gain undeserved power, and with that power they will debase cultural standards and undermine social hierarchies of class and status.

But though celebrities receive a lot of attention, they have little real exercisable power. Alberoni defines stars as those "whose institutional power is very limited or non-existent, but whose doings and way of life arouse a considerable and sometimes even a maximum degree of interest."[16] Today celebrities can use their spotlight to hawk products on television or to bolster favorite political causes. They can use their fortunes, derived from attention, to support pet projects or charities. This type of power was not yet available to seventeenth-century players, though some actors, such as Edward Alleyn, founded hospitals or, like David Garrick, applied their income and revenue-generating ability to a pension fund for "decayed actors," and many are lauded for their private charity. Players had minimal political and certainly little religious influence; no actor used his stage career as a springboard into an oratorical career by standing for Parliament, though Richard Brinsley Sheridan, by virtue of his birth and position as a theater manager, could make this move.

But by the end of the eighteenth century, some performers had achieved the status of cultural authorities. A few, like Sarah Siddons, enjoyed enormous wealth, hobnobbed with the great, voiced respected aesthetic opinions, peddled influence, and were revered as moral models. In their massive modern biography of David Garrick, George Winchester Stone and George M. Kahrl describe Garrick's important position as a patron of visual arts.[17] Even those whose private lives lead to public disapproval can go on to relatively respectable careers, such as Mary Robinson

who, after her affair with the Prince of Wales, became a poet and literary critic, passing judgment on the poetic efforts of others. However, this limited influence was contested throughout the century; some critical assessors such as Charles Churchill deplore performers' artistic authority: "DOTH it more move our anger or our mirth / To see these THINGS, the lowest sons of earth, / Presume, with self-sufficient knowledge grac'd, / To rule in Letters and preside in Taste?"[18] The "low" and self-taught should not be cultural arbiters for the "high," though this is what increased public attention seems to encourage. Such controversies, however, only serve to focus public attention even *more* on these celebrities. The celebrity biographies studied here concern themselves with and ultimately help increase the performer's cultural power, though they sometimes participate reluctantly.

Performers' status increases somewhat over the course of the eighteenth century because of the ways in which perceptions of actors intersected with changing social power structures. Out of the many eighteenth-century thespian biographies, I have chosen to focus on those that wrestle with the issues that establish or deny new authority for the actor or actress. Over this turbulent period of social change, thespian biographies reflect and participate in the efforts to place performers within unstable hierarchies of cultural, literary, scientific, and financial order. Staging royal and popular public spectacles became an important method of manipulating public opinion and consolidating power, as Nancy Klein Maguire and Paula Backscheider have shown.[19] Not only the dramas they performed but the players themselves were implicated in late-seventeenth-century struggles for power. Players had always inspired suspicion; after the Restoration, their status was even more complex as women joined their ranks and as the two patents brought them under direct control of the Lord Chamberlain and Master of the Revels as sworn royal servants. As succeeding monarchs proved themselves less interested in the theater than Charles II, the court connection, while still extant, weakens. Performers become more businesslike, more self-reliant, more professional. Such half-royal, half-public servants join other cultural anomalies such as the writer torn between aristocratic patronage and the opportunities of the free market, or the physician positioning himself between classical university learning and empirical deduction. As Geoffrey Holmes has shown in his study of changing concepts of professionalism from 1680 to 1730, discussions of

these emerging professionals often question their appropriate social position in a society and cultural hierarchy that was not structured to accommodate them.[20] Holmes does not discuss performers, but we can easily extend his observations to the disputed social claims involving this line of work. Biographies of actors and actresses often uncomfortably situate their subjects between the public admiration that makes readers demand their life stories and assures them a certain amount of regard, and the class suspicion that makes the authors and narrators of their life stories assume condescending or even hostile tones. Yet by the end of the century, Samuel Johnson could remark of Garrick, "here is a man who has advanced the dignity of his profession," thus acknowledging that Garrick participated in a recognizable profession as well as in that profession's changing status.[21]

Until the beginning of the eighteenth century, biographers primarily concerned themselves with famous historical figures, rulers, saints, warriors, and clergymen. Biographies written of contemporaries were often published as funeral orations and eulogies. Classical and English writers are well represented in the genre, many appearing as prefaces to collected works. Literate seventeenth-century writers would be familiar with classical historians and biographers as well. Plutarch's *Lives*, Diogenes Laertius's *Lives and Opinions of the Philosophers*, and Procopius's *Secret History* were biographical works that readers might know in their original languages or in the English translations that appeared in the late sixteenth and seventeenth centuries, such as Dryden's 1683 translation of Plutarch and the accompanying account of the classical writer. Martha Walling Howard has listed the numerous editions of the *Lives* in the eighteenth century, implying a continuity of interest from the work's first English translation in 1579.[22] Gildon's references in his *Life of Thomas Betterton* to several anecdotes reported by Plutarch shows his familiarity with them and suggests that he expected his audience to be similarly knowledgeable. Yet Plutarch and other classical biographers wrote of socially advantaged men, or at least men of renown: emperors, orators, philosophers.

Given this emphasis on the traditionally famous in biographies, we can draw generalizations about the kinds of content most seventeenth-century writers considered appropriate. The majority of biographies present only the public characters and actions of their public subjects. Most considered prying into personal life of elevated men to be unseemly for the dignity of the subject and unnecessary to the biography's didactic aims. Francis

Bacon's impersonal narrative of Henry VII included in his *Advancement of Learning* (1605) relates the monarch's political actions and does not mention his private life unless it directs public action. Perhaps this type of biography is appropriate for royalty, who lived on public display. But biographers of other eminent, less public men also believed mention of private behavior to be taboo in biography. For example, Thomas Sprat refused to print personal letters in his *Life of Cowley* (1668): "The truth is, the Letters that pass between particular Friends, if they are written as they ought to be, can scarce ever be fit to see the light. . . . The very same passages, which make Writings of this Nature delightful amongst Friends, will lose all manner of taste, when they come to be read by those who are indifferent."[23] Dryden states that Plutarch provides "a descent into minute circumstances, and trivial passages of life," yet twenty-first-century readers searching for domestic detail will find little.[24] Sprat's and Dryden's comments indicate that the seventeenth century's boundaries between public and private do not correspond to ours. Several seventeenth-century and classical *Life*-writers did address the private lives of their subjects: John Aubrey's *Brief Lives,* Roger North's *Lives* of his three brothers, and Izaac Walton's five *Lives.* Such attention has gained them a popularity with modern scholars that skews our sense of the generic conditions of the period. Readers would not have encountered the works of Aubrey and North until they were first published in 1813 and 1742–4, respectively, though they may have known Walton's work. In any case, the public/private debate in biography continues through the following century at least, as we see in reactions to Boswell's *Life of Johnson.*

As important as the biographical content with which thespian biographers would have been familiar is how that content is presented. Most writers and thinkers of the late seventeenth century assumed an essential stability of character that remained constant over one's life: a person was bound by the lines of class, religion, and gender. The writers of the popular genre of the "character," for example, attempted to codify types of individuals in short descriptions to capture their immutable natures. Other common types of *Life*-writing, spiritual biography and autobiography, presented another pattern for human narratives, linear movement from sin to repentance. We will see how conceptions of the individual either as unified and stable, following a predetermined linear path, or as a fluctuating and developing person affect the biographies of performers,

people whose professional lives turn on contemporary concepts of identity. In a society that usually assumes a stable identity or a clear moral trajectory, how would a writer transcribe the life of a person whose job requires him or her constantly to change identities and moral positions? If the person already performs onstage for all to view, what could a biography add?

Earlier in the seventeenth century, Montaigne's diligent self-scrutiny of his own motivations and growth had encouraged thinking about the sources and motivations of personal development. Increased attention among *Life*-writers to subjects' youth, education, and training allow inquiry into the sources of exceptional talent, misbehavior, or eccentricity. Joining the ranks of the respectable biographical subjects was a significant number of socially marginal people, especially criminal types including robbers, murderers, bawds, and traitors. Hal Gladfelder's recent work on criminal narratives shows their implications to conceptions of identity: "The singularity of the individual is transgressive in itself, inescapably deviant in its origins and enactment. That is, in choosing to live out a singular, self-authored history, the individual willfully breaks with the sanctioned and self-effacing narratives of identity which were the common cultural inheritance of the period."[25] Biography, or the history of an individual, breaks from the character, or the history of a type, as well as from spiritual autobiography with its predictable narrative line. Thus this very act of expressing an individual life is transgressive, linking all autobiographical or biographical subjects to the criminal. The first actor biography, the anonymous *An Account of the Life . . . of the Famously Notorious Mat. Coppinger* (1695), and several successors show strong overt influences of criminal biography. The subsequent movement of many texts within the thespian biography genre toward respectability might indicate that individuality was no longer understood as transgressive.

To have early thespian biography so closely aligned with criminals throws suspicion not only on the subject but also on the motives for writing. In his *History of the Worthies of England* (1662), Thomas Fuller gives five reasons for writing biography: to give glory to God, to preserve memory of the dead, to provide an example to the living, to entertain, and to allow a small profit to the writer. Roger North exclaims against the last: "[T]he very lucre of selling a copy is a corrupt interest that taints an historical work, for the sale of the book must not be spoiled by the dampness

of overmuch truth, but rather be made vivacious and complete by over-much lying."[26] Like the criminal biographies written for profit immediate-ly after the subject's execution, such as the famous accounts of the ordi-nary of Newgate, thespian biographies are almost without exception written for "lucre," and most of them do strive to be "vivacious" in their inclusion of jests, their emphasis on sexual escapades, or their outlandish narrative styles. North perceptively recognizes the hype and exaggeration that accompany fame in a commercial system.

Since celebrities may do little to acquire their biographical renown in comparison to the traditionally famous and great, they can still be "just like you and me" for their fans. Many eighteenth-century players came from low beginnings and had to toil in strolling and provincial companies before they succeeded in a London or Dublin house (if they ever did). Popularization of this career trajectory not only hints that other "low" people can achieve wealth and fame—an unsettling intimation for some, hopeful for others—but it also produces a familiarity that encourages a feeling of intimacy with the celebrity. This intimacy fuels and is fueled by public discussion of a player's public and private lives, a significant depar-ture from customary biographical treatment. As in the twenty-first centu-ry, audience familiarity often leads to audience control, since players must please audiences to earn their livelihood. Eighteenth-century audiences frequently volunteered to prove to actors and theater managers just who was really in charge: audiences rioted and ransacked theaters for reasons ranging from unpopular politics to unskilled performers to the raising of ticket prices. Disturbances often arose when a player insulted his or her social superior, as one of Tate Wilkinson's leading actors, Mr. Murray, dis-covered. Having inadvertently affronted a gentleman in an inn, he was then called onstage to apologize in public for this private offense, and his refusal caused a riot "from nine o'clock to near one."[27]

Audience members of all classes considered themselves superior to performers, since they paid for theater admission or, in the print arena, since they purchased the biography. Players become increasingly depend-ent on the wider public, becoming "humble servants." They were still sub-ject to audience tyranny in the early nineteenth century, as the sixty-seven nights of the Old Price Riots at Covent Garden Theater show. In order to sell performers' intimate stories to this public, a similar act of "humbling" occurred. For example, in her *Apology for the Life and Conduct of Mrs.*

Mary Wrighten, the narrator, Wrighten herself, excuses her literary endeavors: "The life of an individual is so uninteresting to the public, that it would be a blamable piece of intrusion to lay it before readers of discernment without the offer of an apology. Theatrical characters, though denominated public, may possibly of all others be deemed less worthy of the appellation."[28] Through their purchasing power, readers could partially control images and expectations of actors and actresses.

This relation quickly assumes a Foucauldian circularity, as the celebrity develops into someone whom the spectator aspires to emulate and mutual "controlling" mechanisms result.[29] Paradoxically, performers were not "just like" their fans, since they possessed something special that set them apart from their audiences, and by which they in turn could control their audiences: their talent. After all, audiences acknowledge celebrity power by their very attendance at the theater, and eighteenth-century theatrical histories are rife with anecdotes about people who thought they had acting talent or thought that anyone could act—and who, after testing their skills on the boards, failed. For example, Wilkinson reports "stage struck" applicants (the term is his), "who recommended themselves for the stage without any one requisite or idea, excepting impudence in the extreme."[30] The development of player biography and performance criticism is testimony to the fact that, in contrast to earlier times, acting talent was now widely acknowledged to *exist* and was accordingly esteemed. Biographies explored the upbringing and education that revealed or trained this talent, while critical evaluations such as Aaron Hill and William Popple's *The Prompter* (1734–6), James Boswell's articles in the *London Magazine* (1770), or Denis Diderot's *The Paradox of Acting* (written in the 1770s; published 1830) attempt to define and describe it. In addition, biographies also began to establish the familiar myths of the discovery of this talent and the rags-to-riches trajectory of upward mobility. Such narrative lines would be familiar to eighteenth-century readers of the stories of heroes and saints, but their application to actors and acting talent was new.

Players' talent, the crystallization of this talent into the narrative lines of biography, and the attention that resulted from both provoked admiration—and resentment. The social position of players had never been clear, and their ability to consort with royalty while leading reputedly dissolute lives had always been unsettling. Their public exposure set them up as easy targets for abuse, but since their very jobs guaranteed them attention, they

are also often cosseted by those who either respected their talent or who wanted attention themselves. The resulting social displacement is sniffed at by Lady Woodvill in George Etherege's *The Man of Mode* (1676): "'Tis good breeding now to be civil to none but players and Exchange women. They are treated . . . as much above their condition as others are below theirs."[31] This class confusion is apparent in Samuel Johnson's contradictory comments on actors, Garrick in particular; it is also evident in the comments of those who considered players' salaries exorbitant (even though those salaries were sometimes unpaid). Kristina Straub comments that "[c]lass is a prominent issue in the representation of actors throughout the eighteenth century. Actors occupied a liminal position in relation to the English class structure that even Garrick's immense success and widespread recognition in the 1770s could not completely resolve into respectability."[32]

Yet it is precisely players' ability to confuse social expectations and transcend many conventions of class, morality, and decorum that attracts the type of public attention that helps produce celebrity. Their situation develops from the undifferentiated class of all social anomalies: as Gladfelder points out about criminals, "narrative attention on the deviant subjects of the various criminal genres responded in part to a desire for social control and the containment of rebellious drives. But this concentration on the malefactor responded equally to a desire to be bad."[33] Readers were both repelled and attracted, and soon celebrities became distinguished from other criminals and deviants as they achieved social authority, allowing readers to indulge more comfortably in "being bad." Performers fit awkwardly into existing social categories both high and low; thus a new cultural formation arose to describe the type of person who fraternized with—even married into—the upper classes, while doing a job that still legally defined its practitioners as vagrants.

To understand these social anomalies, the public thirsted for knowledge of players' intimate lives, knowledge available about few other people. As Richard Sennett has argued, the late seventeenth and early eighteenth centuries were times when men assumed and were expected to assume public roles distinct from their private identities. The theatricality of such an existence is emphasized by the actual theatrical experience: "The performer's social rise was based on his declaration of a forceful, exciting, morally suspect personality, wholly contrary to the style of ordinary bour-

geois life, in which one tried to avoid being read as a person by suppress-ing one's feelings."[34] Actors projected the importance of an emotional life, as their profession was based on affective talents. They become loci of shared emotion as, in Cowen's words, "The fame of celebrities creates a collective space in which fans share their emotional and aesthetic aspira-tions."[35]

Performing required an actor to adopt multiple emotion-laden identi-ties which, as seventeenth-century antitheatricalists noted, raised ques-tions about that person's "real" identity as well as about the sincerity of that person's emotions. As the private "real" information surfaces, it becomes part of the public identity. This is then reinterpreted as part of the public role itself, which must then be further investigated to find the realer "real" identity. This circular "celebrity inquiry" is self-sustaining. In his study of modern celebrity culture, Schickel comments that the films in which movie stars appear begin "to be perceived . . . as incidents in a larg-er and more compelling drama—the drama of the star's life and career."[36] And the same occurs for eighteenth-century stage players, as Lavinia Fen-ton becomes identified as the leading lady of *The Beggar's Opera*, "Polly Peachum"; a novel based on Garrick calls him "Ranger," after one of his successful roles; and Mary Robinson is referred to as the Shakespearean "Perdita."

Biographical treatment may lead to greater admiration or moral con-demnation, a desire to emulate or castigate the subject, and thus the dis-cussion of stars grows since they "are those members of the community whom *all* can evaluate, love or criticize. They are the chosen objects of col-lective gossip."[37] A writer for the *Gentleman's Magazine* asks in "Biograph-ical Memoirs of Mr. Kemble, Brother to Mrs. Siddons," "What is the rea-son, that the moment our understanding bows to the open display of a man's public talents, our curiosity should begin so busily to pry into the retired scenes of his private life?"[38] The readers of celebrity material are here indicted for their voyeuristic interest, which in turn is incited by gos-sip publications. Though many biographies include information about players' private virtue and public achievements, many more focus on sex-ual exploits, criminal adventures, financial ineptitude, and other sensa-tional material to feed the print machine, like supermarket tabloids and confessional memoirs today.

Both Sennett and Jürgen Habermas have described the eighteenth

century as Britain's last period of meaningful public life, before the valorization of personality and expressiveness (according to Sennett) or before a consumerism propelled by capitalism (according to Habermas) undermined the formal decorum that fosters rational public discourse.[39] Both Sennett and Habermas have identified a significant shift in public life, and media-generated celebrity participates in blurring these distinctions between public and private. Performers' biography clearly supports both theories: the emotional importance of the thespian subject generates interest in collective emotional experiences, while the subject's material commodification as a book indicates market control of players' lives. My story of the development of thespian biography intersects with a larger narrative about the changing boundaries of areas of human existence.

This study of thespian biography and authority begins in chapter 1 with the earliest English actor biographies, which include very little private information and instead focus on public presentation of the player both as actor and as man. He is depicted as either rogue or gentleman, characterizations that engage with several contested class and culture debates of the late seventeenth century. The contemporary controversy between the "ancients" and "moderns" as scientific and cultural authorities that occurred on the Continent and in England permeated many disciplines. One of them was theater, not only in drama theory, as Joseph Levine's nuanced analysis has shown, but also in the characterization of performers, their talent, and their function vis-à-vis society and the dramatic text.[40] The first actor biographies in English represent two different conceptions of the actor that apply to acting the two implied sources of authority debated by the ancients and moderns. By showing criminal or roguish protagonists, *An Account of the Life, Conversation, Birth, Education, Pranks, Projects, and Exploits, and Merry Conceits, of the Famously Notorious Mat. Coppinger* (1695) and Tobyas Thomas's *The Life of the Late Famous Comedian, Jo. Hayns* (1701) present the actor as someone who relies on individual talent and not received wisdom, questioning inherited authority. Charles Gildon's *The Life of Mr. Thomas Betterton, the Late Eminent Tragedian* (1710) shows an actor and his art linked to classical models and a strictly hierarchical organization of theatrical and social authority. These first biographies are critical to understanding the poles of authority between which later discourse on performing celebrities will swing: can an actor claim authority through eccentricity, antisocial tendencies, and mar-

ginality, or through social respectability, prominence, and traditional structures?

The rogue/gentleman dichotomy collapses gradually over the next hundred years. One significant moment in its transformation occurs in the three biographies of the original cast of *The Beggar's Opera* published following the play's success in 1728. The popularity of the play and its attractive cast helped encourage a growing consumer market for theatrical information and memorabilia. This new market was unlocked by a play that seemed to level social differences—showing whores preening like fine ladies and implying that fine ladies were no better than whores—just as acting did. As had long been acknowledged, an actor could play a king one night and a beggar the next. Like the criminals portrayed and politicians lambasted in *The Beggar's Opera*, eighteenth-century actors and actresses began to evoke a vision of a transcendent lifestyle free from conventions of class- and gender-linked behavior, the idealized lifestyle of the celebrity.

The biographies discussed here in chapter 2, however, do not admire but instead disapprove of this new route to fame and prosperity, which they consider an empty and morally corrupt form of cultural heroism. Gay's slippery satire, as critics have found, is often ambiguous in its intentions, but the biographies that followed the play clearly interpreted the play as subversive and tried to control its seductive, socially unsettling force. Yet what could they achieve by adding more publicity to a media mechanism, celebrity, that feeds on publicity? In their diverse responses to *The Beggar's Opera*, these biographies only helped to establish the new authorities they condemn.

In chapter 3, I examine two versions of the life of the actress: the first actress biography (*The Life of Lavinia Beswick, Alias Fenton, Alias Polly Peachum*, one of the *Beggar's Opera* biographies, 1728) and the first actress autobiography (*A Narrative of the Life of Mrs. Charlotte Charke*, 1755). Since women in eighteenth-century England were, to some extent, always actresses, the important difference in the textual descriptions of their life performances is who gets to write the role. In the first actress biography, we see the stable, seamless gendered subject required by a patriarchal gender system that required women to adopt one stable role. In the autobiography, we see a polysemous, disrupted, performative subject reflective of Judith Butler's theoretical work on gender construction—a type of subject that exposed the difficulty a public woman had of containing herself

within her society's gender expectations and presenting herself to the reading public. As we will see throughout this study, female celebrities encounter presentational difficulties that do not often arise for male subjects. Examining these two texts together allows us to see ways in which thespian biographies can reinforce or subvert assumptions of gender authority.

Chapter 4 moves to another collision of biography and biology that links to other social challenges to authority. Barton Booth, a famous actor and theater manager who died in 1733, was, like other celebrity subjects, treated to multiple biographies. One, Benjamin Victor's *Memoirs of the Life of Barton Booth* (1733), includes a gruesome autopsy report describing the possible effects of ingesting mercury—a particularly appropriate treatment of someone engaged in the "mercurial" business of acting. The circumstances surrounding this report show how Booth's death was embroiled in a controversy over medical legitimacy as the medical profession slowly attempted to separate real healers from mere impostors: thus the trope of acting connects both physicians and performers. In his stage life, Booth pretended to the authority of statesmen and monarchs, but his opened body was used to debunk the performance of medical expertise by quacks. Booth's body helps raise questions about truth and authority that permeate both the medical and the performing professions in eighteenth-century England. In fact, the controversy surrounding the medical circumstances of Booth's death reiterates the ancients and moderns debate of chapter 1: what type of knowledge should claim authority, and who are the fitting possessors of that knowledge?

Similarly, chapter 5 examines struggles over *literary* authority: who deserves it and for what type of work? Before 1740 histories, dramatic criticism, prologues and epilogues, and thespian biographies show that actors and authors often chafed against each other, each claiming control of and responsibility for the aesthetic object, the theatrical production. After all, in the theater, the written word is not the final word: it must be performed. This chapter takes up the various ways in which biographical texts served as battlegrounds for establishing literary authority. In autobiography, specifically, an actor must defend literary aspirations. The uproar over Colley Cibber's popular *An Apology for the Life of Colley Cibber* (1740) engages with eighteenth-century renegotiations of the cultural category of "author," as Cibber defends his writing and his version of the theatrical

past against those who would deny an actor this type of public voice.

Cibber's autobiography seems to have tapped not only a large market of potential readers about theatrical lives and history, but it also showed many writers, both those involved and not involved with the theater, that this market existed and could be further cultivated. The most immediate followers of Cibber were his children, Charlotte Charke and Theophilus Cibber. Charke has already been considered in chapter 3; I turn to Theophilus in chapter 6. Reading his *Serio-Comic Apology* (1748), one sees a desperate bid for patrilineal power, which Theophilus assumed was his birthright. Denied his father's position as theater manager, as well as his success as a dramatist and comic actor, Theophilus's text speaks of tense negotiations with two textual fathers: Cibber and the infamous bookseller Edmund Curll. Theophilus suffers from an anxiety of influence that leaves his autobiographical presentation unresolved and as fragmented as his sister's—though for different reasons. Other thespian biographies of this time also look for textual "fathers" and find them in the unusual narrative experiments of the day—mimicking *Tristram Shandy* or Fielding's narrators, invoking John Cleland's *Memoirs of a Woman of Pleasure,* or trying to build on Cibber's own literary and historical legacy. Most celebrity biographers use these techniques to restrain the narrative of social mobility that celebrities endorse, through condescending narrators and suggestion of the fictionality of the celebrity subject. These biographies employ literary authority to suppress other nascent forms of authority.

Most of the biographers concerned with celebrity authority are also concerned with the growing wealth of their subjects, and they write their books in part to guide readers in the appropriate valuation of performers. In chapter 7, we examine how acting is linked to finance through these biographies. Throughout the century, performers are accused of being overpaid—indeed, the question of players' value was a hotly contested one, linked to questions of the social value of their jobs and their personal popularity. The economic contributions of acting are difficult to perceive when compared with other services and manufactures, and their worth seems to waver, depending on theatrical events, assignment and success of plays and roles, private scandals, and changing assumptions about the functions of drama and theater in society. Performers were often assumed to be notoriously profligate, as confirmed by the debt-ridden adventures

19

of the protagonists in *Memoirs of That Celebrated Comedian . . . Thomas Weston* (1776) and George Anne Bellamy's *An Apology for the Life of George Anne Bellamy* (1785). Actresses were assumed to have a special relationship with money: they sold their bodies to the gaze of the audience or in more private performances. Do these performers deserve what they receive, and is their relationship with money an acceptable one? Biographies focus on how these performers acquire and use their money, to help determine the social value of these new economic forces. The mid-eighteenth century was a time of changing relationships to money, as the country adapted to an economic system dependent on credit and debt on both the national and personal levels. Through stock and fluctuating market value, money could "act," or pretend to be worth more than it was, just as actors could be something other than they were. Currency provides an appropriate metaphor for the celebrity.

The most famous eighteenth-century actor, David Garrick, was rumored to be selfish and greedy. The *Town and Country Magazine* reported that "his greatest advocates must own that he loved money, and to the lust of gain must be ascribed his continuing upon the stage when many of his powers had deserted him."[41] However, such statements did little to undermine the praise in his biographical treatment. Garrick was an acclaimed actor and a successful playwright, and the biographies written of him continue to examine this by-now familiar split between actor and author: Thomas Davies cast Garrick as the great professional theater man in *Memoirs of the Life of David Garrick, Esq.* (1780), while Arthur Murphy instead portrayed his sometime antagonist as a literary man in *The Life of David Garrick, Esq.* (1801). Yet in these books, as well as in other less substantial efforts, this split is not acrimonious—literary authority is not used to trump the authority of the actor. Chapter 8 argues that Garrick's undoubted talent, his fortuitous timing, and his regulation of his image during his lifetime allow many of the disruptions in the celebrity discourse I have discussed in this book to be harmonized. The jostling for cultural authority does not disappear, but Garrick's biographical representations show that the opportunity for a performer's cultural prominence does exist at the end of the eighteenth century—at least for the exceptional player.

Garrick was the British stage's first true celebrity. Preserved in the documents and biographies that memorialize him is a record of a new type of

social presence and power. His appearance helped establish a trend in which theaters relied increasingly on star performers rather than on full companies. Although it tempted readers into familiarity with players, players' increased print exposure simultaneously made the theater seem a self-contained society into which only the particularly lucky or gifted would be admitted. Handbooks such as David Erskine Baker's *The Companion to the Play-House* (1764) and *The Thespian Dictionary* (1805) began to appear, in which theatergoers could access information on these citizens of this special world in alphabetically arranged capsule biographies. Training manuals such as *The Spouter's Companion* (c. 1770) were written to help wannabes enter the profession. Schickel has commented that celebrities appear "to the noncelebrity to fulfill . . . a dream of intimate, almost familial connection among figures of glamour and authority."[42] Though an eighteenth-century audience member could still drink with an actor at a local tavern, print, especially through biographical discourse, takes the first step in sequestering players into their own glamorous, specialized culture, with its own rituals and established hierarchy.

Throughout the eighteenth century, the stage and print worlds sustain as well as antagonize each other. Theatrical topics depart their ancillary status in moral debate and history of drama to become topics of interest in and of themselves. Theatrical discourse emerges, with much of its vocabulary and many of its concerns deriving from player biographies. These biographies foreground questions of actors' and actresses' identities, of social positions, of professional standing and personal conduct, of the success and originality of performance—and all of these elements help create new space in preexistent authority structures, themselves in flux. This new type of attention, born of the media, social uncertainty, and the paradoxes that actors and actresses represented for their society, is what we today recognize as celebrity.

CHAPTER 1

Rogues and Gentlemen

THE ANCIENTS AND MODERNS TAKE THE STAGE

Amongst those who will be objecting against
the doctrin I lay down, may peradventure
appear a sort of men who have remember'd
so and *so*; and value themselves upon their
experience. I may write by the *Book* (say they)
what I have a mind, but they *know* what will
please. These are a kind of *Stage-quacks* and
Empericks in Poetry, who have got a *Receit* to
please: And no Collegiate like 'em
for *purging* the Passions.

THOMAS RYMER,
The Tragedies of the Last Age (1677)

T HE BEGINNING of a history
of a genre is necessarily arbitrary. Though I start with what
I identify as the first three actor biographies in English in this chapter,
these texts had been preceded by other
forms in which some biographical
information about actors had been

lodged: characters, elegies, jest books, laudatory and satirical verses. Some of the same concerns articulated in the biographies are anticipated in these earlier forms, but I begin where I do because integrity of the independent text seems to affirm the independent life. The very publication of an individual actor's biography is a claim to authority: this person is substantial enough to demand readers' attention.[1]

These first biographies differ significantly from each other, so much so that they may not seem even to belong in the same category. Two describe the lives of their protagonists as roguish picaros involved in many kinds of scrapes, impersonations, and even crimes: the anonymous *An Account of the Life, Conversation, Birth, Education, Pranks, Projects, and Exploits, and Merry Conceits, of the Famously Notorious Mat. Coppinger* (1695) and Tobyas Thomas's *The Life of the Late Famous Comedian, Jo. Hayns* (1701). In contrast, Charles Gildon's *The Life of Mr. Thomas Betterton, the Late Eminent Tragedian* (1710) casts its tragedian subject and acting itself as respectable, even genteel. Yet all three presume to describe the lives of popular performers. What explains their differences?

The main aim of this chapter derives from that question, in part because these differences will persist throughout the biographies of the ensuing century. These first biographies do trace the lives of players who lived very differently from each other, which is the most obvious reason for the books' differences. But the most *significant* difference—for these texts, their cultural context, and for understanding the biographies that follow—is how each engages with forms of authority. The texts' subjects are people who perform as kings and queens, nobles and martyrs, figures of deepest consequence; they also play villains and fools. Audiences applaud and encourage them and sometimes court their company; they condemn actors as vagabonds and lowlife. This public presence that causes both respect and disgust, this dual reaction, is expressed in and reinforced by the differences within the emerging biographical genre.

This chapter examines the different claims to authority implicit in these biographies. The examination will show how their claims to authority actually reflect and contribute to a larger cultural discussion of the sources of authority: the late seventeenth-century controversy between the ancients and the moderns. This controversy continued in most areas of intellectual life from the late seventeenth to the mid-eighteenth centuries, pitting those who supported the veneration and study of classical Greek

and Roman authors against those who believed that modern empirical methodologies and inquiry could add usefully to the store of knowledge. Joseph M. Levine has brilliantly explicated this controversy, which I must necessarily simplify here.[2] The moderns suggested that, at least in some fields, seventeenth-century Englishmen could use their own native genius to build on the achievements of those who went before. Those supporting the ancients observed the ineffectual striving of the sciences and the poor imitations of ancient beauty. Comparing the moderns' work to the profound originality of the ancients, they believed that the time for great natural genius was past, and attempts to outdo the ancients' accomplishments were merely presumption. In chastising "sufficiency," or pride, Sir William Temple rebukes the man who overreaches his abilities: "his pride is greater than his ignorance, and what he wants in knowledge, he supplies by sufficiency. . . . His own reason is the certain measure of truth, his own knowledge, of what is possible in nature."[3] So at the center of this controversy lies at least one discrepancy in assumptions about human capacity for useful innovation. The moderns assumed that their contemporaries could contribute from their own fund of natural genius. To a certain extent, they acknowledged individual contribution and the power of inherent rather than inherited talent. As Curt A. Zimansky summarizes, "faith in reason, belief in the idea of progress and increased capabilities of mankind belonged to the moderns."[4] In reply, the partisans of the ancients assumed a poverty of modern ability, predicting only failure and cultural degeneration if contemporaries relied solely on their own aptitude.

Joseph Levine has explained: "Apparently, everyone was profoundly concerned about the authority of classical antiquity, and everyone had to fix a position with respect to it before taking the plunge into modern life; and apparently, there was no subject, from art and literature to philosophy and science, from religion to politics, that was exempt from its concerns. It does not seem too much to say that there was then an obsession with this single overriding problem."[5] Neither were dramatic conventions and production exempt from this controversy, which may help explain the increase in published acting and dramatic criticism and history. Along with other cultural and artistic forms, the theater and the state of national drama were reassessed during this time, as Levine shows in his discussions of the quarrels between Dryden and two adversaries, Shadwell and Rymer.[6] This chapter's epigraph, taken from Rymer's *Tragedies of the Last*

Age, for example, opposes critics who assess drama by "*experience*" (the moderns) and those who judge "by the *Book*" (the ancients). What was the position of the Restoration theater, in reference to the classical theater of Greece and Rome? And what about the actor's art and position? If the actor takes on some role of public authority onstage and seems to be gaining in social importance, then from where does this authority and importance arise—from the classical past or from modern sufficiency, from natural talent, the influence of the ancients, or simply cultural perversion? All of the early biographies implicitly or explicitly address this question, and their responses not only help describe the player's type of authority but also help deflect the accompanying threat.

In 1615 John Stephens printed a hostile character sketch, "A Common Player," which was answered by another written by "a friend of the actors" and printed in Sir Thomas Overbury's 1615 collection of characters. [7] Stephens claims that an actor is "*a slow Payer, seldome a Purchaser, never a Puritan*. The Statute hath done wisely to acknowledge him a Rogue: for his chiefe Essence is, *A dayly Counterfeite*: Hee hath been familiar so long with out-sides, that he professes himselfe, (beeing unknowne) to bee an apparent Gentleman. . . . Take him at the best, he is but a shifting companion: for he lives effectually by putting on, and putting off." The other writer answers Stephens: "Whatsoever is commendable in the grave Orator, is most exquisitly perfect in him [the actor]; for by full and significant action of body, he charmes our attention. . . . I value a worthy Actor by the corruption of some few of the quality, as I would doe gold in the oare; I should not minde the drosse but the purity of the mettall."[8]

These contradictory reactions reveal two extreme assumptions about what an actor actually is, and where his power lies. Is he, as Stephens worries, a "rogue," only an "apparent Gentleman," a prodigal member of society who gains his hold via mere impersonation—a Matthew Coppinger or a Jo Hayns? Or, in Overbury's view, is the actor a descendent of the classical and respectable orator (with a few bad examples), who awes us with his rhetorical prowess—a Thomas Betterton or a Theophilus Keene? Kristina Straub has also noted this dichotomy: "Throughout the century, the actor is déclassé, sexually suspect, effeminate, like a 'moor,' or (worse) Irish; alternatively, he is a gentleman, chaste (within limits), manly, and proudly English."[9] Both views of the actor build on the assumptions of authority proposed by the ancients and moderns controversy. The biographies

attempt to explain the source of the player's power over his audience, they hold implications for the status of the actor in society, and they depend not only on reviewing stage performance but on interpreting the performer's whole life.

THE ROGUES AND THE MODERNS: MATTHEW COPPINGER AND JOSEPH HAYNS

Both *Account of Coppinger* and *Life of Hayns* owe much to their generic predecessors in related forms of criminal/rogue biographies, picaresque fictions, and jest books. Of course, the books also owe much to their respective subjects. Both were nominally comedians. Coppinger was a stroller-turned-mountebank-turned-criminal, and all extant information on Hayns describes him as a buffoon, a practical joker, and a rogue—official documents confirm at least fourteen suits recorded against him for debt.[10] Imposture and trickery are common elements in criminal biographies of the time, but these biographies introduce the innovation that Coppinger and Hayns are employed to impersonate, and thus they engage with crucial long-lived debates over the purpose and value of acting as employment, to which we will turn in chapter 7.[11] But these biographies do not focus on the two actors' residence with their acting companies. Depicted as free agents, sometimes legitimately employed but often not, these two protagonists assert their power over those they trick through their own personal talent, not through the vehicles of patented acting companies. And though Joseph Roach has provided much of the physiological background for seventeenth-century explanations of how acting actually works, none of that information appears in these biographies— the ability simply appears, mysteriously.[12] In this, their source of power, we can see their essential (if tenuous) alignment with the "moderns" side of the controversy, though the proponents of the moderns certainly did not have shilling pamphlets in mind when defending modern learning. Yet the biographies, seemingly amused by their subjects' destabilizing power, eventually tie this power to more traditional and established sources, to contain the harm that actors can inflict.

Account of Coppinger makes little effort to differentiate its subject from the career criminals of hundreds of other such biographies. Coppinger was

a little-known strolling player who seems never to have been a member of a London company. Capitalizing on his execution at Tyburn in February 1695, this twelve-page pamphlet comprises almost all the information we have about Coppinger.[13] Each chapter relates one of Coppinger's "merry conceits," organizing the book like a chronological collection of jests. He robs his mother to join a strolling company, tricks a servant into sleeping with him and then flees the country when she becomes pregnant, cheats a Dutch merchant, wounds "a Turner in *Fleet-street*", and is finally condemned to death for stealing a lady's watch and £7. He does not confess or repent, and the reader hoping for what the title page promises—"an Account of his Behaviour in *Newgate* after Condemnation and his Dying words at the place of Execution"—is disappointed, as none of this information appears in the book. The narrator, while sometimes condescending to his subject, is primarily detached; the narrative structure provides what small moral (if any) this book teaches: acting leads to crime, which leads to the gallows.

Paul Salzman observes that rogue narratives were often catalogues of adventures through which the reader could enjoy vicarious violence or licentiousness. Peter Burke, however, argues that such literature helps defuse antisocial energy that might otherwise be spent in progressive action. Lincoln B. Faller extends this argument to the structural incongruities of criminal fiction which, he says, "were not accidental. It was convenient that complex and important questions, difficult and disturbing questions, be lost in a welter of stuff and nonsense. . . . the typical thief's life sought not to enucleate the truth or even to suppress it, but rather to avoid it. Such lives, it seems to me, were designed to please an audience that found the various social, political, and moral implications of crime against property too often at the margins of consciousness, and too ready to intrude. The typical thief's life kept such matters comfortably at bay."[14] By telling Coppinger's story as a rogue narrative, the book participates in this containment process. Now, however, the threatening presence to keep "at bay" is the socially disruptive comedian, whom some considered a type of thief, taking money from the poor through seductive performances and earning more than his frivolous occupation deserved.

The unarticulated implications of Coppinger's biography reside in the depiction of his acting. The book does not mention any stage performances or roles; he uses his acting skills not to improve his stage performance

but to enable his criminal life. This presentation confirms a main fear articulated earlier by antitheatricalists and noted by Jonas Barish and others: if society allows—even praises—actors for their impersonations, who knows how far they may go? The sordid story of Coppinger's life raises and answers this question. Actors may prosper temporarily from their roguish ingenuity, but impersonation is a slippery downhill slope into antisocial behavior and eventually to execution, the ultimate spectacle in which collective national power is acted out on the bodies of the poor. If individual presumption and pride in one's own abilities are left unchecked by deference to traditional forms of inherited authority, criminality and social anarchy will result. Peter Linebaugh maintains that "Tyburn was at the center of urban class contention," and Coppinger's death restores social order to remind readers of the dire consequences of trusting one's own native power enough to disguise one's true social position.[15] Thus this interpretation of the ancients and moderns controversy has serious social implications, as reliance on native ability was linked to the success of people who because of their class would not normally have received formal education, and who may even have been criminals.

Account of Coppinger's anonymous author would certainly agree with John Stephens: as portrayed here, Coppinger is only an "apparent Gentleman." In fact, Coppinger's attempts to be considered a gentleman by exposing his learning and literary expertise are suppressed by this biography. One of the few other pieces of information we have about Coppinger is that he also wrote poetry. In 1682 he published *Poems, Songs, and Love-Verses upon Several Subjects,* a collection that through its choice of pastoral and classically inspired subjects shows pretensions to genteel learning.[16] Another verse effort, *Session of the Poets* ("By Matthew Coppinger, Design'd to be Published before his Execution"), was apparently known before his execution but was printed ten years afterward. Coppinger himself thus seemed to realize the need to link himself to traditional authority structures through advertising a genteel education, but his biographer negates those attempts.[17] Could the biographer not have known about these literary efforts? Was the biographer interested only in a racy rogue tale? Or was the clash of criminality and gentility, "modern" talent and "ancient" learning—and the attitudes toward authority both positions imply—too complex to juggle? While the answers are unknown, the implications are not: in the work that describes his life, Coppinger is a

28

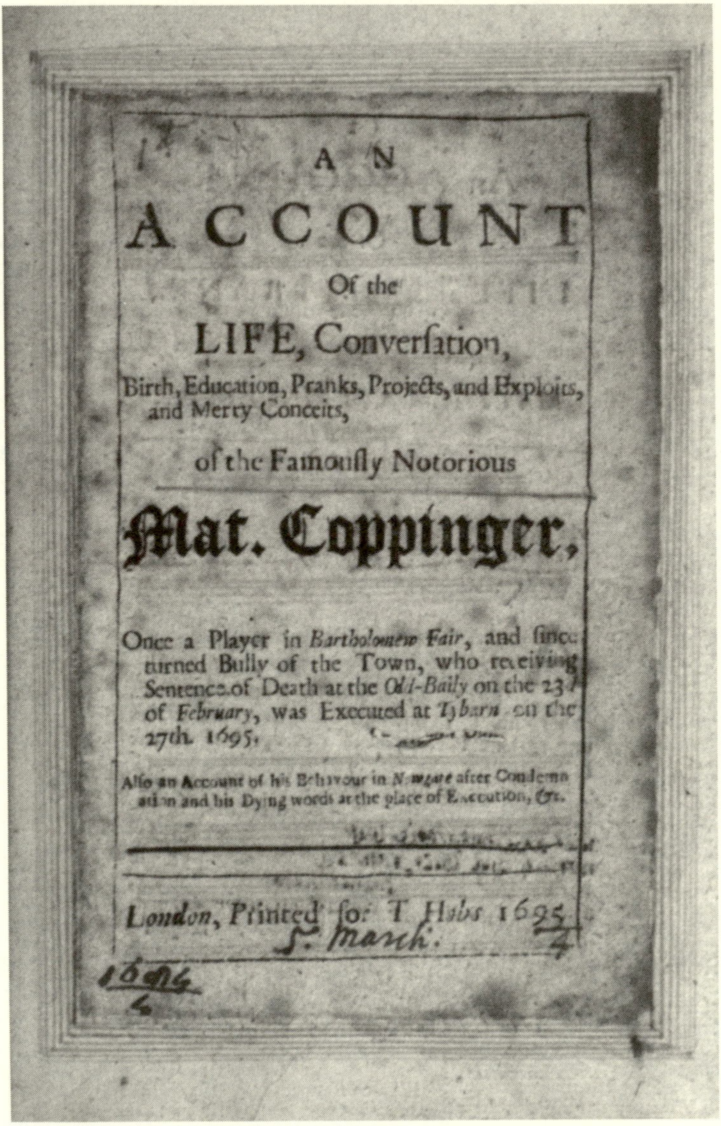

AN
ACCOUNT
Of the
LIFE, Converſation,
Birth, Education, Pranks, Projects, and Exploits, and Merry Conceits,
of the Famouſly Notorious
Mat. Coppinger,
Once a Player in *Bartholomew Fair*, and ſince turned Bully of the Town, who receiving Sentence of Death at the *Old-Baily* on the 23 of *February*, was Executed at *Tyburn* on the 27th. 1695.
Alſo an Account of his Behavour in *Newgate* after Condemnation and his Dying words at the place of Execution, &c.

London, Printed for T. Hobs 1695.

Fig. 1. Title page of *Account of Coppinger*.
REPRODUCED WITH PERMISSION BY ROSENBACH MUSEUM AND LIBRARY, PHILADELPHIA, PENNSYLVANIA.

"masterless man," a criminal whose inappropriately channeled talents lead to his ruin, preserving the structures of society. By omitting biographical information, *Account of Coppinger* seals its subject's association with uncontrolled and dangerous power.

Account of Coppinger's bid for power and its differences from *Life of Hayns*'s approach are evident in the two physical artifacts. Although both books use blackletter type and rule borders on their title pages, typographical styles beginning to lose currency in this period, *Account of Coppinger*'s text is much more sloppily printed, with broken type throughout, and the compositor was forced to reduce type size on page eleven when he realized the text would not fit into the twelve pages allotted. In contrast, *Life of Hayns*'s neatness, more extensive length, and consistent modulations between roman and italic type set it apart from other criminal narratives.

Account of Coppinger's title page lists the book as "Printed for T. Hobs." Indeed, this book, like Coppinger's life, is nasty, brutish, and short, but as I have not been able to locate another text with this imprint name, I suspect it may be false. This biography, like some later actor biographies and contemporary criminal biographies, was a shadowy publication from what Michael Harris calls the "alternative book trade," or those booksellers and printers who operated outside of the legitimate world of the Stationer's Company records, copyright (such as it was), and other criteria of printing respectability. On the other hand, *Life of Hayns*'s imprint line reads, "Printed for J. Nutt, near Stationers-Hall," and John Nutt is one of the best-known publishers of the early eighteenth century.[18] Thus *Life of Hayns* from the outset claims a slightly different subject position for its protagonist: he is within the purview of the professionally recognizable.

Whereas *Account of Coppinger*'s subject is indeed a criminal, and its author subsumes the actor's skill to the criminal's purposes, *Life of Hayns*, the biography of a popular (if troublesome) London and provincial comedian, adopts the style, structure, and some characteristics of criminal biography to illuminate Hayns's acting talent. Coppinger's life shows an escalating seriousness of crimes; Hayns's is a sequence of practical jokes, like the collections of jest books that continue in popularity throughout the eighteenth century.[19] *Life of Hayns* does not end with the actor's execution (he died a natural death); in fact, Hayns does not even die at the end, he just exits with some bad verse. Most important, Hayns doesn't steal physi-

cal property. Thomas reassures any readers who might find Hayns's powers of imposture menacing that Hayns's "Designs and Strategems,
aspir[ed] more to an Aiery Feast, the pleasure of a Light Jest, than from
any sordid hunger after an Avaritious Cheat. . . . His Over-reaches were no
Notorious Invasions of Right and Property; He made no extraordinary
Incursions, excepting only into the Female Quarters."[20]

The potential threat of Hayns's imposture is lightened by Thomas's
assertion that Hayns does not overstep the social bounds of "right" nor
does he commit capital crimes against property, like Coppinger. Donald
Hay, Lincoln Faller, and other criminologists of this period stress its growing urge to relegislate and enforce penalties for crime against property primarily as a way of separating poor from rich, governed from governing.[21]
That *Life of Hayns* exempts its rogue-protagonist from this—except, of
course, his "Incursions" upon the propertied bodies of women—significantly removes him from association with the menacing criminal class.
Like a gentleman who eschews working for mere gain, Hayns uses his acting skill only for his and others' amusement, assuming a casual, aristocratic attitude toward his talent. Hayns's acting is not "real" work, but neither
is it crime. His effortless native talent does not contribute to economic
production, but neither does it undermine that system.

Like *Account of Coppinger, Life of Hayns* is fundamentally a chronological sequence of Hayns's supposed pranks. Echoing early novelists and
other biographers, Thomas assures readers of his text's veracity, stating he
will "assert nothing in this following Account, but what many who knew
him, and are still alive can attest, and which I have had from his own
Mouth." He has "inserted several of his [Hayns's] own Lines as they were
made, and on what occasion, whereby you may believe that his Memoirs
are not fictitious" (A4r–A4v). However, Kenneth M. Cameron and the
editors of *The Biographical Dictionary* have concluded that *Life of Hayns*
"contains such a mixture of quixotically recorded fact and merely incredible fiction that perfect separation of the two is not now possible."[22] Indeed,
Tom Brown agrees in his *Letters from the Dead to the Living* (1702), when
he addresses Hayns: "a Thousand stories of other People he [Thomas] has
father'd upon you, and the truth on't is, the Adventures of thy Life, if truly
set down, are so Romantick, that few besides thy acquaintance would be
able to distinguish between the History and the Fable." Brown continues

by reassuring Hayns that "after this rate the Lives of all Illustrious Persons, whether Ancient or Modern have been written."[23] Jokingly, Brown links this biography to the history of the genre as well as to the "Illustrious," who are the usual subjects of biography.

Hayns's adventures begin with a brief description of his youth. We learn little—not even the year of his birth. Hayns "was put to St. *Martin's* School, where his extraordinary progress raised admiration in all that knew him, Wit, Memory, and all that is capable of making a learn'd Man were found in him, which mov'd some Gentlemen, to have him sent to *Oxford*, here he lost nothing of the Applause he had before attain'd to, but adding dayly to it . . ." (1-2). This breathless sentence runs for another page, after which Hayns takes his degree "which scarce had he perform'd, when down comes certain strowling Players" (4). Hayns joins them.

Thomas does not describe the early blooming of Hayns's talent. The strolling manager, John Coysh, simply sees Hayns and guesses "which way his Genius might tend" (4); asking Hayns to join his company, "he no sooner proposes but *Hayns* embraces: *Metamorphoses* his Cap and Gown to a Plum[e] of Feathers, and a *Persian* Robe; sees a large Prospect of felicity in his future journying from Town to Town, when he may indulge himself in Wine, Women, and other such moderate things" (5). Thomas casts Hayns's ambition not in terms of his need to act, but his desire to lead the roguish life acting would allow. An anonymous elegy similarly stresses the reasons Hayns uses imposture:

> High were thy Thoughts and soaring thy designs,
> Above thy Station, not above thy Lines.
> Thy various Postures in all Plays were such,
> Exceeding *Monsieur, Spaniards,* and the *Dutch.*
> In Potent Glasses when the Wine was clear,
> Thy very looks declar'd thy mind was there.
> Awful, Majestick, on the Stage at sight,
> To play, (not work) was all thy chief delight:
> Instead of Danger and of hateful Bullets,
> Roast Beef and Goose, with harmless eggs of Pullets.
> These were the Wars in which he did Engage,
> Began with courage and so left the Stage.[24]

Like Thomas, this poet mitigates Hayns's threatening conduct: though he has social aspirations, he is still not "above" his stage lines; he acted only in order to procure better meals for himself.

The biography tells little of his subsequent training: for example, that he performed with the Hatton Garden company, which, as the *Biographical Dictionary* tells us, was the "nursery" for both patent companies.[25] Readers learn that Hayns merely presented himself at Drury Lane and became an instant success when he replaced John Lacy as Bayes in *The Rehearsal*. The implication is that this actor's—and perhaps all actors'—talent is inherent, unschooled, "natural." His "Wit, Memory," and inventiveness seem to be all that is necessary for an acting career. These qualities instantly impress others and spur his upward mobility, allowing him to play some of his higher-class impersonations. This text explores Hayns's position on the social continuum stretching from criminal/rogue to gentleman and, even as it records his roguish exploits, distinguishes him from "vagrants" such as Coppinger.

Hayns never works at his craft in this book; indeed, its adventures mostly describe his time away from the London stage, the time that English readers would presumably know least about. He dances to great applause for the French court; he masquerades as a French count, a duke, a "Lord," and an attorney. The pope himself is so pleased with Hayns that he causes Hayns's picture "to be drawn, by one of the most Famous Painters *Rome* then afforded, holding the Pope's Picture in his hand, and smiling on it" (60–1). The biography states that "*Hayns* could humour all Personages, and accommodate himself to all Places" (8). Though Thomas also depicts Hayns adopting "low" roles, he most often shows how impersonation lets an actor slip seamlessly into higher social classes. At one point, Thomas speculates on Hayns's social motivations by projecting Hayns's thoughts after he has returned from the Continent: "What? Says he, I who now drink my *Burgundy* and *Champaign*, revel with the Peers of *France*, and riot with the most Renown'd Ladies of *Europe*; can I be content to be reduced to Belch, be a Companion to every Rope Dancer, and be my own Footman? No, No!" (6). Such a soliloquy shows consciousness of the actor's ambiguous social status and the dissatisfaction that arises when once someone in the lower orders tastes high pleasures. And though Hayns himself never permanently possesses these pleasures and never becomes anything besides a popular performer, the narrative suggests the

heights achievable through one's native talent and proposes other avenues to status besides birth and politics. By surreptitiously encouraging unsanctioned ambition, Hayns's claim about actors' potential is more unsettling than Coppinger's. Though Thomas protests otherwise, the instability of Hayns's social position wrought by his mercurial natural talent serves to undermine social hierarchies. The textual Hayns demonstrates that social authority is, in fact, merely a performance on a broader public stage.

An example illustrates these points. Hayns once masquerades as theatrical authority, a patentee. After Hayns returns from a company-sponsored foray to France, he is obliged by an irritated leading actor and manager of the company, Charles Hart, to play a minor role. Hayns, "being vex'd at the slight Mr. Hart had put upon him" (24), mocks Hart during the performance, which earns him one of his numerous dismissals from the company.[26] As revenge, Hayns impersonates a theater patentee to hire a parson for the company. This parson unsuspectingly enrages the players—Hart in particular—by ringing a bell through the players' street in the early morning, calling them to prayers. When Hart informs this parson how Hayns has manipulated him through his patentee performance, the parson complains to his brawny son, who then challenges Hayns to a duel. Hayns escapes by impersonation once again, by pretending to be an invincible duelist.

This anecdote dramatizes the conflict between the renegade actor and the theatrical establishment, represented by Charles Hart. Michael Quinn has argued that the modern celebrity disrupts the organization of the acting company because this person cannot work in ensemble structure; because he or she "threatens to subvert the economic structure of authority" within a company's budget; and because the presence of a star performer upsets critical evaluation of the aesthetic whole.[27] Hayns's tumultuous relationship with the Drury Lane company displays all three of these elements. Hayns's history with the London companies was one of sporadic employment and frequent desertions and dismissals, as far as we can tell from the extant records. Yet Hayns assumes that his native talent reserves him the privilege of choice stage roles, and when this privilege is denied, he exacts personal and economic retribution. He uses that acting talent against the acting authorities. When the king hears the parson story, he, "being mightily taken with the contrivance, sent for *Jo.* who gave him an account of the whole business; upon which the King remanded him back

to the playhouse" (32). Hayns's ridicule of theatrical hierarchy actually becomes his (re)entrance ticket to that hierarchy. Since this whole anecdote turns on Hayns's pretending to be various authorities, the text warns spectators of their own credulity and vulnerability to the performance of authority. Even people in the business, like Hart, can be duped, and even those charged with maintaining authority, like the king, may be amused into disrupting it, thus showing a problematic critical reception of the performance, in Quinn's terms.

This text's juggling of roguery and respectability and its resultant questioning of public performances of authority suggest a relationship with other negotiations of theatrical authority occurring near the time of its publication. Recent events had thrown into question who really *was* in charge of the theater and what ends it served. In 1695, the same year *Account of Coppinger* was published, a group of leading actors including Thomas Betterton but not, apparently, Jo Hayns, broke from Christopher Rich's tyrannical management of the united company over issues of wages, benefits, and assignment of roles. As the 1694 "Petition of the Players" states, Rich's policies were "tending to the ruine and destruction of the Company & treateing us not as we were the Kings & Queens servants but the Claimers slaves."[28] And the character Critick from *A Comparison between the Two Stages* (1702)—no friend to actors—describes Rich as "a snarling old Lawyer Master and Sovreign; a waspish, ignorant pettifogger in Law and Poetry; one who understands Poetry no more than Algebra."[29] Both accounts characterize him in terms of abused authority and ignorance. Since Rich held the two royal patents granted by Charles II, the actors needed a special license to perform, which they received. So while this rebellion acknowledges the crown's control over the theaters, the Lincoln's Inn Fields cooperative actors answered now primarily to themselves and their audiences rather than to businessmen and speculators.

Actor-managers would soon dominate some of the most successful companies of the eighteenth century. Other outsiders angled for theatrical control in other ways. The controversy arising from the publication of Jeremy Collier's *Short View of the Immorality and Profaneness of the English Stage* (1698) raised questions as to the morality of contemporary stage productions and personnel and asked, by implication, who should regulate them.[30] A newer genre, theater criticism, allows the self-appointed authorities in the pit to try to sway public opinion to regulate the theater. There

is a sense that control of the theaters and the enigmatic acting force was up for grabs, amenable to all kinds of influences.

We can understand actor biography as a type of theatrical criticism, in which authors attempt to express, define, and judge actors' talent and the extent of their growing cultural authority, both in the governance of the theaters and in the ordering of the larger society. Even the texts' authorship contributes to our understanding of these critical aims. *Account of Coppinger* was anonymous, like many criminal biographies. But *Hayns's* author Tobyas Thomas was himself an actor.[31] We know that Thomas and twenty-one others were to be sworn as "comedians in ordinary" on 23 February 1702 as part of the Drury Lane company, and the *London Stage* lists him as part of that company from 1696 to 1700, playing various minor roles.[32] In Tom Brown's *Letters from the Dead to the Living,* one of Hayns's living friends at Will's coffeehouse writes, "since you left this Upper World, your Life has been written by a Brother Player, who pretends he received all his Memoirs from your own Mouth a little before you made a leap into the Dark; and really you are beholding to the fellow, for he makes you a Master of Arts at the University, tho you never took a Degree there."[33] Perhaps Thomas was a friend of Hayns, or perhaps he was merely trying to cash in on Hayns's recent death—or, most likely, both.[34]

Thomas was the first insider to pen a version of the theatrical life, to add the performer's voice to the chorus of external observers (moralists, investors, politicians, drama historians) vying to control the image of the performer and the social role of the theater. In *Life of Hayns,* a *player* presents a player and his talent. The mystification of this talent—its vague origins, its antisocial expressions, its development without training—helps reserve the professional acting arena for those already in the know. Hayns's one possible credential—his invented degree—is immediately exposed as a scam. Paradoxically, then, by using the popular genre of the rogue biography, *Life of Hayns* keeps secret the actual methods of acting from its readers (though not its sometimes distressing consequences for the naïve). For all of its differences from *Coppinger, Hayns* also demonstrates the alarming "sufficiency" of actors who serve as their own authorities and sources of power.

Neither *Account of Coppinger* nor *Life of Hayns* addresses the ancients and moderns controversy directly, and thus neither overtly claims the authority of either ancient precedent or modern knowledge. There are no

Latin tags, classical references, or comparisons to Roscius—those we will see in the next section. Yet the way in which each biographer stakes his subject's claim for attention connects each text to the controversy. The protagonists of these two biographies do not need the classical training and examples of ancient texts. Since no formal acting manuals existed, the "ancients" position on the art needed to be constructed from oratory and anecdote, from the classical dramatic texts themselves, and from the writings of ancient aesthetic philosophers. This led in part to the kind of stilted oratorical declamation about which post-Garrick critics will complain and label "old-fashioned," for example, in reference to the acting style of James Quin. The rogue-actor biographies construct their subjects' successes out of their own inherent talent, not through inherited authorities. As the author of *Hayns* writes, Hayns's life was "all of a Piece, the Comedian both on and off the Stage" (A3r)—and, one might add, on the page. As described in these biographies, the rogue-actors' talent is honed on the street, through experiment and escapade, through the empirical attempts of life that sometimes fail. Their talent is not even closely identified with the playhouse, where they would take their places in the company power structures and mouth the lines of others. This type of "modern" power, disconnected from traditional hierarchical structures, is what gives these narratives their vividness and begins to suggest the unconventional power of the celebrity.

But what happens with this "modern" form of actor authority is another story. Both texts' uneasy need to contain their protagonists' energy suggests the dangers of following one's own talent and warns the society that allows individuals to ignore established authority. In *Coppinger,* inherent talent is viewed as uncontrolled and antisocial, destructive to property. In *Hayns,* the "message" is less punitive, since Hayns, of course, did not hang at Tyburn. The narrative downgrades crime into tricks harmless to property or to the authority it symbolized and portrays Hayns as a jester with genteel pretensions rather than as a criminal. *Life of Hayns,* in fact, best supports Hal Gladfelder's rereading of criminal texts as something other than containment narratives. He counters, "the ideological burden of most criminal biographies is, as both Faller and Richetti demonstrate, to reaffirm the legitimacy of legal authority, but that this constitutes their principal interest, even on the level of ideology, is questionable." Pleasure in reading these narratives comes from their "stirring up of . . . very

subversive possibilities."[35] His analysis cannily describes nascent celebrity, the figure who appeals yet repulses. These two biographies admit to the power of the actor and speculate as to its source in a manner that seems both fascinated and fearful. The next thespian biographies published posit a different source of authority, though they share in the same conflicted responses.

38

THE GENTLEMEN AND THE ANCIENTS:
THOMAS BETTERTON

Charles Gildon's *The Life of Mr. Thomas Betterton, the Late Eminent Tragedian* (1710), the main focus of this section, shows a much clearer appeal to authority than the two rogue biographies. Wilbur Samuel Howell, Joseph Roach, and others have traced Gildon's French and classical sources for *Life of Betterton,* concluding that most of this work was "borrowed" from other authors.[36] Gildon quotes classical authorities, suggests that readers admire and emulate these authorities, and attempts to return his contemporary theater to the luster of the classical past: to "raise the Stage from the present Neglect it lies under."[37]

But while its many classical antecedents and components have been acknowledged, no one has yet discussed how all of this material affects the actor's cultural position as projected by this text. Though we may disagree about the book's generic categorization, Gildon does call it a "Life," and we need to look at it asking the same questions we would ask of other biographies: What kind of life does it show? What are its implications for the type of person it depicts? And, in the context of this present study, what are the claims to authority that this version of a life raises and deflects?

Unlike those of Coppinger and Hayns, Betterton's life was not represented mainly by his biography. The *Biographical Dictionary* shows the wealth of information extant on this gifted and public-minded man.[38] Most contemporary print sources praise him. Even the splenetic Critick of *A Comparison between the Two Stages* admits Betterton's merit, although deploring his forays into playwriting: "*Batterton* [*sic*] is a very honest Fellow, and has all along been bred on the Stage; he's not only a good Actor, but in the number of wretched Poets now a Days, he may pass, at least for a good Judge of Poetry; and I shou'd not ha' scrupled him my particular Favour, if he had not play'd the Fool, and writ himself."[39] Except for some

of the verse satirists, writers about the stage admired Betterton's professional and private lives. John Downes, who knew Betterton for over forty years, praises him throughout *Roscius Anglicanus*.[40]

Written nine years after Thomas's *Life of Hayns*, Gildon's *Life of Betterton* does not acknowledge *Life of Hayns* as a precursor and seems not to owe anything to its example. Indeed, the rogue-actor image *Hayns* presents is precisely that which *Betterton* wants to disavow. Like *Account of Coppinger* and *Life of Hayns*, *Life of Betterton* uses established—if very different—generic models, but the later biography presents its subject as a moral and respectable gentleman who makes important improvements to stage scenery, marries prudently, and becomes the leading actor of his day. Betterton is born on page five and dies on page eleven; the rest of the 176-page *Life* flashes back to a supposed visit with the aged actor during which "Betterton" lectured on emotion, gesture, and speech. Gildon then appends Betterton's play, *The Amorous Widow*.

Through the Betterton lecture, Gildon defines and thus defends acting skill in terms of rhetoric and oratory, just as Overbury countered the injurious image of Stephens's "common player" by comparing the actor to a "grave Orator." Gildon excuses his use of Betterton as a rhetorical device by calling on classical precedents: "*Plato* and *Xenophon* introduce *Socrates* in their Discourses, to give greater Authority to what they say. . . . I shall, therefore, make the same use of Mr. *Betterton*" (3). Readers could alternatively see Betterton as reduced to a device for Gildon's words, or they could view him as ascending to the hallowed seat of Socrates.

The words Gildon places in Betterton's mouth mostly come from turn-of-the-century advocates of the "ancients," primarily French neoclassical critics and their followers. Gildon declares on his title page that he will present "[t]he Judgment of the late Ingenious *Monsieur de St. Evremond*, upon the Italian and French Music and Opera's." Levine has decisively shown that Charles St. Evremond, like many intellectuals of the time, embraced elements of both the moderns and the ancients, showing the two sides' complex interdependency:

[I]t seems that [St. Evremond] preferred the moderns from the outset. . . . Apparently, the exile whose political career had more than once been compromised by the criticism of authority, never did become reconciled to the importance of the rules. Nor did Saint-Evremond ever lose his taste for

the theater. From the very beginning, he was an ardent admirer of Corneille, who, of course, had had his own memorable battle with the Academy. . . . Corneille wished to reconcile the teaching of the ancients with the conditions of the modern stage, to pay homage to the rules and yet preserve a modest freedom for the artist to invent and experiment. Moreover, like most of the ancients, he defended almost every innovation with an appeal to classical precedent![41]

Wilbur Samuel Howell notes that one of Gildon's sources was the English translation of Michel La Faucheur's *Traitté de l'action de l'orator* (1657), and Roach has argued that Gildon also took much from Thomas Wright's *The Passions of the Minde* (1604).[42] Gildon defends himself from accusations of plagiarism from the French by passing the buck: "but then the *French* drew most of them [rules of oratory] from *Quintilian* and other Authors" (ix). He sees himself as a popularizer of such theories, and he adds modern appeal by supplying his readers with more relevant English examples, "[o]bservations more peculiar to the present Age" (x), primarily Shakespeare. He admits the poverty of serious writing about acting, which forced him "to bring my Examples from *Oratory* more than from the *Drama*. But if this [book] meets with the Approbation of the Learned, I may perhaps publish a Treatise for the Stage alone" (x).

Gildon's borrowing should not diminish his accomplishment and innovation. While oratory, rhetoric, physiology, and acting had always been linked from classical times, Gildon is the first to appropriate the English respect for high literary traditions to rearrange the hierarchy of importance so that acting took center stage among these related topics. No English writer before him had considered acting worthy of sober and detailed treatment or presented it as an *art*: "As I am (as far as I know) the first, who in *English* has attempted this Subject, in the Extent of the Discourse before you, so I am apt to believe, that I have pretty well exhausted the Matter; and laid down such *General* and *Particular Rules,* as may raise the Stage from the present Neglect it lies under" (vii).

Gildon's passion for rules, itself a neoclassical tendency, is evident in the formal systems of his numerous critical works, such as *A Grammar of the English Tongue* (1711), *The Complete Art of Poetry* (1718), *A New Project for the Regulation of the Stage* (1720), and *The Laws of Poetry* (1720). Writing about dramatic composition, Gildon upheld the ancients' rules and

unities, in opposition to the irregular moderns. As he states in *The Complete Art,* "To discourage such [pretenders to playwriting], and inspire those to whom Nature has given a *Genius,* I publish these Rules, which if the Managers of the House cou'd understand, and would study, we might hope to see a glorious Stage."[43] The rules comprising the body of *Betterton* begin with "Gildon's" similar complaint to "Betterton" about the present theater managers. They cannot teach acting to their employees because they themselves are not masters of the art: "I have often wish'd, therefore, that some Men of good Sense, and acquainted with the *Graces of Action* and *Speaking,* would lay down some Rules, by which young Beginners might direct themselves to that Perfection, which every body is sensible is extremely (and perhaps always has been) wanted on our Stage. . . . a System of *Acting,* which might be a Rule to future Players" (17). Gildon's complaints and his call for external control of acting by "some Men of good Sense" may simply reflect his disgust at having his plays spurned by the three actor-managers then controlling the only theater in London. Gildon thus appeals ultimately to authorities outside of the theatrical establishment—perhaps, modestly, to himself or to other much-maligned critics and dramatists, such as John Dennis, a sometime collaborator.

Betterton worries that young men "vainly imagine themselves Masters of that *Art,* which perfectly to attain, requires a studious Application of a Man's whole Life," and so he implores them to "study the Graces of ACTION and UTTERANCE" (15, 16). Betterton states, "A Mastery in these two Parts is what compleats an Actor" (33). The purpose of the player's twofold mastery is to "vary with his Argument, that is, carry the Person in all his Manners and Qualities with him in every Action and Passion; he must transform himself into every Person he represents, since he is to act all sorts of Actions and Passions" (34). He elaborates on the appropriate use of gestures and describes the "*Government, Order,* and *Balance*" of the whole body, then the head, eyes, eyebrows, face, hands (57). Next he considers the qualities and defects of speech. The orderliness of his elaboration contrasts starkly with the concept of acting portrayed by the rogue-actor biographies: for Thomas, acting was an impromptu art of life itself, enabling Hayns to scramble through his rollicking adventures; for Gildon, acting is a noble public art, an extension of rhetoric used to control emotion and elicit proper audience response from the stage.[44]

Yet while Gildon focuses on system and rule, he also admits that they

are not all that is necessary for good art of any kind. Betterton states that "those, who have any true Genius to *Playing*, will find such particular Instructions, as may be of very great use to them; and this Art, as well as most others, but especially *Poetry*, delivers such Rules, that are not easily understood without a *Genius*" (57). In supporting such arguments, Betterton refers to stage contemporaries in addition to classical writers. To prove the interdependency of "Genius" and learning, Betterton shows how Elizabeth Barry's talent could save a bad play. Acting opposite her for many years, he can affirm that her "[a]ction is always just, and produc'd naturally by the Sentiments of the Part, which she acts, and she every where observes those Rules prescrib'd to the Poets by *Horace*, and which equally reach the Actors" (39). Though Gildon does not explain how an actress like Barry might come by a familiarity with Horace, he notes her habit of leaving the action of the part to nature and warns: "Tho a great Genius may do this, yet Art must be consulted in the Study of the larger Share of the Professors of this Art" (41). As *Life of Hayns* made concession to traditional authority, so does *Life of Betterton* admit the necessity of something other than blind imitation of the ancients. Gildon's type of acting treatise, emphasizing "Rules," continued to be published throughout the century, joined by other works that stress the "Genius" of individual performers and performances. In biography, as these texts demonstrate, different forms of authority collide and combine.

Over the course of Gildon's own life, his position vis-à-vis the ancients and moderns controversy contained elements of both sides. Gildon's efforts to advance French neoclassical criticism in England have been remarked by J. W. H. Atkins in *English Literary Criticism*, but his admiration for Dryden and other modern writers, as J. C. Maxwell has shown, and his revisions to Langbaine's playlists, as Paulina Kewes has shown, places Gildon with the "moderns." My reading of *Life of Betterton* can perhaps soften G. L. Anderson's claim that Gildon was innovative in his earlier work, but his "transition from 'modern' to 'ancient' is virtually complete by 1710."[45] The key lies in Gildon's own negotiations with cultural authority. While trying to establish a proper social space for players, Gildon himself was struggling for position at the time of *Life of Betterton*. Dismissed by many as a hack and linked until his death to the infamous bookseller Edmund Curll, Gildon not only exposes his own classical learning, but he shows his good taste by dedicating his biography to Richard

Steele, who, though later a dramatist and theater manager, was in 1710 promoting refinement through the cultural conduit of the *Tatler*. Gildon's rhetorical methods recall exactly those he employs within the biography itself: trying to raise his writing and his reputation as a writer to respectability through association with acknowledged, if contested, cultural authorities.[46] Like his subject Thomas Betterton, Gildon was caught between his self-presentation as a learned writer and his profession as an author, writing for money.

In *Life of Betterton*, at least, Gildon was able to counter some of the unsavory associations of acting by stressing particular qualities of Betterton's character. Classical learning comprised the bulk of education for upper-class males. Most actors would thus have been denied this type of education because of their class origins, and even as late as 1798, writers would comment on the effects of its absence: the biographer of the actor John Palmer states, "His defects were ascribable to the want of a classical education, hence his mind manifested occasionally a lamentable want of taste and discrimination, and animal powers were often resorted to" instead of intellectual powers.[47] Gildon's biography took the radical—shall we say modern?—step of presenting the actor as a gentleman, by showing Betterton's conversation and bearing informed by classical authority and by providing his subject with other accoutrements of gentility. Gildon's Betterton is modest and self-effacing. Like a true gentleman, Betterton has never allowed his plays to be published, as Gildon notes. When he lectures, Betterton reads not his own work, but a paper "by a Friend of mine" to which, however, "I confess I contributed all, that I was able" (11). Although he quotes Greek and Latin authorities, he admits that he cites translations because of his own educational deficiency (17), acknowledging his limitations and eliminating the threat of an overeducated, uppity actor from whom some readers may have been reluctant to take instruction.[48] Though Thomas claims an Oxford M.A. for Hayns, we never see any textual proof of his educational accomplishments. But through educated references, Betterton is depicted as an authority in a great chain of deference to other authorities, thus palliating the threat of class anarchy suggested by actors like Hayns. Betterton even decries the crass upward mobility encouraged by recent national prosperity: "[T]he multiplying Avenues to Wealth, whose Number increasing, increase likewise the Number of those, who are drawn into the Pursuit of Riches; which as it spreads a mean and

private Spirit, of necessary Consequence makes the love of the Public more weak and Languishing" (13). *Betterton* develops the strain we noted in Thomas's comments on Hayns's "Over-reaches," that Betterton is intelligent and respectful enough of the social order not only to control his own power of imposture but to instruct others in maintaining their own social positions. One becomes worthy of a more respected position in the hierarchy by exhibiting respect for that hierarchy, not by brazen ambition or rebellion.

Gildon's genteel Betterton recommends proper conduct both on and off the stage for all players. Citing debauchery and other problems, Betterton says, "When I was a young Player under Sir *William Davenant,* we were under a much better Discipline, we were obliged to make our Study our Business, which our young Men do not think it their duty now to do" (15). (This is fairly amusing when one considers that Hayns was one of his contemporaries, though not in Davenant's company.) Actors must take the "greatest and most nice Care of their reputation imaginable" because "the Lives and Characters of those Persons, who are the Vehicles, as I may call them, of these Instructions [plays], must contribute very much to the Impression the Fable and Moral will make" (19, 20).[49] Collapsing the distinctions between a player's public and private lives thus makes *all* of the player's existence a public performance, as Betterton himself admits: "In short, I would have them keep a handsome Appearance with the World; to be really virtuous if they can, if not, at least, not to be publickly abandon'd to Follies and Vices, which render them contemptible to all" (22). Unlike Hayns's life of performance, Betterton's is, in Foucauldian terms, well disciplined through the public gaze of performance and print, an internalized set of rules to create roles that maintain rather than disrupt "Appearance" and social order. These internalized rules are encouraged through society's supposed system of rewards, and Betterton promises that such conduct would allow actors "more Leisure to study their Parts, raise their Reputation, and Salaries the sooner, and meet with Respect from all Men of Honesty and Sense" (22). Well known for the decency in which he and his wife lived, Betterton is the perfect dramatic persona to deliver these admonitions to the players.

However, Betterton's gentility is an unstable stance. With the proper words, like those Gildon provides for Betterton, the actor can very comfortably "appear" in the role of the distinguished, knowledgeable gentle-

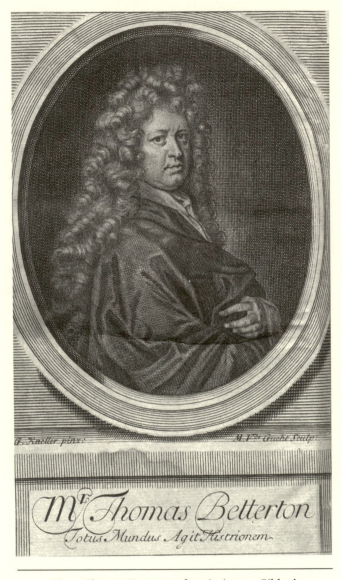

Fig. 2. Thomas Betterton, frontispiece to Gildon's
Life of Mr. Thomas Betterton.
REPRODUCED WITH PERMISSION BY THE EDWIN FORREST
COLLECTION, ANNENBERG RARE BOOK AND MANUSCRIPT
LIBRARY, UNIVERSITY OF PENNSYLVANIA.

man. *Life of Betterton* surreptitiously questions how much being a gentleman relies on the performance—on manners, posture, and correct speaking. What else constitutes gentility besides an appropriate and convincing performance? As Pierre Bourdieu has shown for twentieth-century France (though he does not use these terms), social class depends on knowing the correct lines, attitudes, and props to perform well one's social position.[50] What happens when a society allows a member to acquire all of this performative cultural capital without the actual standing that should support it? Will society be safe if that private life is not also well disciplined? Questions about social performance are raised unceasingly by actor biographies.

Life of Betterton's answers to these questions lie in its relation to its readers. While the handbook is most obviously for public performers, Gildon's systemization makes acting's method transparent, and so his text serves spectators as well as actors.[51] By translating and explaining his classical references, Gildon is able to speak to a wider range of readers than merely the well educated. In order to decode the gestures of performance, nonactors need to know what those gestures mean. To "raise" the stage, not only must the art's practitioners improve but so must the public's understanding of the art, so they can judge good performances from poor, especially as the theater audience drew from many social backgrounds besides the classically educated. If spectators know acting's rules, they will be less vulnerable to manipulation by tricksters like Coppinger and Hayns, who duped their gullible audiences. Gildon's approach to acting removes the threat of imposture—both onstage and in "real life"—by giving spectators its key. It empowers spectators, allowing them to see beyond the stage roles the actor played; biography encourages this intrusive speculation in private life so that actors will exhibit appropriate behavior.

Gildon's book educates both audience and actors because it responds to what Gildon views as a national theatrical crisis. The English stage is contrasted throughout with those of Greece, Rome, and the contemporary Continental stages to show its supposed sad decline. Despondency over the sorry state of modern arts in contrast to the glory of classical times was not new (and is still with us today). As Thomas Rymer claimed in *Tragedies of the Last Age* (1677), dramatic "[p]oetry is not now the same thing it was in those days of yore."[52] If the stage declines, a potent method

of inculcating cultural values (according, at least, to the moralists) also disappears. Thomas Betterton stands at the end of a noble tradition that Gildon hopes to reinvigorate: "[I]t may be said of Mr. BETTERTON, that he was the last of our *Tragedians*" (1). He grieves "the Loss of a Man so excellent in an Art that is now expiring, and for which Antiquity had so peculiar a Value" (2).

Gildon presents Betterton as the English Roscius to emphasize the crisis of the stage through the loss of one individual actor whose classical predecessor instructed famous Roman orators. Betterton tells readers: "'Twas the Skill the ancient Players of *Athens* and *Rome* had in this [action], which made them not only so much admir'd . . . but rais'd them to the Reputation of being Masters of two of the greatest Orators that *Athens* or *Rome* ever saw" (26). In the epilogue for Betterton's 7 April 1709 benefit that prefaces Gildon's *Life*, Mrs. Barry speaks: "What he has been, tho present Praise be dumb, / Shall haply be a *Theme* in Times to come, / As now we talk of ROSCIUS, and of *Rome*" (xiii). Gildon in fact excuses his biographical enterprise by explaining that in ancient Rome, "every Body was concern'd for the Death of *Roscius* the *Comedian*" (2), and thus a commemoration of his life is fitting. "Whether or not Mr. *Betterton* or *Roscius* make a just Parallel or not in their Merits as Actors, is difficult to know," considers Gildon, because "our Player excelled in both *Comedy* and *Tragedy*, the *Roman* only in the former, as far as we can discover" (2). This comparison enforces the notion of a lineage from classical times to the present; although actors are often reviled, the best of them deserve respect for the antiquity of their profession and the illustrious figures it produced in the past. By reminding readers that classical actors trained the orators, Gildon's comparison of Betterton to Roscius helps show that actors are the true "ancients."

Gildon's book may not have heralded a new age of improved British theater, but it did provide a new model of the actor for later biographers to emulate. While none of his successors identify *Life of Betterton*'s influence overtly, and none include the massive amount of oratorical information of Gildon's book, we can see the same attempts to capitalize on the genteel classically inspired image, for many of the same reasons.

The title of the next actor biography published, *Memoirs of the Life of Mr. Theophilus Keene, the Late Eminent Tragedian* (1718), closely recalls

that of Gildon's biography. A leading actor in the early years of the century, Theophilus Keene still remains for us a fairly shadowy figure. We know the stage roles he was assigned—Claudius in *Hamlet*, Bajazet in *Tamberlane*, Clytus in *The Rival Queens*—as the *Biographical Dictionary* says, roles of the "heavy, blunt sort."[53] The five-page biography section emphasizes Keene's dignity, and the eight following commemorative verses encourage respect by invoking the lineage of great actors Gildon's book suggested:

> But Time has shew'd in a preceeding Age
> The Ruins of the Fam'd *Athenian* Stage;
> And Death has in a different Series view'd
> *Roscius* and *Betterton* a-like Subdu'd.[54]

Keene follows Betterton, who follows Roscius. The Roscius reference becomes a commonplace comparison in biographies of gentlemen-actors. For example, in Benjamin Victor's *Memoirs of the Life of Barton Booth* (1733), Booth's schoolfellows honor him by referring to their young companion as Roscius, and Victor himself states, "Cicero observes, there are so many Qualifications requisite to make an accomplish'd Actor, that he thought it almost impossible to meet with them in one Man; yet, says he, I had the Happiness of seeing this Prodigy, *Roscius!*—We who have seen Mr. *Booth,* have enjoyed a like Happiness with Cicero."[55]

Though oratorical lessons separate from biography in most later theatrical texts, biographical uses of Roscius continue until the end of the eighteenth century, when "Roscius" has become almost synonymous with "Garrick."[56] Anointing one actor as Roscius establishes a hierarchy within the acting profession—a hierarchy, remember, that *Life of Hayns* had questioned. Yet the champions of Roscius and these gentleman-actors understand it as a meritocracy of disciplined talent and decent private life, not of arbitrary authority within the theater world—and certainly not of the unpredictable, rebellious trickery of *Coppinger* or *Hayns*. J. C. Maxwell states that "Gildon was certainly an accurate mirror of the intellectual fashions of the moment."[57] His *Life of Betterton* straddles the concerns of ancients and moderns in a conflicted bid for legitimacy, both for himself and for actors.

CONCLUSION: CONTAINING THE
CONTRADICTORY ACTOR

The gentleman-actor biographies demonstrate much stronger ties to the mainstream theatrical world (both classical and contemporary) than the rogue-actor biographies. Gildon indulged his opinions on theatrical topics from acting method to opera, while Thomas focused on Hayns's dramatic performances outside of established venues. Each work familiarizes its audiences with the player and with acting in a different manner: using the criminal narrative tradition, *Account of Coppinger* and *Life of Hayns* pull the actor out of his professional position into the broader context of society; using classical and continental authorities and gentlemanly posturings, *Life of Betterton* pulls that reader into the select world of the theater. Each narrative stance closes the distance between the reader and the actor, making the actor's native "modern" talent less threatening (in the rogue-actor biographies) and capitalizing on the ancients to increase respectability (in the gentleman-actor biographies). Each offers a way to explain and contain the actor's bid for cultural authority.

Levine speculates that the quarrel between the ancients and the moderns "was finally a draw in which the field was pretty much divided—the ancients commanding the humanities, and the moderns the sciences."[58] Though subjects of thespian biographies continue showing roguish traits, more of these texts follow the claims to respectability that *Life of Betterton* and *Memoirs of Keene* propose. These claims are made, however, through an innovative modern genre, thespian biography, and enabled by the modern invention of printing.

But it is not the modern or the ancient stance, the rogue or the gentleman image *alone* that is important, rather the presence of *both*. The tensions arising between the two open a new cultural space for those who could be—in the words of *Account of Coppinger*—"famously notorious" or for those who, like Betterton, could be common actors yet Roscius's heirs. Just as elements of the ancients and moderns controversy continued into the nineteenth century, representing different types of authority, so did these two images of performers persist, as biographers and critics continued to question the sources of acting talent and the implications for the exercise of that talent in society. The actor can be both rogue and gentleman, low and high, in the collective imagination. Individual actors will

accrue often conflicting elements to their public images: Hayns, for example, is a good-natured trickster, but he is also depicted as a malicious sharpster in Theophilus Lucas's *Lives of the Gamesters* (1714). Betterton could be Roscius, yet still be reprimanded for abused authority, as "Hayns" says in Robert Gould's "The Playhouse":

> Our Sharers, now so insolent are they,
> We Under-Actors must like Slaves obey;
> And toil and drudge, while they divide the Pay.
> Not *Busby* more Tyrannically Rules,
> Than *Be*——*n* among his Knaves and Fools.[59]

The image of a performer thus enters popular mythology and there, like the images of statesmen, military leaders, and others, accumulates comment and gossip, is used for partisan purposes, and takes on a public life of uncertain relation to the private person.

Through expanding print media, the images of actors and others become dissociated from their real-life referents. As Richard Dyer says about twentieth-century film stars, "The star phenomenon consists of everything that is publicly available about stars. . . . Star images are always extensive, multimedia, intertextual."[60] In present-day U.S. culture, characters from Sherlock Holmes to the *Star Trek* cast, from Oprah to Tom Cruise, accumulate public presences that, within certain rough boundaries, absorb many, sometimes contradictory, qualities.[61] But unlike the modern star, who can sue over unlicensed usage of his or her image because it has been defined as property, the eighteenth-century public figure can only watch as others profit from his or her image and ponder whether to retaliate in kind. The emerging capitalist order is not yet prepared for figures on the margins of society to control their own public presentations.

The actor's ability to be a rogue and a gentleman, high and low, and to draw from the authority that both stances enable, itself becomes a defining element of the player's presence in eighteenth-century discourse. This ambiguous, contradictory presence is what I claim to be a defining element of celebrity, one that the biographies surrounding *The Beggar's Opera* define much more clearly.

CHAPTER 2

Three Stories of Celebrity

The Beggar's Opera "BIOGRAPHIES"

Surely there is some secret magic in the
Beggars Opera, for ever since they first acted
it, which is thirty years ago, scarce a winter
has passed away, without its contributing to
make some actor famous, who
before was nobody.

*Authentic Memoirs of the Celebrated
Miss Nancy D*ws*n* (c. 1760)

WHILE ADDISON'S *Cato* (1713) and Cibber's *The Non-Juror* (1717) incited vigorous public commentary, the influence of *The Beggar's Opera* is unprecedented among eighteenth-century plays. The play not only had a spectacular first run, but it inspired many ballad opera imitations and vigorous public commentary. One other sign of its influence was its magical power, as the epigraph above notes, to turn

"nobodies" into "somebodies." The play's main characters and the actors who portrayed them were celebrated in verse, reproduced in prints, and advertised as appearing on china, screens, and fans—some of the first theatrical memorabilia.[1] Most important, they inspired the next group of thespian biographies: of Lavinia Fenton (Polly Peachum), of "Mackheath" (a mock biography, only slightly connected with Thomas Walker, who played this role), and of James Spiller (Matt o' the Mint).[2] The three performers concerned were not particularly popular, like Hayns, or bastions of theatrical authority, like Betterton. In fact, none of them had stellar theater records—until *The Beggar's Opera*. This play changed both their lives and the genre of thespian biography. Somehow, it transformed average performers into figures who received exceptional attention, and this chapter examines the play's celebrity alchemy.

The main difference between these texts and those of the previous chapter lies not only in their resulting from the play's success, but also in the way in which their narrators treated their subjects. We might expect the biographies written about such a popular play to be fawning and adulatory, but we would be wrong. These narrators handle their subjects harshly. The biographies were not written for the usual eighteenth-century reason, to honor their subjects. Instead, using different forms of discourse—sexual, political, cultural—these biographies respond to the success of *The Beggar's Opera* and try to suppress the popularity of their star-subjects. Kristina Straub in *Sexual Suspects* suggests that such texts negotiate a changing sexual landscape and reveal a new source of control over players in the audience's gaze. She does not mention the biographies derived from *The Beggar's Opera*, but her argument applies to them: their authors are concerned about this perceived shift of theatrical control to the audience's debased tastes and about the theater's role in reinforcing these tastes. Like Gildon, these authors respond to a presumed national crisis in values, as manifested in the theater and in those employed there. These books respond to as well as provoke some of the first appearances of new cultural heroes and the transgressions associated with figures who challenge traditional authority to succeed in nontraditional ways.

In its parallels of criminals and statesmen, *The Beggar's Opera* investigates authority through its society's definitions of leaders and heroes (or

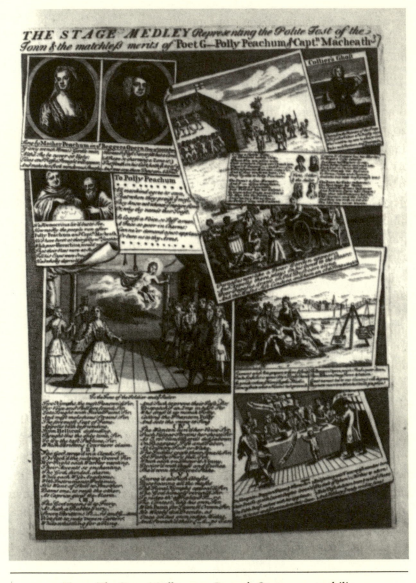

Fig. 3. *The Stage Medley,* rare *Beggar's Opera* memorabilia.

asks whether such categories are even possible), and so do these biographies. Interrogating concepts of heroism was nothing new to a country that had endured the power and leadership struggles of the seventeenth century. One source of such definitions is the classic literature familiar to the educated, where commemoration of a hero's life resulted from eventual triumph after lengthy trial. Nathan Bailey, for example, defines "hero" in his *Universal Etymological English Dictionary* (1721): "A great and illustrious Person, a Person of singular Valor, Worth, and Renown, among the Ancients, who although he was of mortal Race, was yet esteemed by the People to partake of Immortality, and after his Death was reckoned among the Gods."[3] For these heroes, as Richard Schickel writes, "it was understood that there was a logical progression to their achievements."[4] Although Leo Braudy reminds us that "Golden Ages of true worth and justified fame never existed" outside of the media that produced the fame, many believed in such ages.[5] Yet works such as Richard Steele's *The Christian Hero* (1701) and *The Conscious Lovers* (1722) and George Lillo's *The London Merchant* (1731) begin to celebrate heroes who lacked the prerequisites of noble blood or military glory. James William Johnson notes that eighteenth-century writers "made it possible for many men, many women, and many children to be heroes; and the life of anyone could provide examples of heroism."[6] Not everyone welcomed this "democratization" of the hero, as the ancients and moderns controversy continued in this questioning of cultural leaders.

Helped by the expanding print market, the "new hero" assumes unfamiliar qualities. Fame's transience was always a common theme for poets and religious writers, and this hero fulfilled their prophecies by claiming public regard for a month or year, rather than "eternal fame." As Pope writes in "An Essay on Criticism":

> No longer now that Golden Age appears,
> When *Patriarch-Wits* surviv'd a *thousand Years*;
> Now Length of *Fame* (our *second* Life) is lost,
> And bare Threescore is all ev'n That can boast.[7]

Like Hayns and his demonstration of native talent, these new heroes owe their fame more to luck or audacity than to diligence and virtue, and they

are not born into noble families where regard accompanies station. Public attention may be provoked by some singular act, but these figures continue in the public eye through the expanding popular press, eager for new material. Such attention initiates a kind of feedback mechanism, in which knowledge or gossip feeds the curiosity and desire for more knowledge or gossip. The resulting cumulative "media image" often becomes divorced from the incident that originally propelled the person into public notice—even from the person him- or herself—detaching the signifier/signified from the referent. Braudy contends that, by the twentieth century, "the ancient belief that fame was the crown of achievement had been replaced by the conviction that it was the only thing worthwhile at all," a process beginning at least in the eighteenth century, as we read of starstruck young people eager for the attention that the stage confers.[8] In 1785 George Anne Bellamy testifies to the lure of the theater: "The letters I received . . . from itinerant players applying to be engaged, amounted to an incredible number. They generally wrote in such as style, as to shew they all thought themselves Garricks and Cibbers."[9]

My general answer, then, to the question of how *The Beggar's Opera* encouraged these biographies is that they emerged from the play's elevation of performers to new social "heroes." They reacted to the nascent social category of the celebrity, whose fame derives more from the media than from worthy deeds. Both Isaac Kramnick and, more recently, J. Douglas Canfield have argued that *The Beggar's Opera* criticizes emergent capitalism, and these biographies reinforce such criticism in that they deplore the type of heroes created by a market-driven capitalist economy.[10] Cowen explains that "fame for actors and other entertainers increases relative to fame for moral leaders" because "commercialization provides better and more accurate standards for evaluating and discussing entertainers and other commercial figures than for assessing preachers."[11] Commercial success begins to become the measure for all forms of success. My paradoxical conclusion about the biographies' cumulative effect, however, is that the very act of protesting celebrities—disparaging their trivial personal problems, harmful influence, and unearned cultural power—only solidifies their public presence. Thus, unwillingly, the biographical spin-offs of *The Beggar's Opera* enable the creation of new cultural upstart "somebodies."

THE ACTRESS AS GOLD DIGGER: *The Life of Lavinia Beswick, Alias Fenton, Alias Polly Peachum*

The actress was a public woman in a society where that concept was fraught with ideological difficulties, since all women were intended to inhabit the private sphere. Modern scholars have only recently addressed this problem. Tracy C. Davis exposes Jürgen Habermas's gendered formulation of the public sphere by describing actresses' problematic relationship to the division between public (gendered male) and private (gendered female) realms: "They cannot be fully members of the public (in the sense that men can), they cannot be in the public without implicating their private and/or intimate status, they rarely form an effective counter-public resisting hegemonic ideology, they cannot retreat to a fully private existence, and their intimate lives become fair game (whether on the basis of speculation or fact) for public exposure."[12]

In early biography, an actor could be a gentlemanly "eminent tragedian" or a roguish "celebrated comedian," but public exposure of the actress consistently highlighted one particular aspect of her intimate life, her sexuality. As Claire Johnston has explained in her study of modern cinema, "the basic opposition which places man inside history, and woman as ahistoric and eternal" allows men more roles than women. Laura J. Rosenthal agrees: "Smith cannot act, Lee is a fool, Goodman is ugly and a thief, and Jervens eats too much. But the women all have the same flaw."[13] Merely by being a public woman, the eighteenth-century actress is a contradiction that encourages resolution into an "ahistoric, eternal" role: the whore. The first *Beggar's Opera* biography, *Life of Fenton*, uses and reinscribes this role for the play's female lead to undermine the actress's achievement and authority.

Deborah C. Payne has considered the two prominent critical views of eighteenth-century actresses, as victims or as emergent professionals.[14] Examining Robert Gould's "The Play-house" (1685), which is often cited by scholars who embrace the actress-as-victim position, she questions the use of Gould's poem as evidence for victimization, since Gould's career was undermined by his hostility toward some of the major actresses of his day. However, hostile responses to actresses, such as comments in the anonymous *Comparison between the Two Stages* or in the anonymous "Satyr on the Players" (1684–5), share Gould's detraction of actresses' sexu-

ality and unearned social position (though often expressed less severely). And most eighteenth-century actress biographies repeat attitudes that Gould's poem voices:

> An *Actress* now so fine a thing is thought,
> A Place at *Court* less eagerly is sought:
> As soon as in that *Roll* [*sic*] the Punks engross'd.
> Some Reverend Bawd does thus the Drab accost,
> *Now is the Time You may Your* Fortune *raise,*
> *And meet at once with* Pleasure, Wealth, *and* Praise;
>
> ·
>
> Th'Advice is took; and she hurries on,
> Fond to be kept, and in her Chariot shown;
> While Vulgar Drabs must meanly Trapes the Town.
> Against the Consequence she shuts her Eyes,
> For none at once were ever lewd and Wise:
> Thoughtless (like merry *Andrew* in his Pride)
> The higher Mounted we the more deride.
> In short the *Stage* (as *Dorset-Court* assures)
> Is but a *Hot-Bed* rais'd to force up Whores.[15]

In Gould's poem and the writings of numerous later commentators, actresses' presence in the public sphere is attributed to an aberration of their intimate life—their greed and sexuality—instead of to the qualities of other, male, participants in the public sphere: lack of talent, intellect, or education. The stage is a "Hot-Bed" that cultivates the lewdness potential in all women and "forces up" ambitious whores. Writers like Gould vilify actresses for using their sexuality to facilitate upward mobility.

Yet the actress who preserves her reputation for chastity is accused of acting above her station, as though actresses had the special social duty to be promiscuous. Numerous insinuations were printed about Anne Brace-girdle, who apparently did not confer many sexual favors. Colley Cibber reports the abuse suffered by an actress (Hester Santlow, later Booth) when, comporting herself modestly at the opera, she is accosted by a "military Gentleman" who took offense when she preferred to listen to the music instead of his advances.[16] The actress, like a criminal, misuses private property, but here the property is her own body. Her body, however,

is not hers; it is (or should be) the property of a man. Or, because it is the body of an actress, it is now the property of all men who can pay her price—admission to the theater. Actresses' successes are thus often attributed to the intervention of men, usually men who have possessed their bodies. For all of her excellence, Elizabeth Barry, for example, had a "bad ear" that could not be rectified without the ministrations and lessons of her lover, the earl of Rochester.[17] Straub explains: "Unlike actors, who are often touted, in the emergent professionalization of acting, as being 'of a good family,' actresses are most frequently presented as the 'property' of a higher class. This representation 'explains' their transgressions [of class and gender roles] in terms of a dominant class ideology without claiming an inherent class-based respectability for the feminine side of the profession."[18]

While narratives of gender can redefine even transgressive women as property, the acceptable method for a woman to advance socially was to consign her body and sexuality to marriage, as in Samuel Richardson's *Pamela* (1740–1). But even then, feminine upward mobility threatened some eighteenth-century readers, as reactions to Richardson's novel show. The protagonist of Fielding's *Shamela* is a "sham," or performance, because she fakes innocence to use her body for social climbing. Even Gildon's *Betterton* advises that actresses should "remember, that tho it may happen, that their parting with their Honour, and setting up for Creatures of Prey on all that address to them, may bring them in mercenary Advantages, yet that by keeping their Reputation entire, they heighten their Beauties, and would infallibly arrive at more Happiness (if not Wealth) in Marriages" (22–3). According to Rosenthal, this specter of inappropriate matrimonial matches is precisely what *caused* the emergence of the whore image: by imagining the actress as the unmarriable whore, society would be protected from such social climbers. [19] Gould's poem, Fielding's book, "Betterton's" kindly advice, and the biography of Lavinia Fenton contribute to a discourse that derides and blocks women's social aspirations.

Because of her sweet voice, her beauty, and the sympathy evoked by her character in *The Beggar's Opera*, Lavinia Fenton soon drew the attention of spectators, writers, and artists. The author of a prefatory biography to Gay's works (1760) informs us: "The person who acted *Polly*, 'till then obscure, became all at once the favourite of the town; her pictures were

engraved, and sold in great numbers; her life written; books of letters and verses to her published, and pamphlets made even of her sayings and jests."[20] Printers recognized a good market: the fictional printer "A. Moore" produced at least seven pieces of *Beggar's Opera* literature, including *The Life of Fenton* and the *Memoirs of Mackheath*, discussed in the next section.[21]

Because Polly lived in a dramatic world of deception and knavery, perceptions of Polly—and of Fenton herself—have always been conflicted. Is she an injured innocent or a wily manipulator? Toni-Lynn O'Shaughnessy argues against William Empson's cynical reading of Polly by showing that some writers of the 1730s remembered Fenton's first portrayal of the role as sweet and virtuous, and by noting Gay's completely unironic reprise of the character in his sequel *Polly* (1729).[22] However, O'Shaughnessy does admit that even in the play's first season, Fenton's Polly was also seen as a sexual predator. Smutty verse was attached to the Polly name in *The Twickenham Hotch-Potch* (1728) and in *Polly Peachum on Fire* (1728). The title page of the latter warns:

> Tho' the *Cocks* are all *running,* there's not enough Water,
> For the Girl is brimful of combustible Matter:
> Then play with your Buckets, and work for your Soul,
> Or the best Toast in Town will be burnt to a Coal.[23]

The *Craftsman* of 29 June 1728 announced the publication of "The Beggar's Opera Screen," which displayed engravings of "the principal Captives of the All-conquering Polly, . . . and on the Reverse their Amorous Letters and Declarations to that celebrated Warbler of Ribaldry." Polly receives "Amorous Letters" and warbles "Ribaldry": these sexualized views of Polly/Fenton result not only from contemporary views of actresses and the sexually charged world of *The Beggar's Opera,* but also because of Fenton's liaison with the duke of Bolton, for whom she left the stage on 19 June 1728. Social discourse, play character, and the actress herself merge to create a media image called "Polly" that holds in tension the innocent, modest Polly of the stage with the presumably sexual and socially ambitious actress who portrayed her. Fenton, as Rosenthal explains of all actresses, "threatened to blur the distinction between marriageable and unmarriageable women, ladies and whores, and even marriage and prostitution

itself."[24] The tension between the two actress images and the resultant role confusion parallels the rogue/gentleman division we examined in chapter 1.

The biography omits mention of her departure with the duke of Bolton, even though another advertisement from the 29 June *Craftsman* states the biography had been published by then. Though *Life of Fenton's* anonymous author tells us that "it cannot be said by her greatest Enemies, that she was ever a common Prostitute, as some would insinuate" (14), the book portrays "Polly" (it does not call her Fenton) as a good-natured harlot, unconcerned with modesty or morality, a characterization we examine more closely in the next chapter. The image of Polly thus is sexually charged even before she becomes Bolton's mistress. Through a series of amours (which may or may not be true), Polly escapes a low and illegitimate birth, gains entrance to the Lincoln's Inn Fields theater company, and wins the lead in *The Beggar's Opera,* though the famous play itself is barely mentioned in the book.[25] After leaving the stage, Lavinia Fenton never reappeared there: ironically, her success as a public career woman bought her freedom from publicity and career, allowing her to return to the "natural" private life of the eighteenth-century woman, as the kept "property" of an aristocratic male, in a later marriage that reestablishes traditional gender authority as it compromises class divisions. Very little about Fenton herself was published after the early 1730s, though she lived until 1760. However, the "Polly" mystique she established continued, turning "nobodies" into "somebodies."

What is the purpose of *Life of Fenton's* unyielding stress on its subject's sexuality? Above all, it denies her public achievement and condemns her path of upward mobility. As Laura J. Rosenthal has perceptively argued of actresses' representations on and off stage, "As long as the actress could not claim virtue, she could not parley her professionalized seductiveness into class mobility."[26] *The Life of Fenton* implies that low-born women should quietly remain low, instead of taking advantage of stage and print to publicize their availability. Polly's exaggerated lasciviousness does not produce a grotesque portrait but a humorous caricature of a sexual woman, mirroring the effect of *The Beggar's Opera,* in which lustful whores and predatory thieves provoke not fear but laughter. The humor deflates the threat of the actress, denying her any real captivating power, just as the narrator of *Life of Hayns* attempted to tame the antisocial tendencies of his

acting talent. *Life of Fenton* eschews the bitterness of Gould's satiric verse, employing comedy instead, which John J. Richetti notes as a dominant tone of contemporary whore biographies.[27] The few references to her acting talent focus on her ability to impersonate genteel manners: she now "lives in Ease and Plenty, keeps her Servants, and appears abroad in as much Magnificence as a Lady" (33); "I think she may pass for an accomplish'd worthy Lady, *if the Publick will allow an Actress the Title*" (47). The satiric tone betrays an unwillingness to "allow" her such a title, whatever the "Publick" might think. Though the prostitutes in *The Beggar's Opera* commend each other decorously, the audience never confuses them with "fine ladies"—that is why this joke works. *Life of Fenton's* narration mimics *The Beggar's Opera* by underhandedly insisting on some essential difference between actresses (low life) and ladies (high life), whom actresses can only impersonate, never be. The starstruck audience member reading this biography to discover what Lavinia Fenton is "really" like finds her a mere whore, artificially forced up into society. Yet, paradoxically, such a description of a vastly popular actress's talent may have had the unintended effect of proving that theatrical fame is available to any woman pretty enough for public display—who is also willing to have her reputation compromised, whether or not she actually misbehaves sexually.

The narrator's bemused stance toward Polly creates a pact of condescension with the reader, in which both agree that her acting talent need not be taken seriously. *Life of Fenton's* narrative voice creates a tension between specialness and averageness that haunts the celebrity's appeal. Braudy, Schickel, and Richard Dyer have all noted the simultaneous belief by audiences that stars are exotic creatures who possess rare talent, and that they are also "just like you and me," "average" people who have received lucky breaks and with whom we all can "identify."[28] An uncomfortable friction develops in the twentieth century when celebrity, according to Braudy, "in part . . . celebrates uniqueness, and in part . . . requires that uniqueness be exemplary and reproducible."[29] *Life of Fenton's* narration assumes that Fenton is indeed special because of her extraordinary (unfeminine) sexual drive; she is ordinary because, after all, lustfulness is expected of a woman in the public realm. Her rise is special because it is meteoric; it is average because she uses tools any woman possesses. Davis points out this contradictory and confusing status of all early actresses: "Because of their sex they are not allowed the public, yet they themselves

go about in public and embody publicity. They may convey the normative ideology of the private/intimate sphere yet they clearly do not confine themselves to it. *They are* neither *private citizens in the public sphere nor private women in the intimate sphere.*"[30] The actress's status thus embodies the social oppositions of *The Beggar's Opera.*

This first *Beggar's Opera* biography and its characterization of Fenton as sexual property disciplines the anomalous life of the popular, self-propelled actress into something understandable and familiar: in modern terms, a gold digger. *Life of Fenton* and other Polly memorabilia project a celebrity image that, as Dyer suggests, encapsulates certain poignant quandaries of celebrity culture. The image reflects "contradictions in ideology—whether within the dominant ideology, or between it and other subordinated/revolutionary ideologies"; the image can suppress a side, or "magically" reconcile the two, or hold them in tension.[31] "Polly" signifies the problematic social presence of the eighteenth-century actress. Though unconcerned with their subjects' sex lives, the two *Beggar's Opera* texts with male protagonists raise similar concerns about celebrity and its threat to social stability.

THE LURE OF CELEBRITY: *Memoirs concerning the Life and Manners of Captain Mackheath*

Unlike *Life of Fenton,* which ostensibly described a real person, the "memoirs" of "Mackheath" do not deal with the actor Thomas Walker, who played the original Macheath, but with the character Macheath. An example of the eighteenth-century genre of satiric or mock biography, this text continues the play's attack on Walpole and moralizes against political rapacity. The anonymous author deplores the harmful effects of *The Beggar's Opera* but hopes to use its characters and popularity to counter some of them. Collier worried about the effects of portraying corrupt clergy onstage; in the *Spectator,* nos. 65 and 75 (1711), Steele railed against spectators' admiration of Etherege's suave hero, Dorimant; in later centuries, we fret about television viewers imitating the Three Stooges, Murphy Brown, or Beavis and Butthead. Critics of *The Beggar's Opera* warned that its glamorous depiction of criminals would encourage criminality. In his preface to *Seven Sermons on Public Occasions,* Thomas Herring cites evidence:

"[S]everal Thieves and Street-robbers confessed in *Newgate*, that they raised their Courage at the Playhouse, by the Songs of their Hero *Macheath*, before they sallied forth on their desperate nocturnal Exploits."[32] Many others, including Daniel Defoe, spoke out against the dangers of this attractive highwayman.[33] The author of *Memoirs of Mackheath* is similarly preoccupied with the romanticization of both high and low criminals. In effect, this is a concern over the influence of celebrities.

Memoirs sustains the play's loose satiric identification of Macheath with Walpole. Advertised in the opposition journal, the *Craftsman,* on 18 May 1728, the book may have been written by a contributor. *Memoirs* chronicles "Captain" Macheath's career of cheating on his own band of thieves, perpetrating frauds, and hiding his wealth overseas—crimes against property. The narrator warns Macheath that his crimes will be detected, and of his inevitable punishment in the afterlife (an appeal to an even more powerful traditional authority). However, the narrator is more uneasy about the society that elevated such a figure to the status of "hero."[34] The book inquires "into the Degeneracy of our Morals: Let us see then how, and by what Degrees, a brave, a great, and a generous People became so corrupt, to be capable to look on and laugh at Fraud and Rapine, and to mistake a Highwayman, for a Heroe" (9). The book's first chapter attributes England's slip into "degeneracy" to the ascension of the Hanoverians and the Whigs, thus providing a political explanation for the rise of improper hero figures.

According to this writer, Macheath is an example of the pernicious new hero who gets ahead through unscrupulous methods, denying his true social station and avoiding honest work, criticism also leveled at the acting profession. The author exposes Macheath's evil actions "to undeceive my Fellow-Citizens, before whom he has been lately set upon the publick Stage as a Character of Heroism, if not Virtue" (7). This character's evil derives from the view of society he shares with his stage counterpart. After "the Captain" had "dissipated both his Morals and his Fortune . . . he saw no Reason why Property should be so unfairly distributed" (16–7). To remedy this unjust state, he decides to "remit himself to the Original State where all Men had a Right to all Things" (17). Disregarding the property rights so virulently defended by new legislation in the 1720s, Macheath advocates redistributing inherited wealth, which the narrator of *Memoirs* interprets as a return to Hobbesian barbarism.[35] Macheath's "large and

formidable Body" of gentlemanly dissipates will reorganize society: "not only the whole Community, but any Part of it, had a Right to dissolve it self and to erect another" (18). The threat of Macheath is that of Walpole and the Whigs: each would reconstruct the social order in nontraditional ways. This biography suggests the criminal consequences of such a realignment.

Memoirs shows the personal character of Macheath/Walpole to be as despicable as his socially destructive project. Macheath steals and betrays, but the book suggests that any kind of ambition could be immoral or criminal: "[T]he direct Paths to Happiness are Integrity and Content, however Mankind are led astray in the Search of it, among the Glare of Wealth and imaginary Dignities" (60). The book characterizes Macheath as someone who has "degenerate[d] from [his] Blood and Principles" (7), and so he does not live up to his social position. One must peacefully accept one's allotted place, whether low or high, rising only through integrity, and keeping one's elevated status through responsibly genteel conduct. Highwaymen and thieves—and players—can impersonate statesmen and nobility, but that does not change their essential natures. Those who act, whether in the theater or on the larger stage of life, endanger their societies, as antitheatricalists had warned for centuries.[36]

Memoirs, like *Life of Fenton* and, even earlier, *Account of Coppinger*, disapproves of (in fact, criminalizes) new ways of succeeding in society and reinforces the status quo. *Memoirs* criticizes the Walpolean method in serious tones, worried that audiences have missed the satire of *The Beggar's Opera* among its music and humor. The narrator of the anonymous *Thievery a-la-mode; or, The Fatal Encouragement* (1728) is similarly alarmed, noting that its young protagonist "could go into no Company, hear no Discourse, but what was taken up with the charming Characters of Captain *Macheath* and *Polly Peachum.* . . . Good God! cry'd he, as often as any Testimonies of this nature reach'd his Ears, of what use are now the great Examples drawn from the Heroes of Antiquity, or the more lively Instances of the present Worthies? . . . The Conquests of our fifth *Henry*! the Piety of the sixth! and Valour of the fam'd *Black Prince*! are Subjects too dull for the modish Conversation of these Times."[37]

Like *Life of Fenton*, *Memoirs*'s uneasiness over the conflation of highwayman and hero shows a concern with celebrity. The book reveals the real character of Macheath/Walpole to correct the glamorized image pop-

ularized by *The Beggar's Opera*. The media excitement surrounding the play obscures Gay's satire, and this author hopes to clarify Gay's point in the sober forum of prose. The author worries about the effects of celebrity: that handsome Thomas Walker as the dashing Macheath will blind spectators to the criminality of such socially destructive rogues as Walpole. Gay seems to have felt similarly, for in *Polly* he makes sure that no one will mistake the craven Macheath for a hero. The third *Beggar's Opera* biography takes pains to disabuse credulous spectators and readers in its demystification of its celebrity protagonist.

THE ROGUE REVISITED: *The Life of Mr. James Spiller, the Late Famous Comedian*

Like the other two biographies, George Akerby's *Life of Spiller* incorporates satire, though this text adds artistic achievement (or lack thereof) to the other targets of political and class ambition. Spiller avoids duns, pilfers a play from William Pinkethman as they relax over drink, and befriends a group of bibulous butchers who later name a tavern after him. He spends time in the Mint, and after Parliament dissolved that haven of protection in 1723, in the Marshalsea. Akerby acknowledges predecessors in biography, citing Plutarch as an authority for recounting lives of illustrious people and adding that "*British Heroes* of the ROAD communicate a Share of their own Glory to *Captain Alexander Smith,* the learned *Preserver* of their Exploits and immortal Fame. . . . Under the Encouragement of such notable Examples, I have ventur'd on the following Piece of *Biography*" (5–6). Akerby thus ironically emphasizes the shift from traditional heroes to the new hero, exemplified by Smith's models (he wrote the *History of the Lives and Robberies of the Most Noted Highway-Men* in 1713 with an additional volume in 1720) and now by Spiller.

We know little about Spiller beyond what Akerby tells us. Mostly, we have records of his stage roles. Like Hayns or his nearer contemporary William Pinkethman, Spiller played low comedy (specializing in old men). His most recent stage success was Matt o' the Mint in *The Beggar's Opera,* which Akerby incorrectly tells us was Spiller's last role before his death.[38] Sven M. Armens maintains that Matt is the character "who voices most explicitly the Beggar's social protest" against unfair distribution of wealth, even though he speaks only a few lines.[39] But the biography of the actor

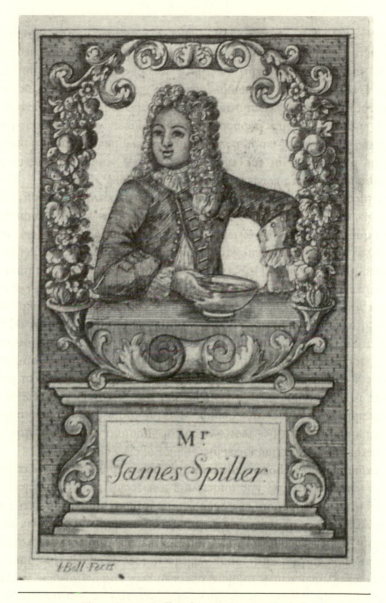

Fig. 4. James Spiller, frontispiece to Akerby's
The Life of Mr. James Spiller.
REPRODUCED WITH PERMISSION BY ROSENBACH MUSEUM AND LIBRARY,
PHILADELPHIA, PENNSYLVANIA.

who played that character supports the opposite view. Like *Memoirs of Mackheath, Life of Spiller* undercuts social protest and criticizes nontraditional methods of achieving higher social status. In the play, Matt inverts the belief that thieves, like actors, do not "work" for their money when he remarks distastefully that upper-class gamblers are just as bad: "Of all Mechanics, of all servile Handycrafts-men, a Gamester is the vilest. But yet, as many of the Quality are of the Profession, he is admitted amongst the politest Company. I wonder we [Macheath's gang of thieves] are not more respected."[40] He reduces genteel play to "Mechanics" and "Handycrafts," his disdain exposing his own code of social distinction. In *Life of Spiller*, Akerby opposes radical interpretations of these remarks by reducing Matt to Spiller, a scapegrace actor.

Akerby comments ironically on Spiller's upbringing and career. Like Fenton, Spiller had humble beginnings: his father was a Gloucester carrier resolved to raise James as a gentleman, "if Persons may be allowed to be such, who practice the Liberal Arts" (6). Spiller may please audiences of all ranks, but Akerby never allows Spiller to get "above" himself, constantly returning him to the lower classes of debtors and rogues. Though "some Persons of the first Rank have not thought an Evening ill spent in so good Company" as Spiller's (37), the actor should not mix socially with his betters. For example, one night, the duke of Wharton had "an unaccountable Frolick come into his Head of obliging every Man in Company to disrobe himself at ev'ry Health that was drank, of some Part of his Covering, first a Peruke, then a Coat, and afterwards a Waistcoat." This game reveals that Spiller is wearing no shirt, and so he was "expos'd in his *Buff* to the whole Company" (38), causing much hilarity for the gathering. Akerby turns his subject's discomfiture into a lesson in social order: "[H]ow much happier had it been for him to have contented himself that Evening, with the humble *Conundrums* of some of the Peers of his own House, who might have been in the same Condition with himself. But this cursed Ambition leads a Man into numberless Inconveniences" (38). This physical stripping replicates the purpose of the biography itself: *Life of Spiller* exposes the star actor as just another social impostor. Akerby's criticism is always based in class.

Akerby derides his subject throughout the book. He ridicules Spiller's married life and prints Spiller's love verses with snide commentary (37). Yet he still plays the principled, selfless biographer, claiming: "The Liberty

I have taken with Mr. *Spiller*'s Character in these Reflections on his Moral and Political Conduct, may, perhaps, seem very surprizing to those who are acquainted with the Intimacy that has been between us for near twenty Years: But the Regard I have to Truth, and my own Reputation as an Historian, compels me even to break through the Bands of Friendship" (25). Akerby uses a standard defense—that in betraying his friend he serves a higher responsibility to truth—to excuse his narrative of titillation and self-aggrandizement.

While Akerby also undermines Spiller's claims to be a poet by printing some of Spiller's verses and according them ironic praise, his ambivalence toward his subject is most clear in his treatment of Spiller's theatrical accomplishment. Akerby commends Spiller's comic powers: "His Looks, his most significant Shrugs and Gestures, would oftentimes set the whole Audience a laughing before he had spoke one Word" (7). While he was a stroller, "into whatever Place he came, or in whatever Play he acted, he was, at all Times, the Life of the Performance, and the greatest Support of the *Company*" (7). Yet he also points out that Spiller uses his talents to mock the government from the stage, a practice of which he disapproves.

Spiller's greatest stage role was in *The Beggar's Opera*. Akerby praises the play, but ironically. By printing a letter supposedly written by Spiller, Akerby shows Spiller's ingratitude toward Gay, who had written Spiller's most popular role. In this letter, Spiller accuses Gay of plagiarizing *The Beggar's Opera* from Christopher Bullock's 1715 revival of *A Woman's Revenge* (20–1). While somehow appreciating the literary achievement of the play, Akerby condemns its characters and those who perform them. He hints that Spiller's success as Matt is attributable to his true, low nature: "I am not insensible that those Persons are not wanting, who either wantonly or maliciously report that Mr. *Spiller*'s doing so much Justice to his part of MATT *of the* MINT is to be attributed to the Fondness he frequently shew'd of resorting, in Company with his Brother *Pinkethman*, and other Comedians of the same Note for a polite Taste, to the *Taphouses*, or *Lodges* of most of the Goals [*sic*] in *London*" (44–5). Spiller is not only damned when he presumes to consort with the upper classes, he is also damned for mixing with the low.

Akerby notes the widespread adulation of Spiller (and other players) as new heroes and hopes to disillusion the gullible public through disparagement and satire. Like the authors of *Life of Fenton* and *Memoirs*, he wishes

to show readers what these actors "really" are. Through Akerby's ironic narrative, Spiller appears as a clown, with little real acting skill. For Akerby, even Spiller's long, steady theatrical career and his success in *The Beggar's Opera* were not enough to dislodge social condemnation.

CONCLUSION: THE INFLUENCE OF *The Beggar's Opera* BIOGRAPHIES

Biographies such as *Life of Fenton, Memoirs of Mackheath,* and *Life of Spiller* take part in a larger process of commodification and commercialization of theatrical pleasure. The young gentleman of *Thievery a-la-mode* strolls by "a great Picture-shop" where "he saw the Prints of Captain *Macheath* and *Polly Peachum* hanging in the Windows with those of the first Quality of both Sexes in the Kingdom."[41] Robert D. Hume suggests that the success of *The Beggar's Opera* identified a previously untapped London theater audience that opened a market share for new houses such as the Little Haymarket and Goodman's Fields.[42] We can see the same process occurring in the print world—the play helped create a new consumer market for theatrical information and memorabilia, a market that had existed in potential for quite a while, but had not been exploited.

This new market was unlocked by a play that seemed to level social differences just as acting did. As had long been acknowledged, an actor could play a king one night and a beggar the next. Like the criminals portrayed and politicians lambasted in *The Beggar's Opera,* eighteenth-century actors and actresses began to evoke a vision of a transcendent lifestyle free from conventions of class- and gender-linked behavior. As Straub states, "Players are pervasively represented as transgressive of social and moral boundaries."[43] The nine players' *Lives* that appeared in the six years following *The Beggar's Opera* probably owe their existence to the reader interest that the play and its products inspired.

Unlike the first thespian biographies, however, these texts do not admire their subjects, nor are they even neutral toward them: these narrators are condescending, hostile, disapproving. In modern celebrity studies, Fred and Judy Vermoral describe how they "were astonished by the degree of hostility and aggression, spoken and unspoken, shown by fans towards stars. Later we realized this was one necessary consequence of such unconsummated, unconsumable passion."[44] These performers inhabit an

appealing world that their biographers do not, and the biographical hostility may be explained by jealousy or by the intensity of attraction that the biographers feel—and resent. Faced with a play that disrupted social positions—showed them all to be social *roles,* in fact—and faced with a cast of mere role-players who were gaining as much publicity as "the first Quality of both Sexes in the Kingdom," these biographers wrote in ways that allowed them to capitalize on their subjects' popularity without compromising their own social integrity. They maintained a satirist's distance from their subjects and also from the frenzied fan interest that their subjects evoked. This snide tone and safe distance will pervade many later thespian biographies, especially those of actresses, whose problematic status in life-writing we address in the next chapter.

The magical power of *The Beggar's Opera* as the perfect star vehicle lay in its ability to juxtapose social types ingeniously; its danger was its seductive suggestion that one can transcend conventional morality and bypass customary trajectories of success, achieving fame and wealth through impersonating what one is not. Gay's slippery satire, as critics have found, is often ambiguous in its intentions, but the biographies that followed clearly tried to control its seductive force. Yet what could they achieve by adding more publicity to a media mechanism, celebrity, that feeds on publicity? In their diverse responses to *The Beggar's Opera,* these biographies only helped to establish the new heroes they condemn.

CHAPTER 3

The Eighteenth-Century Actress and the Construction of Gender

LAVINIA FENTON AND
CHARLOTTE CHARKE

[T]he Irregularities of the Ladies ... rob
them of that Deference and respect, that
their Accomplishments of Person would
else command from their Beholders,
especially when set off to such Advantage as
the Stage supplies in the Improvement of
the Mind and Person. ... Mr. *Harrington* in
his *Oceana,* proposing something about a
regulated Theatre, would have all Women,
who have suffer'd any Blemish in their
Reputation, excluded the Sight of the Play,
and by that means to deter Women from
lewdness, while by that they lost the Benefit
of Public Diversions. If this were push'd
farther, and all Ladies of the House
immediately discarded on the Discovery of
their Follies of that Nature, I dare believe,
that they would sooner get Husbands, and
the Theatre lose Abundance of that
Scandal it now lies under.

CHARLES GILDON,
The Life of Mr. Thomas Betterton (1710)

ACTRESSES were long a favorite subject of smutty verse as well as fulsome eulogies, but the full-scale treatment of *Life of Lavinia Beswick, Alias Fenton, Alias Polly Peachum* (1728) was new. Twenty-seven years later, the first autobiography of an actress appeared. Written by Charlotte Charke, the eccentric daughter of Colley Cibber, *A Narrative of the Life of Mrs. Charlotte Charke* (1755) describes her youthful exploits, her attempts at supporting herself—from London company actress to pastry cook—and her years spent impersonating a man.[1] While feminist scholars have begun reassessing Charke's *Narrative*, they have yet to place it in the context of the emerging genre of celebrity biography, and *Life of Fenton* has been completely overlooked.[2] These texts exemplify two methods of gendering the problematic actress, the female who gained prominence in the male public sphere, and comparing them will allow us to explore the difficulties actresses encountered even in claiming the authority of presenting their own lives to the public.

Straub considers the sexual politics of Charke's cross-dressing on both the stage and the street: what guises the crossed-dressed actress could assume without violating her society's increasingly polarized, heterosexual gender roles. Straub concludes that Charke steadfastly maintains gender ambiguity: "She is 'somewhere else' on the field of sexual possibility, but cannot or will not specify where. Charke raises the question of why she cross-dresses only to refuse to answer."[3] But Straub does not fully explain the sources of this ambiguity. By looking at the *Narrative* in light of its predecessor *Life of Fenton* and of recent work in gender theory, we will see how Charke's book exposes the essentially performative construction of gender—a construction that *Life of Fenton* suppresses by ignoring.[4]

Older theories of gender identity are being revised to problematize some assumed relationships between gender and discourse. For example, Judith Kegan Gardiner has suggested two forms of textual identity that develop from gender differences: a masculine model with the qualities of constancy, stability, and often linear development, and a feminine model that is "less fixed, less unitary, and more flexible than male individuality."[5] But recent writers such as Judith Butler disagree with such a simple model because it assumes that the qualities of the text result from gender differences rather than the qualities themselves *creating* gender. Butler elaborates a crucial distinction between gender as expressive (of some internal, essential reality) or as performative. In arguing for the latter, she states:

"[G]ender is an identity tenuously constituted in time, instituted in an exterior space through a *stylized repetition of acts*. The effect of gender is produced through the stylization of the body and, hence, must be understood as the mundane way in which bodily gestures, movements, and styles of various kinds constitute the illusion of an abiding gendered self."[6]

Regarding gender as a semiotics of action has useful applications for analysis of gendered identities in biographical and autobiographical texts, such as the two I consider here. *Life of Fenton* is a "successful" performance of gender because it unifies its subject's acts into a coherent, integrated gendered character. *Charke* is a more complex, less convincing, and even "bad" gender performance because it exposes those discontinuous acts that cause Donald A. Stauffer to complain that the "narrative pays no attention to time, place, or character. . . . [T]he scenes shift so fast that she never bothers to describe any of them."[7] These same qualities encourage Straub's conclusion of gender ambiguity. *Life of Fenton*'s author shapes the actress's gender in ways more familiar, less threatening, and more stable than Charke shapes her own. The disunity of Charke's textual identity results not from a less rigid and more organic biologically determined "femininity," but from a frustrated attempt to accommodate a phallocentric society's demand for a clearly gendered subject.

Since women in eighteenth-century England were far more rule-bound and role-bound than men, they were, to some extent, always actresses. These two texts present two articulations of the actress's experience, one from the dominant position of the spectator, the other from the objectified position of the spectacle. *Life of Fenton*, with its anonymous author projecting a vision of the actress's life onto the actress, presents us with one-half of the performance situation: the view from the theater's pit, of the spectator expecting to be entertained by the exhibition of a female, with all of the necessary "acts" of femininity intact. If they grow "irregular"—as the epigraph above from Gildon's *Life of Betterton* implies—they will be excluded not only from the stage but also from the audience, and the controlling gaze will remain male, with a particular construction of femininity expected. Only then can the theater be released from the "scandal" it lies under, which, in Gildon's view, seems attributable solely to female performers. Writing her own story, Charke gives us the other side of the actress's positioning—the view from the stage, from the actress herself; that of the woman displaying herself for approval and for her keep.

The performance metaphor applied to these two texts dramatizes the problems of woman as object and as subject of literature, the opportunities for and restrictions on textual identity offered by different genres, and the consequences for women who challenge cultural repertoires of gendered acts. Looking at these two texts together helps expose the struggle for authority in the gendered presentations of thespian identity and returns us to the question raised earlier: Who controls the theater and those who work there? The gendered identity constructions here show part of the struggle to answer this question.

THE VIEW FROM THE PIT: *The Life of Lavinia Fenton*

The life of an actress in the eighteenth century was often precarious and humbling. Not introduced on the public stage until 1660, actresses were subject both to their culture's distrust of players and to its prejudice against women in the public sphere.[8] All stage careers were unstable and maligned, but actresses suffered doubly since they were deprecated by their society and consistently paid less and treated more cavalierly than male performers. They were, to use Straub's phrase, "sexual suspects," even more than male colleagues, because they more overtly transgressed gender boundaries by assuming a public role inconsistent with the time's expectations of their sex. And as we noted in the previous chapter, writers of the period stabilized this ambiguously gendered subject by invariably constructing her as a product of her sexuality. For example, the anonymous author of *The Players: A Satire* (1733) presents a "character" of an actress:

> *Phillis,* her pipkin Maidenhead once crack'd,
> By my good Lord, is to the Playhouse pack'd;
> She lives, inconscious of the Players Art,
> And makes the Theatre a bawdy Mart,
> Coquets, paints, patches, studys every Air,
> To draw in Chapmen for her fly-blown Ware:
> The Stage is elegant, the Dress is nice,
> A glitring Miss commands a glitring Price.[9]

The unfailing emphasis on her promiscuity in verse and prose points to

and reinforces a common eighteenth-century view of the outspoken, pro-fessional, successful public woman: that she is at best immodest, at worst a whore. These writers solve the dilemma of the ambiguously gendered actress by denying this ambiguity, by interpreting her problematic gender as really only an *exaggeration* of a feminine quality, lust. In actress biogra-phies, this exaggeration does not produce a frightening, voraciously sexual female monster but a humorous caricature of a sexual woman. The humor deflates the threat of the actress's authority, denying her any real power to captivate and control.

In the *Life of Fenton*, this denial is manifested in Fenton's appearance as a carefree harlot: her characterization overlooks the hardships of the actress's life and her enigmatic position in reference to the increasingly polarized gender roles of her society. While the anecdotal structure of the book strongly resembles a picaresque narrative, Lavinia Fenton herself is fixed and happy in her harlotry, a stable character with little depth or complexity. Her spectators in the pit—and the main one is her author—construct her as the safe and consistent whore that they and their society had customs and laws to control, not as the resilient individual an actress needed to be at this time.

According to *Life of Fenton*, Lavinia was born the illegitimate daughter of a sailor named Beswick and worked in her mother's coffeehouse while a young girl. As readers follow her astounding rise from oblivion to celebri-ty through *The Beggar's Opera*, they might expect a woman who had gar-nered such acclaim to change as she ascends from trollop to triumph, but Fenton is the same contented woman on the make in her mother's coffee-house at the beginning of the book as she is in high society at the end. For-tune, popularity, and favors from the rich do not affect her character, as her author presents it.

The book follows "the surprizing Incidents" of Fenton's life—that is, her amorous adventures. Early on, her solicitous mother advises her "above all *Things*, to observe this; *That the first Market a Woman made, was always the best; and second-hand Goods would fetch but a second-hand Price*" (15). Her mother saves Lavinia for "a certain ludicrous Knight, known by the name of the *Feather'd Gull*, and the Bargain was made as followeth: That upon the first Surrender, *Polly* should have 200 *l*. in ready Specie, and be deck'd in all the *Mundus Mulieris* at the Knight's Expence; that she should have 200 *l. per Annum* while she remain'd constant, but if

she suffered the Enemy to beat up her Quarters, she was to be devested [*sic*] of all her Ornaments at once, and driven out of Paradise" (15). Even though he is "ludicrous," the place in society he offers to a woman is "Paradise," and he, like an offended deity, can remove her as he chooses. Notwithstanding these terms of agreement, her daughter plans differently: "a *Portugueze* Nobleman, being her only Favourite, she consented, unknown to her Mother, to give him the Prize, which he generously rewarded" (16). We read of how they managed their assignation, and "after some time spent in Raptures at his own House, he brought her to her Mother, and promised *he would make a Provision for her, suitable to the Merits of so fine a Creature*" (16). When he is arrested and confined in the Fleet Prison, Lavinia "took his Misfortunes to Heart" (26) and sold her jewelry to free him.

The rest of *Life of Fenton* elaborates on the qualities evident in this sequence of events: she is wily and willing to provide for herself by her wits and her body; she is sensuous and enjoys her liaisons; she is the "whore with a heart of gold," generous with both her favors and her money. By the book's conclusion, she is cohabitating happily with her Portuguese, whom she periodically rescues from debt and incarceration. The picaresque travelogue of her sexual encounters is linked chronologically by a narrator at once patronizing and admiring of Fenton. The book's structure, its cheery narrator, and the insouciant character of Fenton reinforce a blithe view of the actress's existence, overlooking the poverty, meanness, and social disparagement common to the lives of both whores and actresses. The *Life* implies that women pursue and enjoy such work, instead of being forced to it by economic necessity or even being drawn to it as a venue for performing talent.

Although *Life of Fenton* mentions Lavinia's acting, her stage career is consistently subjugated to her amours. Her acting skill is reduced to "a lively Imagination, join'd with a good Memory, a clear Voice, and a graceful Mein" (27), and her entrance into a London theater company is attributed to the kindness of a "certain Nobleman" (29). The author hints snidely that Fenton "seem'd as if Nature had design'd her for the Pleasure of Mankind, in such Performances as are exhibited at our Theatres" (27), and compliments her resemblance to a notorious prostitute: "Her Amours are not inferior to those of the celebrated *Sally Salisbury*, nor have her Gallants been less generous to her than they were to that once famous Beauty"

(38–9). Indeed, any acting talent she has merely allows her to play the part of the upper-class prostitute more convincingly, since she only "may pass" for lady (47). And although the author tells us that she was never "a common Prostitute, as some would insinuate" (14), this reminder plus the portrayal of Fenton as a whore throughout only affirm this characterization of Fenton by denying it. Such statements and the repetition of Fenton's many amours constitute the performance of those "stylized repetitive acts" that constitute a gender identity.

Fenton's unified character in this *Life* is a public performance, a role for the actress to play that makes her problematic gender easier to understand. The images of rogues and gentlemen in contemporary biographies of male players also perform their masculinity in a similar, seamless way, though without the consistent emphasis on their sexual availability. The author of the first actress biography must look beyond the theater for a profession sufficiently gendered to make the actress understandable, and prostitution is one of the few open to women at this time. As in the whore biographies of the same period, Lavinia's individuality becomes a product of male desire and of male-dominated media, the cheap print industry that encouraged *The Beggar's Opera* souvenir boom.[10] The unity of Fenton's constructed identity in this volume is apparent even in the terms of its publication. It was published while its subject was still living, a circumstance that occurs for actresses much more often than for their male counterparts. It is as though the biographers have already determined the essence and the salient facts of the actress's life, even without the conclusion to the story. The actress's biographical character is evident at all points in her life, since her life is all of a piece.

This exhibition through performance of a highly "feminized" Fenton is reinforced by the explicit references to performance identities in the book. *Life of Fenton*'s author refers to Fenton throughout the *Life* as "Polly," the title of her famous role. Lavinia Fenton and Polly Peachum—real life and stage life—merge in this biography. The author probably chose this name to capitalize on the financial success of *The Beggar's Opera*, but the effect of that choice is to usurp Fenton's own identity and provide a ready-made role with which readers would be familiar. Readers avoid confronting the troublesome identity of the accomplished actress by reading Fenton as Polly, the bewitching trollop, the woman whose performance they purchased at the theater. As the heroine of the "Newgate pastoral" who

bestowed herself on the profligate and bigamous highwayman, Macheath, Polly's actions reflect back on Fenton, as stage roles merge with real life—a common occurrence in development of celebrity public images. While the subject of *Life of Fenton*'s pages lacks the starry-eyed quality of Polly in *The Beggar's Opera*—Fenton as Polly embodies a shrewdness of which Mr. and Mrs. Peachum would have been proud—she is still linked with a strongly gendered female.

Women are vulnerable to a loss of identity through externally imposed conventions of naming, especially in marriage.[11] Appropriating Fenton's identity to the role of Polly further deprives her textual representation of anything resembling the daily, individual life of the particular actress, making her a projection of the spectator's desire. The full title of the book, *The Life of Lavinia Beswick, Alias Fenton, Alias Polly Peachum*, penetrates in its very structure the subject's multiple identities to her eventual stable identity as "Polly Peachum." The subject is first Lavinia Beswick—the name of her supposed natural father who went to sea and never returned to his lover and their child. By stressing her illegitimacy in the title, the author reinforces patriarchal constructs of lineage and naming while simultaneously cashing in on the sensationalism associated with the illegitimacy of an acclaimed woman. The title then provides us with the actress's first "alias," Fenton. But it does not stop there: it continues to "Polly Peachum," her second alias, as though with this name we have finally pierced through her roles and arrived at her true identity (a view the text supports). Though the title seems to promise a complex layering of roles, it functions instead as a stripping away of masks to define the subject as Polly.

"Performing" the actress as a stable gendered identity makes her an easily assimilable object for her society. Objectified and commodified, the actress's life is opened to speculation in its most literal sense: voyeurism is the key to this author's representation of Fenton. The voyeur apprehends an object for titillation and vicarious pleasure; *Life of Fenton*'s compression of the hard life of the actress or the even harder one of the prostitute into the exploits of an eighteenth-century happy hooker distorts reality to satisfy the wishes of its audience. Fenton becomes Other, displayed on the textual stage for the pleasure of her reader/spectator in the pit. Just as she can be bought physically, she can now be bought textually; her private life goes public and is exposed as a salable commodity. And, as Gildon points out

in this chapter's epigraph, such a use of feminine property contributes to the improvement of the stage and, by allowing actresses to "get Husbands," to the traditional authority structure of gender and economy. Gildon advises actresses to take advantage of their public exposure and the male gaze in order to procure for themselves more traditional feminine positions.

Unlike what she may do with her body, however, she does not sell herself in this *Life*—a spectator, an external author creates and then sells her. What happens when an actress is free to sell herself, textually? How does an actress herself construct her textual identity when faced with the demands for gender stability that *Life of Fenton* evinces so well? Examining the first actress autobiography will help answer these questions.

THE VIEW FROM THE STAGE: *A Narrative of the Life of Mrs. Charlotte Charke*

After their childhoods, described as similarly precocious, Lavinia Fenton and Charlotte Charke led radically different lives. Fenton's career was a phenomenal success, Charke's an abysmal failure. Fenton's performance as Polly allowed her to capture the heart of a duke and, while still at the height of her popularity, retire from the stage as his mistress, later to become his wife. Her later private existence affirmed the clear gender identity constructed in her biography. Charke, however, spent her life on the street, always in public, always an enigma. Born into the financially comfortable family of Colley Cibber in 1713, Charke married imprudently, bore a child, and attempted a career in the London theaters. However, her clashes with management, her odd temper, and her connections with Henry Fielding's unlicensed Haymarket company eventually left her shut out of the London companies—and out of the good graces of her father, who was well known for his parsimoniousness, even toward deferential and obedient members of his family, which Charke certainly was not. Charke turned to provincial strolling companies for her living. We have no way of ascertaining Charke's truthfulness, but her catalogue of occupations is staggering: at one time or another during her life, she set up as a puppeteer, a sausage seller (indignantly denying that she ever stooped to selling fish), a pastry cook, a boardinghouse keeper, a waiter, a gentleman's servant, a farmer, and an author. All of her schemes disintegrated.

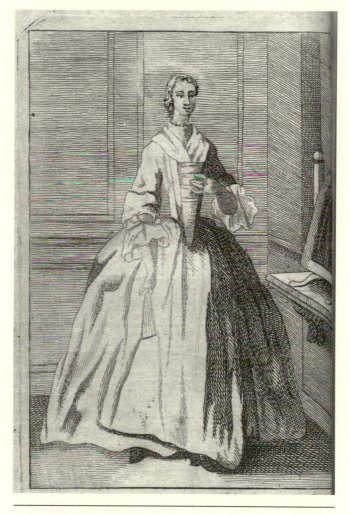

Fig. 5. Charlotte Charke, frontispiece to her *Narrative of the Life of Mrs. Charlotte Charke.*
REPRODUCED WITH PERMISSION BY THE SINGER-MENDENHALL
COLLECTION, ANNENBERG RARE BOOK AND MANUSCRIPT LIBRARY,
UNIVERSITY OF PENNSYLVANIA.

Fenton's success onstage demanded recuperation of her gender identity into a recognizable, stable gendered subject. No author felt obligated to recuperate Charke because she did not garner popular acclaim. Her inability (or refusal) to provoke desire through a feminized role like Polly and her impersonations of men both on- and offstage contribute to the gender ambiguity that intrigues Straub and other modern scholars but not Charke's contemporaries, by whom she was usually derided or ignored.[12] And although I analyze her *Narrative* here as a means she used to recuperate herself to her society's gender roles, Charke wrote the *Narrative* primarily to earn money. Just as *Life of Fenton*'s author created a stable gendered subject to sell more books, Charke's creation of a textual gender identity results from financial pressures.

The identity emerging from this commercial venture reveals the performative, constructed categories of gender. Charke's *Narrative* uncovers the struggle of the actress's life, which *Life of Fenton* suppresses or glamorizes. *Life of Fenton*'s unified gender role is imposed from without, from a society that expects an "appearance of substance," in Butler's terms, whereas the *Narrative* fragments its subject into multiple roles, both in the life described and in the method of description, a series of "acts which are internally discontinuous."[13] Like an actress onstage, Charke is conscious of her many "acts," or roles, and in her *Narrative* she attempts to play all roles to satisfy the disparate demands of her audience(s). But the attempt to perform them all merely accentuates the constructed nature of the performance rather than convincing readers of a unified character, like Fenton. The *Narrative* shows readers the discontinuous acts that social custom usually smoothes over to produce gender roles.

Several scholars have identified the numerous roles Charke plays in the *Narrative*. Sidonie Smith, for example, acknowledges three that Charke's readers would recognize—the sentimental heroine, the rogue, and the prodigal son—and Joseph Chaney has added much to our understanding of the latter.[14] Straub shows how such roles variously engage with different gender associations.[15] These variously gendered acts construct an ambiguous aggregate gender identity, reinforced by the *Narrative*'s rambling disorganization. I have already noted Stauffer's disdain; Patricia Meyer Spacks comments on its "narrative incoherence."[16] Its narratological shifts propel Charke into different occupations and different tones. On one page she's a waiter; on the next she's a mother. With breathtaking rapidity, Charke's

shifting roles change her relations to her eighteenth-century reader: a female transvestite working as a waiter could definitely expect a different reaction than a concerned mother. Sometimes she addresses the reader directly; sometimes she narrates her adventures in the third person.[17]

Fenton was always the predictable harlot whose biographer maintained a consistent bemused attitude toward her; Charke is many people and many voices, primarily because, unlike the author of *Life of Fenton,* Charke cannot or will not simplify the multiplicity of her experiences. She cannot or will not connect the disparate "acts" into one of the increasingly rigid gender configurations offered by her society. Stauffer concludes that throughout all of her adventures, "Charke remains the same strolling-player, careless, wild, irresponsible even in her quotations. The effect produced by her narrative is one of undirected power, thunderous and murky, masculine." Spacks more sensitively ascribes the *Narrative*'s structural disunity to Charke's "manifest difficulty in coming to terms with herself."[18] But both explanations rely on an essential, unconstructed subject: Stauffer's disapproval results from Charke's incorrectly gendered subjectivity ("masculine"); Spacks presumes that Charke has a "self" external to her text with which to come to terms. And Stauffer's choice of the unifying descriptor "wild" dismisses the dislocations and fragmentations of the text as expressions of an uncontrolled temperament instead of viewing them as discontinuous acts for which both eighteenth-century and Stauffer's early-twentieth-century society do not have adequate gender categories.

Some of the divergent roles Charke assumed resulted from her primary model: her father's enormously successful *Apology for the Life of Colley Cibber* (1740), to which we will turn in chapter 5. Cibber was an important public figure—theater manager, actor, dramatist, and poet laureate—who had important enemies to answer, most particularly Fielding and Pope. He wanted to account for his much-criticized life, yet the *Apology* contains little personal detail. Cibber creates a unified professional persona, affecting to confess folly and vanity to disarm his critics. As a wealthy man satisfied with his life, he can afford to admit his follies breezily. He does not need to write to support himself, and he overcomes the few unpleasantnesses of theatrical life he mentions.

Straub discusses Cibber's complex gender negotiations in his *Apology* and points out that Charke's attempt to imitate her father's ambiguous gender model makes her textual gender doubly ambiguous.[19] But the

resemblances do not seem to me to be "parodies," as Straub asserts, but rather bids for masculine power, the power of the father, as Mackie argues.[20] Charke was as audacious as her father in her life, and in her *Narrative* she attempts some of his rhetorical maneuvers. But because she was not a famous wealthy actor but instead a stroller disinherited by her father, and because she was a woman, these attempts sound plaintive and uncertain instead of blustering and self-confident.

What are her rhetorical strategies, and how do they affect the sense of gendered identity created by the *Narrative*? Spacks says that eighteenth-century female autobiographers "sketch a drama of self-defense." Felicity Nussbaum agrees, stating that "[m]ost scandalous memoirs find their genesis in an attack or accusation, and the texts function rhetorically to vindicate the apologist publicly from the charge."[21] Charke writes to defend her character and show how she was in part forced into her outrageous lifestyle. She describes her "unfeminine" education and her permissive parents' reactions to her early mishaps, blaming both for their determining influence on her later life and character. For instance, her tutor "got Leave of my Parents to instruct me in Geography; which, by the Bye, tho' I know it to be a useful and pleasing Science, I cannot think it was altogether necessary for a Female" (26). She tells us that "my Education was not only a genteel, but in Fact a liberal one, and such indeed as might have been sufficient for a Son instead of a Daughter; I must beg Leave to add, that I was never made much acquainted with that necessary Utensil which forms the housewifely Part of a young Lady's Education, call'd a Needle" (17). She prefers the "masculine" activities of shooting and gardening and states that her parents hesitated too long before correcting her misguided education (30). But as usual for Charke, her attitudes toward her education—the source of her gender confusion—are mixed, ambivalent. She recalls her childhood with fondness and amusement, but defending her later life causes her to condemn the laxity that estranged her from other girls. Such inconsistencies pervade the text.

Charke both acknowledges and criticizes her father's authority. She also takes a perverse pride in her eccentricity: her father openly admits his follies, and Charke similarly states that when her readers "know my History, if Oddity can plead any Right to Surprize and Astonishment, I may positively claim a Title to be shewn among the Wonders of Ages past, and those to come. Nor will I, to escape a Laugh, even at my own Expence,

deprive my Readers of that pleasing Satisfaction [of their curiosity], or conceal any Error, which I now rather sigh to reflect on" (13–4). Such attempts at ironic self-scrutiny dissolve into regret for the unconventionality that sets her apart from other women. Her "Oddity" is indeed her inability to reconcile her acts with established gender roles. She defensively attributes her failure in all of her business ventures to eccentricity and error, just as Cibber attributed his success to the same. Oddity, error, and failure, however, were not qualities that would endear a woman to much of the eighteenth-century reading public.

Charke certainly wanted to endear herself to her readers, because she wrote not only to defend herself but to advance other projects. Just as she engaged in her other schemes, she wrote to survive. She often appeals to— and sometimes threatens—her father for succor in her poverty: "if strongest Compunction and uninterrupted Hours of Anguish, blended with Self-conviction and filial Love, can move his Heart to Pity and Forgiveness, I shall, with Pride and unutterable Transport, throw myself at his Feet, to implore the only Benefit I desire or expect, his BLESSING, and his PARDON" (14). She prints the contents of an affecting letter she supposedly sent to Cibber's house, which was returned unopened:

> HONOUR'D SIR, . . .
>
> I Doubt not but you are sensible I last *Saturday* published the First Number of a Narrative of my Life, in which I made a proper Concession in regard to those unhappy Miscarriages which have for many Years justly deprived me of a Father's Fondness. . . . Be assured, Sir, I am perfectly convinced I was more than much to blame; and that the Hours of Anguish I have felt bitterly have repaid me for the Commission of every Indiscretion, which was the unhappy Motive of being so many Years estranged from that Happiness I now, as in Duty bound, most earnestly implore. (118–9)

Cibber did not respond to such blackmail, but Charke simultaneously implores her reading public for financial support by playing the injured daughter to the hard-hearted father. She shows her readers that she has and always has had the best intentions. She scrambles for work in London and then in provincial acting companies, and when she cannot find work as a performer, she enters trade. Abandoned by her husband (who she claimed was a dissolute spendthrift), she raises their daughter on her own,

stressing their hand-to-mouth existence. She hopes to elicit the pity (and generosity) of her readers, and follows up her indirect appeals with overt ones. For example, she puffs a future benefit performance: "[I]f I can obtain a Grant for ONE NIGHT ONLY, I intend to make my Appearance once more as Mrs. *Agnes,* for my own Benefit, at the *Hay-Market* Theatre; on which Occasion, I humbly hope the Favour and Interest of my worthy friends" (65).[22]

Her appeals to her reading public include adopting conventional feminine personae. She appears as dutiful daughter, afflicted mother, and devoted spouse. Yet her attempts at playing such repertory roles are disrupted by the facts of her outrageous life—later actress apologists such as George Anne Bellamy and Mary Wrighten are more successful at playing single, expected female roles, especially victims. While her supplicating tone exhibits the passivity and helplessness required from an eighteenth-century female, she sabotages its effect by listing her failed enterprises to prove her diligence and inventiveness. The very communication of her worthy attempts at self-support might deprive her of readers' patronage by turning her into an inappropriate object of support—an unnatural, energetic woman. She consistently disturbs her "feminine" gender identity with attributions of "masculine" qualities. And indeed, except for her benefit and the sale of her novel *The History of Henry Dumont, Esq; and Miss Charlotte Evelyn* (which she also puffs in her *Narrative*) for a paltry sum, we have no record of her receiving aid or occupation from anyone—but rather a patronizing report that she ended her life in wretchedness and filth.[23]

Of course, the act of publishing her own life story divided her from accepted models of femininity and contributes to the splintered identity of her text. She confronted the stigma attached to female authors and female memoirists. Although many women had begun to write novels, very few autobiographies or memoirs of a woman's own life had been printed, and these were usually of noble or pious women, published for the moral edification of their readers.[24] The woman who wrote of herself was immodest—indeed, unwomanly. Eighteenth-century female memoirists such as Delariviere Manley, Teresia Constantia Phillips, and Laetitia Pilkington were criticized, used as models of what women are not—or should not be. Charke tries to forestall mistreatment: "As the following History is the Product of a Female Pen, I tremble for the terrible Hazard it must run in venturing into the World, as it may very possibly suffer, in many

Opinions, without perusing it; I therefore humbly move for its having the common Chance of a Criminal, at least to be properly examin'd, before it is condemn'd" (1). Her bizarre career had already divorced her from standards of femininity by 1755, and her brazen recording of that life would only further aggravate her ostracism.

86

Mother, daughter, wife, and contrite lady author clash with the role of entrepreneurial jill-of-all-trades. But significantly, Charke eschews playing one particular role in her *Narrative*: the sex object. We have seen how *Life of Fenton*'s author reduces the actress's whole existence to her promiscuity, yet Charke's *Narrative* never touches on her sexual life. Even so eccentric a woman as Charke knew that revealing such information would transgress too far. She says, "I have paid all due Regard to Decency wherever I have introduc'd the Passion of Love" (12). Using sexual sensationalism to sell her book would have undermined its primary rhetorical aims, to flatter or pressure readers into helping her. She states that "I did not prostitute my Person" (139), and her misadventures in male garb always end respectably. However exhibitionistic in her other roles, Charke must not exhibit herself as a sexually active female. But though the exaggerated sexuality that became the main gendering tool of *Life of Fenton* and that readers associated with actresses is absent here, we can imagine that her contemporary readers, conditioned by books like *Life of Fenton,* would encounter her denials of romantic intrigue rather incredulously. Similarly, the contentment of the actress-whore, present in *Life of Fenton,* does not appear in Charke's book. Because of her rhetorical aims, Charke could never portray herself as content. Lynda M. Thompson states of eighteenth-century women's "scandal memoirs" that a reader "quickly discovers that they are less about sex or desire and more about eighteenth-century women's fraught and unequal relationship to money, property, law and 'priceless' reputation."[25] Charke's foregrounding of her numerous occupations and her constant explanations of what she had to do to support herself and her dependents builds on the salacious interest an actress-autobiographer might raise to isolate the true conditions of her existence.

Another of *Life of Fenton*'s methods of streamlining its subject's gender was to adopt the feminized stage role of "Polly." Charke incorporates many more acting roles in her *Narrative,* intensifying the text's fractured effect. As a child, she impersonated a gardener, a physician, and even her

father: all "masculine" roles. Throughout the *Narrative* she often uses dramatic examples as analogies for her circumstances. She often invokes the plays of George Farquhar: when young, she "grew so great a Proficient in that notable Exercise [shooting], that I was like the Person described in *The Recruiting Officer*, capable of destroying all the Venison and Wild Fowl about the Country" (29); later, she describes her relations with her husband as "in the same Circumstances, in Regard to each other, that Mr. *Sullen* and his Wife were" (53). Such layering of dramatic reference only further muddies any possible clear, unified idea of "Charke" as subject. And in Charke's role-playing coup, drama overlaps life when she spends nine years "en Cavalier," dressed as "Mr. Brown" or as a gentleman's servant. She explains that her impersonation was so convincing that women fell in love with her, sometimes requiring "oracular proof" to dissuade them from their mistaken passion. She thus seems to have given her best performance as a genteel or feminized male; her attempts to play the more masculine roles of grocer, baker, and farmer failed.

87

The *Narrative* is thus a complex interplay between roles imposed and roles assumed, contributing to a fragmented gender performance. The *Narrative* presents the actress from the stage of life itself, instead of viewing her from the pit. In a stage performance, the actress assumes the qualities that fit the dramatic role her audience expects. Whereas the successful actress convinces the audience that she has become the role, the actress herself is always aware that she is creating an illusion of a self. Charke's "self" in her *Narrative* does not negotiate the demands of gender performance successfully, and her book presents its readers/spectators with the soliloquy of an unassimilated textual identity.

CONCLUSION: THE TEXTUAL AND ACTUAL ACTRESS

The metaphor of performance applies well to these texts because of the three interrelated performances occurring in them. Not only were these two women professional players—people who assumed other characters as their job—but they were *women*, pressured by the strict gender roles their society prescribed. The combination of these two types of role-playing simultaneously generates tension because of their contradictoriness: if Fenton and Charke were playing the standard life roles of eighteenth-

century women, they would not be actresses. So the third type of perform-ance—in their biographies—is to reconcile the demands of these roles to create a textual identity.

The authors of the two biographies provide two methods of reconcilia-tion, one successful and one not. The author of *Life of Fenton* must account for Fenton's ability to be the social curiosity of the thriving public woman. This author's answer reverts to female stereotypes current even early in the century: that she must have achieved success because of her sexuality, her ability to sell herself wisely. Acknowledging her acting talent would both complicate her unified gender identity as harlot/mistress and implicitly approve of a woman in the public realm. Simplifying the actress's life for biographical ease continues in other biographies of actresses published in the eighteenth century: only two of these others do not present their subjects as sexually promiscuous.[26]

Charke's *Narrative* accommodates the divergent demands differently. She appeals to her audience's expectations of a repentant daughter and a fond mother, she portrays herself as victimized and helpless, she describes her schemes with pride and then embarrassment, she cajoles, pleads, threatens, and accuses. Her textual self is chameleonic, always role-playing, "as changeable as *Proteus*" (40). Her gender performance is as unpredictable as the scene in the *Narrative* in which she and another actress recite snippets of different plays to an ignorant provincial audience: "[W]e both took a Wild-goose Chase through all the dramatic Authors we could recollect" (204). Her multifurcated performance in this scene is an apt analogy for her identity in the *Narrative*. And recent work by Hans Turley shows how the editors of the *Gentleman's Magazine* recast Charke's *Narrative* as a unified biography, with a stable central identity and a third-person narration: in effect, *Fenton*-izing Charke.[27]

Charke may fail at providing an integrated gendered identity, but I do not agree with scholars such as Smith who label Charke a failed feminist.[28] Her "failed" gender performance is really a triumph of a sort. Butler explains how the sustained social performances of gender help to repress "the performative possibilities for proliferating gender configurations out-side the restricting frames of masculinist domination and compulsory het-erosexuality."[29] Perhaps Charke's refusal to conform to gender norms—even those that were beginning to regulate same-sex desire—is a rebellious assertion of a new configuration.[30] Chaney has pointed out the difficulty

of understanding Charke's textual performance as a conscious choice: "Surely Charke can't both want to conform to feminine conventions and then refuse to conform."[31] However, it seems to me that Charke herself would love to conform, but her text (and the identity it constructs) do not. The later actress autobiographers show that unified textual identities can be derived from tumultuous lives. Thus Charke's rebellion is a textual one, not an intentional effort on her part. Perhaps against her own will, she exemplifies the resistant woman autobiographer Nussbaum identifies: "[W]omen's autobiographical writing, organized within prevailing discourses, helped to shape and resist the dominant cultural constructions of gender relations and to substitute alternatives."[32]

Future actresses, however, will not follow Charke's lead and its rhetorical ineffectiveness but will create personae more conventionally feminine and more commercially viable. All of the texts relating to actresses' lives had to confront the monolithic, socially imposed structure of gender authority. *Life of Fenton* capitulates to the required unified feminine identity, and her biography seems to imply that this explains her worldly success. Charke's *Narrative* alternately challenges and bows to this authority, thus assuring her self-presentation an unwelcome response, which can translate to a life of frustration and distress.

Paradoxically, in the eighteenth century, the public woman was the marginalized woman. Exhibiting herself overtly in an age when most female self-exhibition signified immodesty, the actress was available for the projection of desire. By becoming the object of male desire and male gaze, and thus an embodiment of rampant feminine sexuality, the actress in biography exposes her society's construction of femininity. The story of "Polly" Lavinia Fenton shows how the spectator could use social expectations and generic models to recuperate this aberrant woman, to create the actress in a manner that reinscribed cultural gender roles. Intentionally or not, Charke corrected that image by exposing its performative nature. Thus these biographies present two strikingly different versions of the life of the public woman in a time when she was not supposed to exist.

CHAPTER 4

Dissecting the Actor's Authority

BARTON BOOTH'S FINAL ACT

[T]he kingdom is full of mountebanks,
empirics, and quacks. We have quacks in
religion, quacks in physic, quacks in
law, quacks in politics; quacks in patriotism;
quacks in government; high German quacks
that have blistered, sweated, bled, and
purged the nation into an atrophy.

TOBIAS SMOLLETT,
*The Life and Adventures of
Sir Launcelot Greaves* (1760–1)

AFTER THE *Beggar's Opera*
celebrity frenzy but before
Charke wrote her *Narrative,*
numerous other biographies appeared
as an older generation of performers
passed on. Though Colley Cibber
thrived, other stalwarts of the Drury
Lane acting company died and, almost
immediately afterward, were memorialized in biography. Ann Oldfield,

dying in 1730, was honored with two biographies; Robert Wilks, dying in 1732, received three book-length treatments; and Barton Booth, dying in 1733, earned two biographies. This sudden surge in biographical publication points to the influence of *The Beggar's Opera,* yet these 1730s biographies negotiate authority in different ways than the suppression of threats of cultural heroism and gender of the *Beggar's Opera* biographies, in part because these players were not part of the *Beggar's Opera* cast, acted at Covent Garden, and in part because of the higher status of these memorialized players.

This chapter looks closely at two of these biographies, those written about Barton Booth. Booth was famous for being the original Cato in Addison's play, and was also known for his tragic heroes: Cibber states in his *Apology* that "[t]he masterpiece of *Booth* was Othello" (314). Booth's funeral was elaborate; his coffin was carried by six prominent men, and he was mourned by many more. He was memorialized in poems and newspaper pieces as well as in three biographies: one by an anonymous writer published by John Cooper (1733), one by Benjamin Victor (1733) and, much later, one by Theophilus Cibber (1753). These biographies attest to Booth's importance to the London stage by supplying information about the Drury Lane triumvirate management, Booth's performance style, his ability in different roles, his private life and amours, and his strange final illness and death.

The disconcerting circumstances of Booth's demise appear in Victor's *Memoirs of the Life of Barton Booth, Esq.* Victor's sixteen-page account of Booth's life gives way to a seven-page highly detailed description of the autopsy performed on Booth, surveying the extent of the disintegration of the actor's internal organs after a mercury treatment: "The *Rectum,* with the other Intestines, were ript up with a Pair of Scissars, in which was found very little Excrement, but the whole Tract on the inside, lin'd with *Crude Mercury* divided in Globules, about the Bigness of Pins Heads" (23). Such a grisly report is unique in actor biographies of the whole century and very rare in any biography of the time. And, as Peter Linebaugh, Ruth Richardson, Jonathan Sawday, Thomas R. Forbes, and others have shown, postmortem dissection often aroused fear and shame.[1] Why would Victor have included it in this otherwise laudatory biography? Current scholarship has had little to say. Only Straub interprets its appearance as spectators' "desire to know the player physically"—an extension of the prurient

emphasis of some of the thespian biographies of the time.[2] Though the editors of the *Biographical Dictionary* do not explain its appearance either, they do note its dissonance: "The whole wretched business was a most ignominious end for a player who had so loved the dignity of majesty."[3] Booth is presented as a stately if phlegmatic actor, recalling the gentleman-actor biographical tradition. But the grotesqueness of the autopsy undercuts the respectability and authority of the genteel image that Booth inherits. This chapter examines the strains apparent in Booth's biographies to show how the actor was connected to other forms of authority, specifically, in this instance, with the contested images of medical doctor and medical hack.

Victor included this otherwise humiliating public exposure, paradoxically, to *defend* Booth and his widow. To understand why it appears more thoroughly, however, we must investigate the report's provenance. While its source is known, no one has yet unraveled the complex history of its appearance in the biography. The final act of Booth's life was embroiled in a controversy over medical legitimacy, as the intimate hidden secrets of Booth's body became ammunition in a battle between self-appointed medical authorities. In serving in this battle, however, Booth's body helps illuminate questions about truth and authority that permeate both the medical and the performing professions. Knowing where the autopsy comes from and speculating on why Victor placed it in his biography leads us to investigate what it means—to Booth, to biography, to actors, and, most important, to a culture obsessed with questions of order and legitimacy. By tracing the relevant medical controversy, we can identify the concerns about imposture and authority that underlie and tie together physic and acting in the eighteenth century.

THE SOURCE OF "THE CASE OF MR. BOOTH"

Two traditions of anatomizing existed during the period under consideration here. The first can be called "dissection," and is amply discussed in Linebaugh's "Tyburn Riot against the Surgeons," an account of riots against the established and legal practice of the Royal College of Physicians and the Company of Barber-Surgeons using executed felons' bodies for the purposes of anatomical dissection and public lecturing. Such treatment is, of course, part of the punishment and public humiliation of the

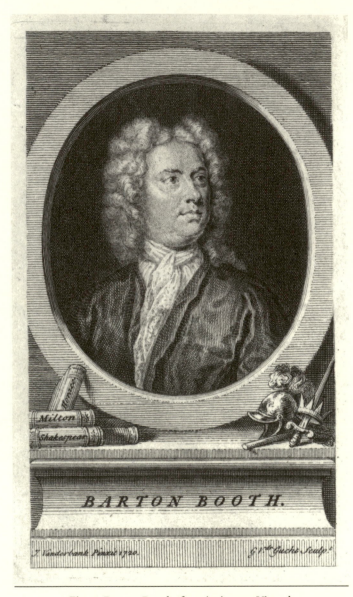

Fig. 6. Barton Booth, frontispiece to Victor's
Memoirs of the Life of Barton Booth.

criminal. Foucault stresses that "the body of the condemned man was . . .
an essential element in the ceremonial of public punishment," and then
notes the ritual importance of dismemberment and dishonor after death:
"Justice pursues the body beyond all possible pain."[4] Thomas R. Forbes
reminds us that "[s]o as to increase the severity of the death penalty, Parliament in 1752 passed an act (25 Geo. 2, c.37) directing that the bodies of
persons executed for murder be hung in chains or be handed over to the
surgeons for dissection."[5] The Anatomy Act of 1832 was passed in part to
stop body snatching for dissection from graves, which incited rumor and
panic, especially among the poor, those whose graves were most often
robbed. Thus autopsy was linked with shame, punishment, suspicion,
poverty, and criminality.

The second type of anatomizing, however, has been much less studied,
perhaps because it holds less attraction for those critics intent on showing
class exploitation. David Harley's work on the history of anatomizing royalty and powerful aristocrats proves such cases made the procedure more
familiar to the British, even though he also shows how its implementation
passed from physicians to the less respected surgeons during the early
eighteenth century.[6] Most of these bodies were opened to establish cause
of death. Lady Mary Wortley Montagu's father, the duke of Kingston, was
autopsied in 1726 as was most often done: in private.[7] Yet pamphlets re-
porting these autopsies of eminent figures were sometimes published. In
An Account of the Dissection of His Highness William Duke of Gloucester,
"the Right Honourable the Earl of Marleborough, one of the Excellencies
of the Lords Justices of England, and Governour to His late Highness was
pleased to give order That the Body should be Opened" by Dr. Edward
Hannes.[8] Descriptions of anonymous postmortems appeared regularly in
medical books of the period. For example, William Oliver's *A Practical
Essay on Fevers* tells how another doctor "was at the Dissection of a Person
who had died of a Fever, who . . . had taken great quantities of Testaceous
Powders," which then "lay in hard lumps like Sheeps Dung in the Stomach
and some of the Intestines."[9] Such autopsies contributed to the empirical
data that helped "modernize" the medical profession away from its "ancient" past.

These descriptions are divorced from the shameful spectacle of public
execution and dissection, but presumably the exposure of the internal
organs of a close family member was still not a desirable circumstance.

Those who conducted autopsy on the upper classes had the same motivations as modern forensic physicians, to remove suspicion of foul play or medical misconduct, and their explorations were usually restricted to one part of the body. However, the bodies of criminals, usually healthy at death, underwent complete dissection for general scientific knowledge, in front of anyone who could pay to attend the lecture at the anatomy hall. Harley stresses the importance of privacy in the postmortem and how it helped calm relatives' doubts about the procedure; the primary difference between the two traditions may be the degree of public exposure through death and immediately afterward.

Booth's report is clearly of the second kind: a description of the anatomizing of a popular public figure. But though such reports were not unknown, the intimate fate of the body after death was not a usual component of eighteenth-century biography. Though we have information that other popular performers were autopsied, no other English thespian biography during the seventeenth or eighteenth century provides an autopsy of its subject.[10] The seven biographies of other actors published over the five-year period from 1728 to 1733 treat their subjects' deaths very differently, if at all. Lavinia Fenton does not die in her *Life,* James Spiller suffers a comic and not graphic death, the two biographies of Ann Oldfield describe her great pain but not the nature of her disease, and the three biographies of Robert Wilks allow him to expire (of the stone, according to two of the biographers) with seemliness. No mention is made of postmortem disposition, except to note the names of famous pallbearers and the place of interment.

Thus though readers may have been familiar with autopsy reports of the rich and famous, they were not accustomed to encountering them in biographies and may have been disturbed by Victor's account. What exactly did it include? "The Case of Mr. Booth" describes his final illness and medication, and summarizes the opening of his body by the surgeon Alexander Small "in the Presence of Sir Hans Sloan," president of the Royal College of Physicians and the very prominent medical figure who would later found the British Museum (19). The autopsy report begins, "His *Liver* was in very good Order, neither hard nor livid, but somewhat larger than usual" (23). However, Booth's gall bladder was "six Times bigger than what is commonly observed, and filled with *Bile,*" and "[i]n the *Ductus Choledochus* was found a Gall Stone of the Size and Shape of a

Horse Bean, which had so entirely stopt the Bile from passing into the *Duodendum,* that not the least Appearance thereof could be observed in the whole Tract of the *Intestines*" (23). The doctor found five other stones as well, and we remember that gall and bladder stones were so dangerous during this period that Samuel Pepys celebrates with a special dinner the anniversary of his own stone's removal—a miraculous recovery, given the danger of surgery and its aftermath at this time. Booth's report escalates in repulsiveness: "I endeavour'd to divide the *Rectum* and tie it, but it was so rotten that it broke between my Fingers like Tinder, and sent forth a most offensive cadaverous Stench" (23). The report continues: "The Inside of the Intestines was not glaz'd over with the Mercury, as you had been told, for they were as black as your Hat, and so rotten, that they would not endure the least straining without breaking in pieces" (23–4).

Victor states that Booth was first struck with a lingering illness in the form of a "violent Fever" in 1727; he was sick for forty-six days (12, 13). He was intermittently ill until his death, especially in 1729, when "he continu'd a considerable time in a very severe and dangerous Condition, being under a constant Visitation of violent Fevers, attending with tormenting Colicks," or intestinal pains (15). Victor identifies the cause of Booth's death as a premature return to the stage, "which was his Bane, being unequal in Strength to the laborious Business of the Stage" (13), though Colley Cibber tells us that Booth himself thought stage work a recipe for health: Booth said "for his Part, he saw no such great matter in acting every Day; for he believed it the wholesomest Exercise in the World; it kept the Spirits in motion, and always gave him a good Stomach" (310).

Booth intended to travel to Holland in order to consult with Dr. Herman Boerhaave, the most famous doctor of the time, "who had before been acquainted with his Case" (14). However, Booth proved too sick to travel, and he was advised by other eminent medical figures.[11] Then, as now, money and celebrity can buy one the best medical care. Since physicians at that time lived in a web of social connections and patronage, they were encouraged to treat and cure famous patients. No legal requirements existed for promoting one's medical skill (licentiateship or fellowship in the Royal College of Physicians was not required in order to practice), so many doctors used testimonials and case histories to prove their efficacy and distinguish themselves from quacks. Rivalry was sometimes rancorous and vicious between members of the Royal College, the Company of

Barber-Surgeons, and unlicensed healers who promoted their nostrums and cures through the increasingly available print media.

One of the most vociferous adversaries of the medical elite of the day was Thomas Dover, with whom Booth was connected.[12] Dover is perhaps most familiar to modern readers of Defoe, who may recognize him as the man who rescued Andrew Selkirk—the original model for Defoe's Robinson Crusoe—from his two years' exile on a desert island. But Dover was also a well-known medical man in the early 1730s, due largely to the publication of his popular home manual, *The Ancient Physician's Legacy to His Country* (1732), a type of publication growing increasingly common. This manual saw eight eighteenth-century editions, was translated into French, and enjoyed notice on the Continent.[13] In it, Dover consistently portrays himself as a well-traveled man of the world, who has by virtue of his travels accrued much more medical experience and knowledge than any mere London physician. He particularly lambastes the medical orthodoxy manifested in the Royal College of Physicians, which had accepted him only as a licentiate back in 1721 (he could never become a fellow because he lacked a Cambridge or Oxford degree). At several times in his life, he was at odds with the establishment of his profession.

In *Ancient Physician's Legacy,* Dover describes and recommends treatments for common ailments: asthma, fevers, diabetes, gout, and many more. For most of these illnesses, he suggests a dosage of metallic or crude mercury, taken orally, which earned him the nickname "Dr. Quicksilver."[14] Kenneth Dewhurst tells of the contemporary legitimacy and long history of mercury cures: "Dover was promoting nothing new by urging the use of mercury, which in one form or another is probably one of the oldest remedies. . . . Before the development of abdominal surgery, metallic mercury was given without ill effect in single one-pound doses in order to relieve intestinal obstruction."[15] Dover volunteers to diagnose even for the deceased great and then use them to puff his medications: "had the late Queen CAROLINA but taken the same Remedy, I will aver, she would have been well in Twelve Hours."[16] Mercury treatment was linked most strongly to syphilis (known in England as the French pox), though patients with this disease and its skin manifestations would usually be treated by an external unction of mercury rubbed on them, leaving them to salivate and sweat. Interestingly, this is a disease that Dover ignores in his manual, though he does prescribe cures for smallpox.

97

The autopsy report in Victor's biography notes that Booth "was resolv'd, after reading Dr. D——r's [Dover's] Book of *Crude Mercury,* and fearing the Return of his Fever, to take the Doctor's Advice: He accordingly sent for him, and from the Encouragement he gave him, . . . on the Day following he began the *Mercurial Course,* as directed, and so punctually follow'd those Directions, that he had taken within two Ounces, two Pounds weight" (19–20). Booth probably had followed Dover's prescription for "Diseases of the INTESTINES," especially that for "the most painful and dangerous Disease, call'd the Iliac Passion; and by some, the *Miserere mei,* from the acute Pains it gives the Patient." For this disease, Dover suggests the patient "take a Pound, or a Pound and half of Crude Mercury."[17]

After Booth began applying Dover's cure, he "began to complain of a very great Pain in his Head, and as great in his Bowels also, with a universal Uneasiness of his Body" (20). Though he hoped to continue his mercury treatment, "Mrs. Booth apprehending the ill Consequences, sent away for Sir Hans *Sloan*" (20), who prescribed bleeding, plasters, purges, glysters, and cordials. Booth died—mercifully—soon after, on 10 May 1733.

Thus we have a famous public figure dying after employing the prescriptions of a pugnacious and cantankerous doctor of the popular press. Did he die *because* of his cure? At least one person seems to have thought it possible. A medical author and member of the College of Physicians from 1711, Daniel Turner made it his personal quest to expose quacks, perhaps to help legitimate his own leap from surgeon to physician.[18] Turner wrote numerous medical books on skin diseases, syphilis, and other topics, such as *The Modern Quack; or, Medicinal Imposter* (1718), in which he debunks the methods of London medical frauds and includes "[a] Catalogue . . . of all the Members of the Royal College of Physicians, residing in Town" for the benefit of patients wanting legitimate, "approved" doctors. As Philip K. Wilson asks, "What did Turner hope to gain from authorship? His prolific writings suggest that he was driven to become recognized as an authority."[19] The self-aggrandizing Dover soon became a target.

Turner answered Dover in *The Ancient Physician's Legacy Impartially Survey'd.*[20] Turner criticizes Dover's trust in the efficacy of metallic mercury. Turner himself never prescribes mercury unless the patient insists, and his final judgment is, "I cannot persuade myself it will do any hurt; and if

it passes not further, which in the far greater part of those who take it, I think it does not. . . . it be not a little doubtful whether it can do good," since almost the same amount that is ingested is also evacuated.[21] In an earlier book, *Syphilis,* Turner warned strongly against the topical use of mercury. He knows that the metal is "prejudicial" to the nervous system, since those who work with it, such as glaziers, have "run mad, and dy'd soon after, under their Convulsions, from no other Cause than the poisonous Steams fixing on the Membrane of the Brain."[22] Even with the less harmful ingestion, Turner believes that relying on mercury cures can do harm by keeping people from sound medical care and by encouraging them to self-medicate.

The celebrated case study Turner uses to prove his point of the ineffectiveness of the mercury cure is none other than "*The CASE of Mr. BOOTH, the famous Tragedian,*" which concludes his book and is virtually the same as the account in Victor's biography of the actor. Turner introduces the account thus: "Having heard that there was something very remarkable discover'd upon the opening of the Corps of Mr Booth, in relation to the Quicksilver that the Gentleman had taken just before; I sent to Mr. Small the Surgeon, who dissected the Body, to desire he would draw me up the Case in Writing . . . which I received in a Letter . . . as follows . . ."[23] This case study or testimonial method of establishing credibility for medical treatment was common at the time and remains so in modern advertising. Turner's title page reveals an obvious attempt to help market his book and bolster his argument via the name of a popular figure—an early instance of celebrity endorsement (though with no benefit to the celebrity).[24] If, as David Harley has asserted, the politicized anatomies of royal and aristocratic bodies helped familiarize the populace with this medical procedure and made it less threatening, then to find the politicized body of an actor in the same position not only suggests an indirect equivalency between these figures but also shows how the market was using the new celebrity "heroes" as it had used traditional ones.

Dewhurst reports that "[t]he quicksilver controversy triggered off a pamphlet war lasting for fifty years. . . . I have traced fourteen books or pamphlets dealing with the medicinal aspects of metallic mercury." The Booth autopsy appears in several of these, sometimes verbatim and sometimes merely mentioned.[25] The main issue for the medical men seems to be whether the mercury caused or hastened Booth's death, though this is

not stressed when Victor reprints the report. Dewhurst explains, "The cause of Booth's death was hotly disputed in subsequent pamphlets, but it would seem that the most likely diagnosis was that of chronic gall stones, and the course of his illness was unaffected by the administration of quicksilver."[26] But a biography of an actor is not a work of medical controversy. What could have caused Victor to pluck this report from the medical realm and place it in his reverential biography?

BOOTH'S BODY IN BIOGRAPHY

One fairly pedestrian reason why Victor may have included this report is, if Booth's case was already known to the reading public and generating reader interest, why not include it? An eighteenth-century reading public would probably be more familiar and comfortable with medical intrusions than we are today. For example, Edmund Curll (of whom more in the next chapter) printed in his *Memoirs of the Life, Writings, and Amours of William Congreve,* ostensibly written by Charles Wilson (1730), an excerpt from the works of George Sewell on medical properties of snails. Even Dover includes a short digression about the medical uses of frogs in *Ancient Physician's Legacy.*

Yet medical information is one thing, an invasive autopsy is another. Victor's use of this material has more to do with his particular social situation than with generic habits. In 1733 Victor was a linen merchant with literary and cultural ambitions. He had published a pamphlet defending Richard Steele's *The Conscious Lovers* (1722), he angled for court positions, and in 1728 he was introduced to Booth. [27] Though he would subsequently become prompter at Smock Alley in Dublin and treasurer at Drury Lane, at the time of the publication of his biography, he seems to have been looking to advance himself by publication, flattery, and drawing attention to his connection with such a celebrated actor. His biography of Booth is the only monograph biography of an actor he published, which is odd, given his closeness to the stage, his apparent interest in publishing, and the increasing popularity of the genre.

Victor later penned two large collections of theatrical history and reminiscences: in 1761 *The History of the Theatres of London and Dublin, from the Year 1730 to the Present Time* and its sequel from 1761 to 1771.[28] In the first volume, he provides a nostalgic retrospective on the players who lived

and performed from 1720 to 1730. His longest biographical sketch is of Booth, but Victor uses surprisingly little of his own earlier *Memoirs*. The unexpected absence of the postmortem signals that its purpose may have been fulfilled at the time of Booth's death. By 1761 the local concerns of ambition that had driven Victor's use of it had diminished, and he did not need to curry favor any more. Victor employed the autopsy in an unusual bid for self-advancement. But how is it possible that including the grisly account was more useful than omitting it? Primarily because Victor sought to ingratiate himself through a chivalric defense of Booth's memory and his widow.

The cause and circumstances of Booth's death were very important to the medical world, as we have seen. But they were also important to Booth's family and to the public, and Victor's publication of the autopsy report fits into a larger pattern of defense of the actor and Hester Booth, his wife, throughout the biography. Immediately before Victor's biography, another account of Booth's life was published, the anonymous *Life of That Excellent Tragedian Barton Booth Esq.*, printed by John Cooper (1733). Discrediting this other biography is one of Victor's main aims.[29]

Both Victor and Cooper present the text of Booth's will, which leaves all his estate to Hester. Booth, who seems to have supported his extended family for some time, feared that they would contest his will. He explains this in terms of his celebrity in Victor's biography: "As I have been a Man much known and talk'd of, my not leaving Legacies to my Relations may give Occasion to censorious People to reflect upon my Conduct in this latter Act of my Life" (26). He states that his present worth does not equal the money his wife brought into the marriage, so he prefers "not to give away any Part of the Remainder of her Fortune at my Death, having already bestow'd in free Gifts upon my Sister, *Barbara Rogers*, upwards of 1300 Pounds, *out of my Wife's Substance*; and full 400 Pounds of her Money upon my undeserving brother, *George Booth*" (26–7). He reveals that he administered these gifts "*at the earnest Solicitation of my Wife*," though "[t]he inhuman Return that has been made my Wife for these Obligations, by my Sister, I forbear to mention" (27). His sister may not have approved of his marriage in 1719, for Booth's intended was a dancer and actress who had also been mistress to James Craggs and the duke of Marlborough, and who had had an illegitimate child by Craggs. Booth's prescient consciousness of public scrutiny of his death caused him to spell out in his will his

past efforts to help his family, his devotion to his wife, and his clear intent to leave his property to her.

Doubts about Booth's mental state during his last years and final illness could call into question the soundness of his will and its problematic contents. John Brydall's *Non Compos Mentis* (1700) and Anthony Highmore's *A Treatise on the Law of Idiocy and Lunacy* (1807) testify to the importance of the sound mental state of the testator: Highmore writes, "[I]t is sufficient for the party who pleads the insanity of the testator's mind, to prove that he was in that situation at any time previous to the making his will; although he do not prove this condition at the very time of making it."[30] Significantly, Cooper's anonymous biography describes the end of Booth's life quite differently from Victor. First, Cooper describes a "violent Fit of Lunacy" during the first attack that caused Booth's long decline. He explains, "'tis generally thought [the fit] was created from Notions of Greatness, which his Performances had instilled into him" (16). In his fits, which continued intermittently until his death, Booth "would generally imagine himself the Hero he had been upon the Stage, and treat his Servants as his Slaves" (20). If Booth had been mentally ill, his illness's severity could affect the outcome of his legacy.

Victor considers these accusations of madness as slander and legally dangerous. To counteract accusations of madness when Booth wrote his will, Victor states that Booth composed it "two Years before his Death" (25), on 2 June 1731. In *The Most Solitary of Afflictions*, Andrew Scull notes how mental illness has historically been humiliating for the sufferer's family, and Victor's account seems sensitive to the vulnerability of Booth's widow.[31] Victor answers the accusations of the Cooper biography by pointing out that during Booth's first illness, "he was delirious but two Nights and one Day: I thought it proper to take notice of this Circumstance, to obviate a false Report, *viz.*, that *He was out of his Senses during the whole time of his Illness*" (13). Instead of describing a man driven mad by his profession, Victor shows, via the hard scientific evidence of the autopsy, a man of great courage enduring a terrible illness with fortitude. And he thus protects Hester Booth's feelings—as well as her inheritance.

We have seen how actress biographies construct their subjects solely as sexual beings. Those of actors are not so one-dimensional, but actors were also accused of sexual profligacy. The autopsy report also works to defend Booth against this charge. The Cooper biography suggests that Booth's cal-

lous rejection of his mistress, Mrs. Mountfort, "threw his Mistress into a violent Fit of Sickness, so that she took to drinking, which, some say, kill'd her" (14). Victor denies this, stressing his subject's honorable conduct. Of the affair, he writes: "I should be inclin'd to leave this Circumstance beneath that friendly Veil, which Humanity directs us to throw over the Failings of the Dead, if Justice due to the Memory of my Friend did not compel me to clear him from some base Aspersions, which have been cast on him, even since his Death, in relation to this Affair" (8–9).

Victor may have felt that Booth and his widow needed protection against assumptions about the consequences of his affairs, especially when it became public knowledge that Booth had followed a mercury cure. This prescription was most strongly linked with syphilis, a disease that physicians complained drove patients to quacks to preserve secrecy. In locating Booth's end in his bowels, Victor worked to remove suspicions that the great actor died in more shameful circumstances. In proving this point biographically, Victor tried not only to clear the record for Booth but to raise his own reputation. His success in securing Mrs. Booth's gratitude and friendship throughout his life is evident from her leaving him fifty guineas when she died in 1773.

That an actor's life and death intersected with controversy over mercury is especially appropriate. Mercury's properties had always been seen as inscrutable and wondrous, used in attempts to change lower metals into gold. The author of the anonymous *A Treatise on Mercury,* one of the pamphlets in the Dover/Turner controversy, states that, "Mercury, according to the Alchymists, is the Proteus of Nature." That author also asserts that its name derives from "its Agility, and the different Shapes it is capable of, alluding to the Character of the Heathen Deity of that Name."[32] Like an actor performing characters, then, this metal fits the various vessels into which it is poured.

But these magical characteristics of both mercury and acting are negated through the anatomical facts of the autopsy. Through those facts, medical writers tried to identify the exact uses of mercury. By negating the report of Booth's madness and by sticking to the clear medical facts of the case, Victor was also struggling against contemporary misconceptions of actors. Cooper's book attributes Booth's mad spells to his position as an actor, suggesting that actors could fall victim to their all-consuming talent, that they were toying with enigmatic, overwhelming powers. Joseph Roach

has noted the anxiety expressed in some eighteenth-century acting theory, which proposed that passions could be easily summoned from lower regions by "voluntary metamorphosis" or "force of Imagination," but they may not be so easily quelled.[33]

However, the evidence of this autopsy recasts this problem as medical rather than mysterious and links the actor's case not only to medical practice but also to acting theory and biography. Cooper implies the dangerousness of acting to those who meddle with the expressive powers of the body, but the autopsy counteracts his irrational fear with somatic testimony. In doing so, this nexus of texts participates in the systematization Barbara Maria Stafford describes in *Body Criticism*: "The task of the enlightened critic was like that of the mathematician. He was to prune this thicket into an orderly, objective, and mechanical nature conceived according to eternal principles. The complex transformation of the physical into the conceptual, or of the probable into the formulaic, required a century to accomplish. In an increasingly specialized, professionalized, and discipline-oriented world, prismatic and indistinct effects ran athwart monochromatic and exact readings."[34]

The "indistinct" potential of Booth's body and its powers was countered by the autopsy's "exact reading" of his final illness. The flourishing new genre of performance and drama criticism, in which Victor later took part, worked similarly, by dissecting the actor's expression of emotion into prescribed, appropriate gesture and movement. In *The Life of Mr. Thomas Betterton*, Gildon has Betterton stress the "*Government, Order,* and *Balance*" of whole body, then head, eyes, eyebrows, face, hands. His precepts are part of the impulse to "prune" the messiness of acting into a formula: "I have often wish'd, therefore, that some Men of good Sense, and acquainted with the *Graces of Action* and *Speaking,* would lay down some Rules, by which young Beginners might direct themselves to that perfection, which every body is sensible is extremely (and perhaps always has been) wanting on our Stage . . . a System of *Acting,* which might be a Rule to future Players" (57, 17).

In *Memoirs of Booth*, Victor prints a letter from Aaron Hill that describes Booth in a way that echoes (but does not exactly imitate) this systematizing, anatomizing approach: "His Gesture, or, . . . his Action, was but the Result and necessary Consequence of this Dominion over his Voice and Countenance: For having, by concurrence of two such Causes,

impres'd his Imagination with the Stamp and Spirit of a Passion, his Nerves obey'd the Impulse by a kind of Natural Dependency, and relax'd or brac'd successively into all that fine Expressiveness, with which he painted what he spoke, without Restraint or Affectation" (33). Hill's description reflects the exploratory approach to acting, the need to find the hidden springs of its paradox. This anatomical approach will also be applied to and then condemned in biography, as Helen Deutsch has shown. Commentators on Boswell's use of anecdote in *The Life of Johnson* stress that "the anecdote's exposure of private and petty details was equivalent to murderous fragmentation, and Johnson's outraged corpse refused to pardon its offenders."[35] An anonymous biographer of Johnson points to the shame that both physical and biographical anatomizing can cause: "With a new and base species of intellectual anatomy, they have laid open his heart after his death, and have produced to the observation of mankind parts of its constituent materials not always creditable to the dead, but what is perhaps of still more consequence, in the highest degree, afflicting to the living."[36] Though Victor includes the autopsy in his book, he is not guilty of this intrusive psychological exposure.

In counteracting tales of Booth's madness, Victor also answers perennial suspicions of the actor's ontological and social status, of the indistinct divide between the actor and his roles. In the early modern period, as Jonas Barish and others have noted, performers were often chastised because they replaced their God-given identities with ones they had themselves chosen, and often those new identities overthrew social hierarchies: a pauper-actor could play a prince; the unknown Booth could play the classical hero Cato. Mad, Booth raises his social prominence and treats others as slaves far beneath him. His roles become conduits of his madness, encouraging that madness to take on disruptively ambitious social forms. Cooper's author is still wary about the performer's social ambitions and so stresses Booth's unreliability through details of his temper, his affairs, and his illnesses. Cooper's Booth is a roguish, unstable character, in contrast to his dignified stage role and the upstanding citizen Victor presents.

In answering the Cooper pamphlet, then, Victor champions the dignity of Booth and thus the potential of all performers. His version of Booth's end implicitly claims actors as professionals who can live sober and socially useful lives, and who die of the same morally neutral diseases as anyone

else. Booth's body, so often displayed on stage for the entertainment and instruction of his audience, was also bared textually for his readers. Though commodified in both media, Booth's bodily performance in his biography connects intimately to these larger issues of the performance of authority and claims actors as "normal" physical human beings who engage in a comprehensible though difficult craft.

CONCLUSION: ACTORS AND QUACKS

Recall that Turner used the case primarily to expose the supposed quack doctor Dover. The word *quack* derived, perhaps, from the Dutch/German *quacksalver,* or mercury doctor (and thus appropriate in at least one way to Dover), it denoted medical practitioners who operated outside most established medical channels, and it implied unqualified and inferior medical practice. Practitioners outside the mainstream could be—or were characterized as being—charlatans and impostors looking to get rich through patients' fear and ignorance; but some, like Dover, claimed that the very fact of not being part of the established system made their care more effective. As he warned in the sixth edition of his *Ancient Physician's Legacy* (the last published in his lifetime), "I would caution unwary People against one Thing, which is, Not to take every Graduate for a Physician, nor a Clan of prejudiced Gentlemen for Oracles. Experience is all in all; and I will venture to say, some Experience has fallen to my Share."[37] Traveling doctors made good livings in the provinces, where they could set up stages and hawk their nostrums. Such quacks performed the role of the physician, though they neither had the accepted qualifications nor, perhaps, the intention to heal. In fact, Tobyas Thomas's biography of Jo Hayns describes how Hayns set up in Hartford as "Signior Salmatius," a famous Italian doctor, who advertised "[c]uring all manner of Distempers incident to Mankind . . . which was believed by the admiring Rabble" (36).[38]

The connections between medicine and performance were many. As Roy Porter notes about attitudes toward quacks, "for many contemporaries, imposture was the heart of the matter."[39] The author of *The Modern Quacks Detected* (1752) rails against "Physical Impostors," "villainous Pretenders," and "impudent Intruders on the Medicinal Province." This

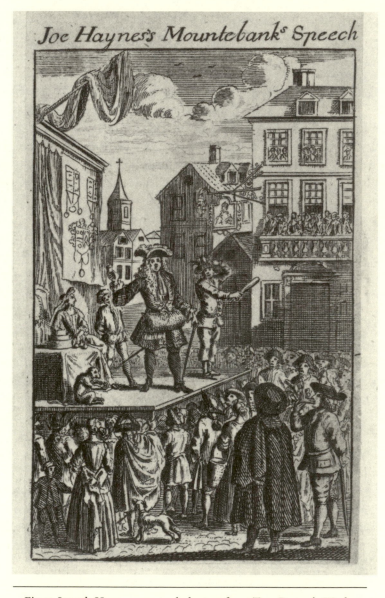

Fig. 7. Joseph Hayns as a quack doctor, from Tom Brown's *Works*.
REPRODUCED WITH PERMISSION BY THE HARVARD THEATRE COLLECTION,
THE HOUGHTON LIBRARY.

author pinpoints the underlying anxiety medical authorities had about quacks: that all people will "let in an Opinion, that the Art [of medicine] itself is a Cheat, and its Professors Men of ill Designs."[40] The danger of false authorities is that they call into question all authorities. Suspected quacks only further undermine public trust in the medical profession, which already had public relations problems, given its perceived tendency to kill rather than heal its patients: "These Gentlemen of the *Faculty* are Pensioners to *Death*, and travel Day and Night to enlarge that Monarch's Empire; for you must know, notwithstanding distemper'd Humours make a Man sick, 'tis the Physician has the Honour of killing him."[41] Public distrust results in economic impact for those licensed practitioners who saw their patients siphoned off by those they considered quacks.

So a central connection between the player Booth and this medical controversy was the concern with imposture. In his stage life, Booth pretended to the authority of statesmen and monarchs, but his opened body was used to debunk the performance of authority by quacks. Victor's biography, then, serves a dual unmasking. Readers desired to know the man behind the roles, and this is what Victor shows them: an upstanding professional man, cleared of the charges of usurping inappropriate social roles. And Victor claims his book, rather than Cooper's, to be the real biographical authority on Booth. The included autopsy report strengthens this validation, as it helps establish the true cause of Booth's death, it helps show the true uses of mercury cures, it helps identify the true physicians, and it indicates the true biographer as opposed to the slanderous hack. The demystification of the body's secrets combines here with the demystification of the actor's art. Stafford enumerates the "[d]igging knives, invading scissors, sharp scalpels [that] mercilessly probed to pry apart and distinguish muscle from bone," and claims that "such excavation stood for an investigative intellectual method that uncovered the duplicity of the world. Discursive thought called upon powers of baring abstraction whereby the lowly particular was mentally separated from the elevated generality."[42] Victor's biography participates in this process; the mysterious art of acting, as we saw in the early *Life of Hayns*, is replaced by an effort to understand the specific physical mechanics of the actor. Stafford's interpretation of new medical methods gives us a tool for understanding how the particulars of Booth's body contribute to the larger body of a general acting theory.

Players will continue to be linked with questions of physiology and health throughout eighteenth-century criticism and biography. Many will be chastised for using illness as an excuse for not acting. Others, usually actresses, will be accused of using their bodies inappropriately, thus endangering the health of their admirers and even that of the nation. The physical is reflected in the linguistic as well. Samuel Foote loses his leg, spawning a host of puns (many by Foote himself). Superstar David Garrick has a Dublin flu unofficially named after him—"Garrick fever"—because its outbreak coincided with his successful appearance in that city and the fan frenzy he caused.[43] Tools of their professional as well as social success, performers' bodies attract attention and suspicion. Writers probe and describe those bodies scientifically, admiringly, and salaciously to discover the sources not only of the performer's art but also of their increasing social attainments.

In the eighteenth century, a "mercury" was also a hawker of pamphlets and news sheets: a meaning of the word derived from Mercury as the god of commerce combined with that of his Greek roots as the messenger-god Hermes. Booth was himself a mercurial Proteus of an actor, whose acting abilities resembled those of the metal. He consulted "Dr. Quicksilver" and ingested the metal; his mercury-laden body became a battleground for "quacksalvers," and the body's postmortem report became the subject of biographers and medical hacks. Their books, in turn, could have been sold by mercuries. Thus the circle of acting and medicine and print is complete.

CHAPTER 5

Actor v. Author

COLLEY CIBBER'S CHALLENGE
TO LITERARY AUTHORITY

This Apology being chiefly intended for the
Satisfaction of future Readers, it may be
thought unnecessary to take any notice of
such Treatises as have been writ against this
ensuing Discourse, which are already sunk
into waste Paper and Oblivion; after the
usual Fate of common Answerers to Books,
which are allowed to have any Merit: They
are indeed like Annuals that grow about a
young Tree, and seem to vye with it for a
Summer, but fall and die with the Leaves in
Autumn, and are never heard
from any more.

JONATHAN SWIFT,
"Apology" for A Tale of a Tub (1710)

AT LEAST TWO of the biog-
raphies surveyed so far were
published by authors who are
as much involved in a struggle for cultural authority as their thespian subjects. Added to the difficulties Charles
Gildon and Benjamin Victor faced are

some of the special problems an actor or actress has in attempting a writing project for him- or herself, as in the case of Tobyas Thomas or Charlotte Charke. This actor-author category exists between the dual sets of cultural expectations for authors and for performers. (And for Charke, the nexus is even more complex because of additional expectations for women.) As many recent scholars have noted, "authorship" itself was in transition at this time; for example, Dustin Griffin traces the unsteady and incomplete shift from patronage to a market-based writing economy in the eighteenth century.[1] The Scriblerians and others tried to maintain a distinction between the genteel poet, properly educated and writing for noble fame and the improvement of his country, and the commercial hack, assumed to be from a low background and writing out of unseemly ambition and for personal gain. Conceptually, in the words of Elizabeth Eisenstein, the eighteenth-century professional author "wavered between the lofty position of arbiters of taste and inspired 'immortals' and the lowly role of supplying for favor or payment commodities sold for a profit on the open market."[2]

Actors are a special case. In the theater, the written word is not the final word: it must be performed. Before 1740 dramatic criticism, histories, prologues, and epilogues show that actors and authors often chafed against each other, each claiming control of and responsibility for the aesthetic object, the theatrical production. Actors who wrote plays often met with disapproval. For instance, Gerard Langbaine's *An Account of the English Dramatic Poets* (1691) includes an entry for William Mountfort that begins, "One who from an Actor, sets up for an Author; and has attempted both Tragedy and Comedy, with what success, I leave to those who have seen his Plays to determine." His description of Thomas Heywood's voluminous output is prefaced by "Tho' he were but an Actor," as if Heywood overcame a serious occupational handicap.[3] In all of his actor-author entries, Langbaine implies that a mere actor should not attempt to scale Parnassus—even only to the lower elevations of dramatic comedy—and when one does so successfully, the feat must have been accomplished either by luck or indulgent patronage. Recall that the anonymous *Comparison between the Two Stages* (1702) said of Betterton, "I shou'd not ha' scrupled him my particular Favour, if he had not play'd the Fool, and writ himself." In this author's view, actor-authors have contributed to the disease afflicting contemporary drama: "The Players have all got the itching Leprosie of

Scribling as *Ben. Johnson* calls it; 'twill in time descend to the Scene-keepers and Candle-Snuffers."[4] Playwriting has already "descended" from the lofty authors to the hireling actors—and who knows to what depths it may fall from there. Before John Downes's *Roscius Anglicanus,* players were not often integral to stage history but more often appeared as necessary evils who transgress beyond their class into more elevated activities such as dramatic writing.

By the late eighteenth century, and with some exceptions, resistance toward players as playwrights seems to disappear. Yet actors' further trespasses on literary ground were still problematic. What happens when an actor writes poetry, or cultural criticism, or—worse yet—considers his own paltry life and opinions worth the attention of a large readership? Describing the ways in which actors collided with changing concepts of authorship is the main aim of this chapter. Examining the results of these collisions not only will lead us to a better understanding of some of the mid-century thespian biographies and their influence on the genre, it will also help us see the impact on a protocelebrity culture, when actors themselves begin to take a larger role in their own image creation.

We turn first to the debut of thespian autobiography in English, Colley Cibber's *An Apology for the Life of Mr. Colley Cibber, Esq.* (1740).[5] In my discussion of Charke's *Narrative* (1755), I mentioned the pivotal role of her father's book as a model and foil for her autobiographical writing. But Cibber not only played this role for his children—his son Theophilus, like Charke, published a self-referential work—he also was one of the first to claim a position between the competing demands on the actor-author. In this chapter, we will consider the *Apology,* its contributions to the thespian biography genre, and its place in the print culture of the mid-eighteenth century. By viewing it primarily as a rhetorical product of print controversy, we can understand its aims better, and we can also see how it managed to anger so many critics.

Cibber's work generated scorn primarily because of its authorial claims. Cibber not only portrayed himself as a knowledgeable theatrical writer with little formal training, he reveled in that role. After many years applauded and heckled on stage as well as in pamphlets and newspapers, observing what sold and what failed in both performance and print, he knew his audience—though he may not have respected it—and he was able to market himself appropriately via his textual presentation. This

autobiographical and commercial self-fashioning allowed any writer to present him- or herself in whatever way he or she chose, an ability of print that was perhaps even more threatening than the performances of actors. As Jean-Christophe Agnew quotes from Shaftsbury, "'An author who writes in his own person,' Shaftsbury warned, 'has the advantage of being who or what he pleases. He is no certain man, nor has any certain or genuine character; but suits himself on every occasion to the fancy of his reader, whom, as the fancy is nowadays, he constantly caresses and cajoles.'"[6] In his autobiography, Cibber embraces this market-driven method of self-presentation. Besides writing a theater history still valuable today, Cibber's contribution was to expand literary roles for his theatrical writing heirs; this was—Swift's assessment of an "apology" and its critics notwithstanding—a legacy from which even David Garrick profited.

CIBBER AND CONTROL OF THE STAGE AND TEXT

In the *Apology*, Cibber presented the theater as a populous, complex world of interdependent roles: players, managers, spectators, dramatists, patentees, financial speculators. By drawing on his privileged position as a powerful theatrical insider, Cibber enlarges the reader's sense of what that "inside" contains, helping to create that specialized celebrity space where theater denizens seem to enjoy a different type of life than other people. Cibber includes short biographies of past and contemporary players within his work. These sketches do not respond directly to earlier biographies and do not recycle any earlier material, but since Cibber refers in the *Apology* to the "hasty Writers" who have followed the deaths of Ann Oldfield, Barton Booth, and Robert Wilks with biographies, we can assume that he was familiar with the quality and format of the biographies of the 1730s. This phrase of disapprobation seems to indicate a desire to modify current biographical methods.

The main goals of his modifications appear to be increasing biographical accuracy (though his detractors would maintain he never attempted this) and including a more thorough exposition of how the professional life of each player, past or present, contributes to the health of the whole theatrical enterprise. Unlike earlier and subsequent writers who capitalized on scandal or who provided only vague insights, Cibber's version of the acting life centers on the theater and on the crucial importance of the

actor—not the dramatist—to the theatrical project. In his characterizations of himself and other players, Cibber proposes that actors should be those in control of the theater and also in control of their textual representations.

Cibber effects reform by basing his sketches of other players on interactions with these players, on observations of performance, and on the anecdotes he has collected through the years: his own personal experience. During his ambitious early years at Drury Lane, Cibber acted, wrote plays, and served as an assistant to the unscrupulous manager, Christopher Rich. Both this experience and his later years as a manager taught him to be a close observer, a skill amply evident in these biographical sketches. Because of the sources of his material and his rhetorical aims, Cibber does not give standard biographical data such as birthplace, education, parentage, or death, *except* as they relate to the particular player's stage career. Cibber concentrates on the public professional life and omits personal material in his sketches, just as he does in his self-presentation. Cibber describes his biographical method in the following passage: "I had once thought to have fill'd up my Work with a select Dissertation upon Theatrical Action, but I find, . . . that all I can say upon that Head, will naturally fall in, and possibly be less tedious, if dispers'd among the various Characters of the particular Actors, I have promis'd to treat of; I shall therefore make use of those several Vehicles, which you will find waiting in the next Chapter, to carry you through the rest of the Journey, at your Leisure" (70).

If he was not pleased with the hackwork of "hasty Writers," he also seems dissatisfied with books like Gildon's, which provide "tedious" lessons that could better please if they instructed through biography. Thus his sketches merge the two earlier methods into pedagogy made more comfortable by use of particular players as "Vehicles." By eschewing Gildonian discussion of systematized "Theatrical Action," Cibber downplays the "high" oratorical tradition and its elite and educated social roots. By avoiding use of scandalous private material, he dismissed the "low" tradition of popular forms such as rogue and whore biographies and their variants in *The Beggar's Opera* books. His selective methodology helps create new discursive positions for the performer, though it also will help provoke the hostile reactions to his book.

What exactly does Cibber have to say about "Theatrical Action"? Cib-

ber chooses thirteen late-seventeenth-century players to present to his readers: "These Actors whom, I have selected from their Contemporaries, were all original Masters in their different Stile, not meer auricular Imitators of one another, which commonly is the highest Merit of the middle Rank; but Self-judges of nature, from whose various Lights they only took their true Instruction" (59). He poses the crucial question, "[W]hat Talents shall we say will infallibly form an Actor?" (69). He acknowledges the importance of training and study but saves his highest commendation for "[t]hat *Genius*, which Nature only gives" (69). He elaborates: "Actors, like Poets, must be born such. . . . Instruction, 'tis true, may guard them equally against Faults or Absurdities, but there it stops; Nature must do the rest" (55). His biographical sketches stress that these are not simply well-trained craftspeople but unique, artistic individuals. Embracing this "modern" perspective on the sources of acting talent, he consistently praises originality as a player's most valuable quality, and each sketch identifies the player's most distinctive feature.

The sketches present a palette of thirteen distinctive acting traits from which others derive. Superlatives abound. For example, William Mountfort was "the most affecting Lover within my Memory," one who also had "a Variety in his Genius, which few capital Actors have shewn. . . . he could entirely change himself; could at once throw off the Man of Sense, for the brisk, vain, rude, and lively Coxcomb" (74–6). Unfortunately, even superior performance is transitory. Betterton is Cibber's consummate actor, yet Cibber despairs of his ability to describe Betterton's art: "But alas! since all this is so far out of the reach of Description, how shall I shew you Betterton? Should I therefore tell you, that all the *Othellos, Hamlets, Hotspurs, Mackbeths,* and *Brutus*'s, whom you may have seen since his time, have fallen far short of him; This still would give you no Idea of his particular Excellence" (60). Cibber uses comparisons in other instances, but for Betterton, a true original, they fall short. He wrestles with this difficulty in his character of the seventeenth-century comedian James Nokes as well, and hopes to resolve it by describing audience reaction: "To tell you how he [Nokes] acted them [his roles], is beyond the reach of Criticism: But, to tell you what Effect his Action had upon the Spectator, is not impossible: This then is all you will expect from me, and from hence I must leave you to guess at him" (83). Cibber tries to capture the ephemerality of acting in the permanence of print, writing his history to "contribute to the

Prosperity or Improvement of the Stage" (8). Cibber provides printed act-ing models but in a less formal and more personalized manner than Gildon did or than Aaron Hill, author of "Essay on the Art of Acting" (1746), was to do. Cibber does not, however, recognize the paradox of his method—providing models of originality for imitation.

Like Gildon's *Betterton,* Cibber's *Apology* serves multiple readerships, the most important of which are actors and appreciative spectators. But while Cibber uses the *Apology* to instruct other actors through his exam-ples, his approach to his nonacting readers is much different than Gildon's. Gildon urged these readers to think of acting as a skilled and respectable art. Notwithstanding his admonitions to his acting colleagues, Cibber shifts Gildon's emphasis and sides with his fellow professionals against "outsiders," especially audience members. Sometimes he merely analyzes how audiences affect what happens on stage, as in his treatment of Nokes. He tells us also how Betterton reacted to applause, explaining that Betterton thought "there were many ways of deceiving an Audience into a loud one; but to keep them husht and quiet, was an Applause which only Truth and Merit could arrive at" (65). In almost all instances, Cibber casts the audience as an object to be manipulated by the talented actor. When trying to explicate differences in dramatic effect, such as that between tragedy and comedy, Cibber again emphasizes the ignorance of the audience in the face of the actor's power. The playgoer can usually explain why he or she weeps at tragedy, "[b]ut it may sometimes puzzle the gravest Spectator to account for that familiar Violence of Laughter, that shall seize him, at some particular Strokes of a true Comedian" (82). Cib-ber may give instructive descriptions of good acting, but he is not willing to dissect the actor's mystery for an unappreciative audience—and he had faced many, both on stage and in print.

Cibber's comments stress the actor's power over the audience, a situa-tion he sees as its proper distribution. When the audience seizes control, Cibber chastises it. He actively blames spectators for unhealthy trends in drama, disruptions of performances, and encouragement of bad acting habits. Sometimes Cibber uses a whole character sketch to explicate actor/audience relations and to teach proper audience behavior. For exam-ple, Samuel Sandford excelled in playing villains and was thus an actor "admir'd by the Judicious, while the crowd only prais'd him by their Prej-udice" (77). He had a "low and crooked Person" and since stage conven-

tion decreed that "such bodily Defects were too strong to be admitted into great or amiable Characters," Sandford "was not the Stage-Villain by Choice, but from Necessity" (77). Cibber adapts Hamlet's theory of dramatic effect, claiming that Sandford could not have possessed the evil qualities of the characters he portrayed, "for had his Heart been unsound, or tainted with the least Guilt of them, his Conscience must, in spite of him, in any too near Resemblance of himself, have been a Check upon the Vivacity of his Action" (80). Cibber regrets Sandford's typecasting and recounts a memorable anecdote about Sandford's once playing "an honest Statesman." The audience, after sitting through four acts without Sandford being revealed as a villain, could not believe him honest and "fairly damn'd" the play. Lois Potter points out that Cibber himself was also often typecast as fops and villains; she suggests that he uses the story of Sandford to "defend Sandford's morals and, by implication, his own." [7] We will soon discuss Cibber's self-defense in more detail, but the identification of an actor with his roles is also a component of celebrity.

Cibber's use of such anecdotes reproves spectators but also reveals how the development of drama lies at the mercy of what happens nightly in the theater between actors and audience. He protests the unfairness of an audience's not allowing a play a hearing because of prejudice against the author, perhaps alluding to the rough treatment some of his own plays received. He explains how loud playhouse "Criticks" intimidate the quiet, well behaved spectators who would allow the play a respectful hearing. Even when he complains about recent actors' "Errors" of rant and "straining Vociferation," he in part excuses them by explaining that the audience rewards such behavior: "I am not yet sure that they [the actors' faults] might not be as much owing to the false Judgment of the Spectator, as to the Actor" (61). Finally, Cibber accuses sweepingly: "It is not to the Actor therefore, but to the vitiated and low Taste of the Spectator, that the Corruptions of the Stage (of what kind soever) have been owing" (67). As a retired actor and a manager who has tried to placate and please, he can now indict the rabble, which often refused to be mollified and to accept the delicacies offered by the theaters. Textually, from his comfortable retirement, he can resist the role of the "feminized" spectacle (in Straub's terms) at the mercy of the audience's gaze.

Cibber thus uses his penetrating depictions of performers and his authorial status as a professional theater man to establish himself as a the-

117

atrical authority who can judge between gentle readers and loudmouth critics and help chasten unruly audience members through cultural intimidation. Cibber sets up standards of proper conduct and discrimination for his readers similar to those his own critics used on him. Instead of the theater being run by gentlemen-actors like himself who have the good judgment to mount tasteful, edifying, and well-acted productions, the theater is controlled by the mob, by anyone who can buy a ticket, by any uninformed wit who calls himself a "Critick": in short, by the market. As with a modern television station that plans its programs for the highest viewership numbers, Cibber blames a commercial need to provide the type of product the low tastes of his customers demand. Cibber prefers a tightly controlled two-theater monopoly for London. "I know it is the common Opinion, That the more Playhouses, the more Emulation; I grant it; but what has this Emulation ended in? Why, a daily Contention which shall soonest surfeit you with the best Plays; so that when what *ought* to please, can no *longer* please, your Appetite is again to be rais'd by such monstrous Presentations, as dishonour the Taste of a civiliz'd People" (56). For their own good as well as the good of the art, then, audiences should submit to the professional wisdom of management, which will guide them in using their new economic influence more intelligently.

Throughout the eighteenth century, struggles for control of the theater occurred as frequently between theater management and the audience as between management and the government. Theaters were destroyed; players and managers were forced to make public apologies. As Straub notes, such exertions of audience control were often physically dangerous to the players.[8] Performers had moved from being Their Majesties' servants to being humble servants of the public: like literature, the theater during this period shifts, slowly and not linearly, from a patronage to a market-driven system. Johnson's famous rueful lines from his Drury Lane prologue (1747)—"The drama's laws the drama's patrons give, / For we that live to please must please to live"—acknowledge this dependence on public opinion, although such reminders were commonplace in prologues that sought to curry audience approval. In the twentieth century as in the eighteenth, numerous writers, such as Richard Schickel, have seen such a shift as an ominous sign: "[T]he older forms of elitism have been all but entirely replaced by a new and deadlier form, a marketplace elitism in which all

success is measured quantitatively rather than qualitatively and critically."[9] Like Pope for poetry—though he would be mortified by the comparison—Cibber is engaged in maintaining an older, more authoritarian elite system for the theater, yet modified in that it would be controlled by informed actors, not Gildon's outsiders, those "Men of good Sense."

Cibber reacts to the spectators' bid for theatrical control by placing the actor—particularly the actor-manager and, even more particularly, himself—at the center of the theatrical world. The player had another strong rival as well, whose authority Cibber also delimits in his book. Many theater historians both before and after Cibber's time base their accounts on the development of the *drama,* and thus view dramatists as the central figures. Cibber champions the player's importance over the dramatist's. For example, Cibber blasts the bombast and absurdity of Nathaniel Lee's *The Rival Queens,* especially its language, asking, "[T]o what must we impute . . . its command of publick Admiration? Not to its intrinsick Merit, surely, if it swarms with passages like this I have shewn you! . . . Where, then, must have lain the Charm, that once made the Publick so partial to this *Tragedy?* Why plainly, in the Grace and Harmony of the Actor's Utterance" (64). Cibber credits the longevity of the play to the power of Betterton's voice. Indeed, a bad play like Lee's can corrupt other authors (encouraging "barren-brain'd" dramatists to compose more in the same "frothy flowing Style"), spectators, and even players, causing them to injure their voices (64). Cibber never blames Betterton, however, for using his extraordinary talent to popularize such trash; Betterton was merely doing his job and doing it admirably. As his discussion of Sandford also shows, players are exempt from moral responsibility in their representations. Moral and aesthetic rectitude are the playwright's jobs; approval of worthy plays is the audience's job.

Cibber's reproof of playwrights indicates his frustrations as a manager who had to read and choose plays as well as deny them. Executing this practical control over playwrights caused him much trouble. Cibber was often, perhaps justly, condemned by writers he received coldly and whose plays he was reported to have rejected with a curt "Sir, it will not do."[10] Himself a playwright, Cibber was also often accused of self-serving ambition and favoritism. My purpose is not to condemn or defend his conduct but only to point out that, since most dramatists of the time were also

pamphleteers and critics, Cibber's tense interactions with writers often showed up in the public presses from 1695, the year he gained some managerial oversight, until the end of his life. These tensions spread, however, from the simple denunciation of his bad taste and bad manners in repertoire selection, to larger concerns about actors' relations to writing. We have seen that Cibber elevates the actor over audience (or readers) and dramatists (other writers), so to these larger concerns we now turn.

CIBBER, AUTHORSHIP, AND PRINT CONTROVERSY

Included in the large group Cibber attempts to subdue to the actor's authority are his many detractors. Indeed, much of the *Apology* that has puzzled or alienated modern readers can be explained by understanding the book in terms of its rhetorical motivation and techniques. Cibber himself describes his book this way: "This Work, I say, shall not only contain the various Impressions of my Mind . . . but shall likewise include with them the *Theatrical History of my Own Time,* from my first Appearance on the Stage to my last *Exit*" (7). Cibber claims to write both autobiography *and* history, but most recent scholars seem to want to see it as either one or the other. Some precedent exists for making such a choice, since many writers who came after Cibber imitated either the historical or the autobiographical sections of the *Apology,* yet choosing encourages readers to miss the book's major function: self-defense. We now turn to what has been the most contested element of the *Apology,* Cibber's own narration.

Undoubtedly, the *Apology* stands as one of the most valuable sources of theater history in English. It provides an account of the London companies from the Restoration in 1660 through Cibber's own days as a manager. Such reference works as the *Biographical Dictionary* depend on Cibber for data; individual scholars such as Leonard R. N. Ashley focus on Cibber's "brilliant" character sketches. Richard Hindry Barker considers the book primarily as a history of the theaters, reducing the *Apology* to a single "thesis": that Cibber wrote to show that the London market could not support two theaters. The most recent editor of the *Apology,* B. R. S. Fone, seconds this thesis, and it certainly accords with Cibber's other efforts in his book to control the theater audiences.[11] Barker ultimately judges that the *Apology*'s "subject matter is rarely of general interest. . . . The *Apology,* in short,

is not a classic: it is a reference book for students and a source book for scholars."[12]

However valuable as a repository of fact, the *Apology* also claims to be, in Cibber's words, a "History of my private Life" (7). Because of such material, other scholars focus on Cibber's life and persona in the *Apology*; they want to view Cibber primarily as an autobiographer. They try to discover his true identity and his "sense of self" in his flippant narration of managerial woes. Most return from their explorations disappointed: Stauffer concludes that there is "something essentially hollow about Cibber's character." Using a puzzling metaphor, Ashley agrees: "In Cibber's autobiography we find no scintilla of the dark night of the soul." Patricia Meyer Spacks claims that Cibber "recognized an identity between story and self," but then shows how Cibber constructs a falsified and uncertain self that suffers from a "deep confusion of values." J. Paul Hunter views the *Apology* as eminently confessional, a successor of Puritan spiritual autobiography, where Cibber "would, in print, record himself as he understood himself to be: no holds barred, no secrets willfully kept, no perceived flaws unmentioned." Yet Hunter admits apologetically that "Cibber was not an especially perceptive viewer of himself," which assumes that the *Apology* was designed to present such a view (and that Hunter himself perceives Cibber correctly).[13] Only Straub, Lois Potter, and Jean Marsden seem comfortable with Cibber's persona in the *Apology*, undoubtedly because they see, in Marsden's words, "the constructed nature of the self he presents": a *role* instead of a "self."[14] These critical divisions are mostly a function of time, however; as more recent scholars apply the concept of the performative identity to autobiographies, the view of Cibber's narrative persona changes.

Considering the *Apology* as history or as autobiography leaves scholars dissatisfied with Cibber's text and, indeed, sometimes asks it to perform in ways for which it was not written. Hunter acknowledges the text's generic complexity when he states that it "represents a viable merger between private and public history, the story both of personal life and of larger events." But Barker comes closest to a satisfactory way of reading the *Apology* when he states that "the book is really Cibber's answer to his critics," although he does not elaborate much on this point.[15] If we approach the *Apology* as a rejoinder, an artifact of print controversy, we will be able to

reconcile the two approaches and avoid their inadequacies. Taking our cue from Barker, we can examine the book according to the rhetorical and tactical demands of a document functioning as an answer to earlier disagreements and attacks and as a spur for later comment and rebuttal.

I use the term "print controversy" to refer to the body of literature, most of it short-lived, that springs up around a topical issue and is fueled by the resources of print culture: pamphlets, broadsides, newspapers, periodicals. In Swift's words, "They are known to the world under several names: as disputes, arguments, rejoinders, brief considerations, answers, replies, remarks, reflections, objections, and confutations. . . . the chiefest and the largest . . . begin to be called Books of Controversy."[16] This discursive formation or subgenre is not of course restricted to theatrical and aesthetic issues; politics and religion are always the most active topics. In the most useful study of the political manifestation of this genre, Robert D. Spector notes that "[e]very crisis—whether an administrative change, a proposed excise tax, an economic scandal, or an outbreak of international hostilities—produced heated journalistic exchanges intended to bolster partisan support, sway adversarial opinion, or nurture opposition."[17] Theatrical controversy frequently accumulated moral and political associations, as in the case of *The Beggar's Opera*. In turn, print activity affects what happens (or doesn't happen) onstage, as in the suppression of *Polly*. Print controversy operates cyclically, accreting opinions and perspectives, not dissimilar to the mechanisms by which celebrity images develop.

Print controversy is a market-driven discursive formation: it presumes that power lies in the consumer of the pamphlet or periodical. Whereas Jürgen Habermas sees this as an indication of a healthy public sphere, and some eighteenth-century writers celebrated it as British liberty, literary reactionaries such as Swift and Pope decried it—often at the same time participating in it eagerly and using it shrewdly. Cibber condemns the audience's economic control over the theaters and drama, but he does not acknowledge print to be one of the prime means by which they have acquired this new power. By involving himself in print controversy, he encouraged the market control that he deplores in the *Apology*, yet by creating a strong, unified narrative persona for himself, he tries to control his readers' reactions in a way that he couldn't as a theater manager when he simply needed to please audiences.

Barker explains how Cibber entered print controversy. Cibber "was sin-

gularly tactless, capable of deliberately antagonizing men with whom he should never have quarreled," and his callousness toward hired actors and hopeful playwrights made him heartily disliked.[18] Cibber's cheapness and superciliousness have been remarked by his contemporaries, yet Barker's comment reminds us of Cibber's social position and how, while it afforded him practical power, it also obliged him to deference and servility. His negotiations of the player's balance of power and powerlessness seemed to invite print comment. Cibber himself rarely launched attacks outside of the occasional play preface or dedication, but he was often the subject of them. Although the *Register of Theatrical Documents* lists only two open letters to the public attributable to Cibber, it records at least forty-two attacks on Cibber and his plays (as compared to five accounts praising him in print and seven fairly balanced commentaries). One of the most vociferous public print embroilments in which Cibber took part was that over his politicized play, *The Non-Juror* (1717): the *Register of Theatrical Documents* catalogues six articles in the London newspapers, five pamphlets, one broadside, and one printed poem.[19]

Most noticeable about the attacks on Cibber are their strong narrators' voices and the intensity of their personal abuse. These were standard narrative techniques. According to Swift, a "disputant" takes on "the true spirit of controversy, with a resolution to be heartily scurrilous and angry, to urge on his own reasons, without the least regard to the answers or objections of his opposite, and fully predetermined in his mind against all conviction."[20] Print sparring becomes a complicated and protracted game of response and parry. The tendency of such productions to reply to each other was something Cibber would have learned and something booksellers may have encouraged to increase business. Edward L. Ruhe suggests cases in which seemingly antagonistic writers and booksellers taking different sides of controversial issues may in fact have been conspiring for mutual profit from the continuing controversy.[21] These practices kept people in the public eye; each disputant claimed to know the "true character" of those involved as, paradoxically, the versions of the "truth" multiplied with each addition to the controversy. Cibber understood these developing mechanisms of print. In responding to Pope, Cibber writes: "*Satyr* shall have a thousand Readers, where *Panegyric* has one. When I therefore find my Name at length, in the Satyrical Works of our most celebrated living Author, I never look upon those Lines as Malice meant to me, (for he

knows I never provok'd it) but Profit to himself: One of his Points must be, to have many Readers: He considers that my Face and Name are more known than those of many thousands of more consequence in the Kingdom: That therefore, right or wrong, a Lick at the *Laureat* will always be a sure Bait, *ad captandum vulgus,* to catch him little Readers" (25). Cibber knew his own value as both subject and object of print controversy.

But what was the controversy in which Cibber's *Apology* took part? The book was Cibber's coup de grâce, a 488-page response to all of the criticism to which he had been subject. It responded to accusations about his conduct as manager, his talent as an actor, and his failings as a man. But the controversy that develops *from* the *Apology* is slightly different, having more to do with the cultural positioning of the book and with his appointment as poet laureate ten years earlier. Recall the many lines Pope devotes to establishing Colley Cibber as the favorite of the goddess Dulness:

> In each she marks her Image full exprest,
> But chief in BAYS's monster-breeding breast;
> Bays, form'd by nature Stage and Town to bless,
> And act, and be, a Coxcomb with success.[22]

One of Cibber's "monsters" that contributed to Pope's scathing judgment is the *Apology*. An anonymous response entitled *The Laureat* (1740) describes Cibber's writing as "obscure, unconnected, and wrapt up and conceal'd in the clinquant Tinsel of Metaphor, and unnecessary Figures," and summarizes it: "[T]he frothy Thing is . . . blown up with tumid Metaphors, spun out with impertinent Deviations, crowded with distasteful Sufficiency, every where abounding with palliated Malice, and open Vanity; in many Places dark, and sometimes wholly unintelligible."[23]

Of course, many scholars since 1740 have pointed out that Cibber sometimes wrote poorly in the *Apology* (and always did in his odes as poet laureate) and have noted the contemporary abuse he received for it. While acknowledging Cibber's striking ability to describe fellow performers, Barker also states that "on the whole the style [of the *Apology*] is that of an undisciplined, even a slovenly writer; it is a style generally lacking in strength and incisiveness."[24] Admittedly, the quality of the *Apology*'s prose is uneven. But such a statement ignores the possibility that his irregular style was part of his persona in the *Apology*, and it also ignores the fact that

124

many of his contemporaries wrote poorly without garnering the indignant response that the *Apology* did. To understand why Cibber's writing has been scrutinized so caustically, we need to look beyond bad style and the well-documented personal animosities with Pope, Fielding, and Mist. Because underlying these grudges is one more reason for abuse: the *Apology* was written by an actor.

Cibber's actor-narrator has been discussed extensively: how he blithely admits and even parades his faults, his obvious pride and vanity, his inability to take himself seriously. Indeed, for an author out to show the importance of the player, he seems to undermine his authority through his own narration. However, like Gildon's adoption of Betterton, Cibber's use of a narrative persona helps deflect the type of criticism he would have had to endure had he presented a serious work of such length (which might have been just as extensive but of a different nature than what he actually experienced). Straub has argued that he attempted to "seize control through a show of giving it up," and that Cibber's ultimate "gesture of control depends upon the self-conscious show of relinquishing authority." As with Gildon's molding of Betterton, Cibber had to fashion himself a role that would best allow him to grant his words authority; unlike "Betterton's" modest deference, the pose of Cibber's flippant persona undercuts any deference he shows. In Straub's words again, "When Cibber makes a spectacle of himself, as he frequently does, he retains a self-consciousness that becomes a central part of the show. The actor, Cibber shows us, is not a helpless object but a professional exhibitionist who watches even as he displays himself."[25]

I believe Cibber's contemporaries recognized the bid for authority embedded in the multiple paradoxes of Cibber's textual self-presentation, especially as a writer of plays and odes and as apologist. Maynard Mack states that "Cibber had come to represent everything [Pope] believed a poet should not be, an enemy both to esthetic standards and to independence of court servilities."[26] Enmeshed in Pope's (and others') personal hostility lie his grudges against new types of people taking up pens—women, threshers, milkmaids. In his edition of Shakespeare, Pope even blames the errors in the plays on Shakespeare's own background as an actor; John Roberts, himself "a Stroling Player," then responds: it is "as utterly unreasonable to call Shakespear's Judgment in Question as an Author, because he was an Actor, as to degrade Mr. *Pope's* Capacity as a Poet because he is

Pope the Editor."[27] According to Pope, some of Cibber's plays had been bad enough—examples of plagiarism, of sentimental crowd-pleasing, or of political lackeyism, according to his critics—but the poetry he produced as poet laureate was unpardonable, both because the verses were so bad, and because an actor shouldn't *be* poet laureate. If Gildon had been concerned over what the state of the stage meant for the state of the nation, what could possibly be England's condition when someone like Cibber was laureate? Of course, many previous players had also been poets: Matthew Coppinger, Jo Hayns, James Spiller, Barton Booth. But many of these men chose not to publish (certainly none sought the laureateship), and those that did often expressed the ambivalence of their position. For instance, Coppinger says he publishes "in Compassion to the *Writing Players* (as having been one myself) and trust, my Example will make 'em fear the Judgments that attend those who Profane so Sacred a thing as Poetry," yet he also refers to "those Paltry Creatures the Poets" and hopes that "the Wits will say I'm a good Poet" after he's dead.[28] The conflicts in his comments reflect those of being a "Writing Player."

Cibber's position as the first actor to treat both his acting and his writing in a first-person narrative is significant in the context of the preceding thespian biographies. First, some of these texts simply ignore their subjects' literary efforts, such as in *Account of Coppinger*. Second, some biographies praise or at least take a benign view of their subjects' work. In his *Life of Betterton,* Gildon says of Betterton's plays, "Three Plays were written or translated by him, and brought on Stage with Success. . . . But he never would suffer any of them to be printed" (11). In his *Booth,* Victor prints a Latin inscription by Booth as a specimen of Booth's learned writing. He follows this with a collection of Booth's poetry, saying: "His Genius for Poetry is evident by the following Pieces, thro' all which there flows the greatest Harmony in the Numbers, and Accuracy in the Stile; but that Modesty which obstructed his Progress in the Poetical way, prevented the Publication, of any thing he wrote, in his Lifetime" (35). Each of these quotations relies on ideological assumptions of class-appropriate behavior. Gildon and Victor highlight their subjects' gentlemanly unwillingness to print their literary efforts, either because of an aversion to soiling their hands with vulgar print or because of their genteel modesty. Their writing was a private act, and they did not claim indiscriminate public praise for it, in contrast to their public performances.

Finally, there are those performers who are condemned for their literary attempts. For actresses, the accusation, predictably, is of impurity. As the narrator of a biography of Mary Robinson entitled *The Memoirs of Perdita* puns, "[I]n order to provide for herself as profitably as she could, . . . previous to her intimacy with his lordship, Perdita had issued proposals for publishing her *poetical works* by subscription; and it was reasonably expected that an edition of her *works* in *sheets* would produce no inconsiderable sum. . . . Whatever success attended her proposals, her works certainly never came into existence."[29] Notwithstanding such pessimism about her abilities, Robinson was able to launch a fairly successful literary career.

Akerby's *The Life of Mr. James Spiller*, discussed in chapter 2, is subtitled, "In which is interspers'd much of the poetical history of his own times." In addition to Spiller's roguish exploits, the book includes attacks on contemporary poets such as Lawrence Eusden, Thomas Moore, and John Dennis while at the same time ironically condemning Pope's *Dunciad* for its abuse of these writers. After discussing poetic criticism, *Life of Spiller* ridicules Spiller's own attempts in verse; Spiller borrowed "Gildon's *Arts of Poetry* for his Assistance, from whence having learn't the Rules of Measure, and furnish'd his Head with as great a Competency of Jingles for the ends of Verses, . . . he brought forth several very pretty Pieces" (31). Akerby prints Spiller's epilogue to his own benefit performance in the Mint, ironically commenting that the "elaborate and circumstantial Critick Mr. *L. T.* [probably Lewis Theobald] . . . designs to publish . . . with such ample Notes, as will make, with the Prolegomena, Testimonia Authorum, and Appendix, two Volumes in a handsome Octavo." Akerby characterizes Spiller's poetry as crimes, saying of the epilogue that "it was the first Piece of Poetry my Friend Mr. *Spiller* . . . was ever guilty of" (29). Akerby implied that Spiller excelled in his part in *The Beggar's Opera* because he knew the criminal milieu intimately, so his infringement on gentlemanly verse also becomes a crime, one of social class. Akerby portrays Spiller as a hack. Satirists implied that men were hacks not only because they wrote for money, but also because they were not born to an educable writing class, so hacks were also a type of impersonator. Spiller's impersonations can thus be condemned through both his job as an actor and his pretensions as a writer.

Enter Colley Cibber and his *Apology*, with a lifetime of ambition,

audacity, and print attacks behind him, combining the threat of the "unauthorized" author with the class ambiguity of the actor and the social status of a powerful manager and poet laureate. Two anonymous authors respond to the *Apology* immediately after its publication in 1740: *An Apology for the Life of T. . . C. . .*, a 144-page "pamphlet" purporting to be a biography of Cibber's son Theophilus, and *The Laureat; or, The Right Side of Colley Cibber,* another lengthy work at 126 pages. Both texts have on occasion been attributed to Fielding, though Martin Battestin mentions neither of them in his biography of Fielding, nor has anyone supplied anything but circumstantial and general stylistic evidence for their attribution.[30] Cibber himself continues the battle by answering these pamphlets in *The Egotist* (1743), in which he skillfully examines how print controversy works and laughs at those who would criticize his writings: of his odes, he writes that "none but Dunces would be serious Criticks upon them, and those you know are unanswerable."[31]

While these two critiques disagree with Cibber's characterizations of other players (especially his two fellow managers, Barton Booth and Robert Wilks) and his versions of theatrical events, and they assail his acting, his singing, and his phenomenal pride, they save their greatest hostility for Cibber as an author (which of course includes all of the above). Cibber considers his actor's life to have been worthy enough to publish, and both authors are appalled at his act of self-aggrandizement. Neither *T. . . C. . .* nor *The Laureat* spares Cibber's birthday odes or his dramatic works. *The Laureat* saves its harshest criticism for the *Apology* itself: its style, its text's structure, its narrative persona, that persona's prejudices. Cibber trespasses on literary distinctions of tasteful diction, appropriate subject matter, and the proper character of an author. *The Laureat* states: "[I]f this Work of his were to be dissected by a good Pen, . . . it would appear a most wretched and imperfect Skeleton, void of almost every Thing necessary either to delight or instruct" (2). This "dissection" by a "good Pen"—a pen held by a man with proper literary training—is *The Laureat*'s aim. Just as Victor included the autopsy of Booth's physical body to find the truth of his ailment and thus judge his life and art fairly, *The Laureat* will dissect Cibber's textual persona to reveal the real Colley Cibber and bring him to judgment. This author states that Cibber's "very Nakedness is a Disguise, . . . *Colley Cibber* is not the Character he pretends to be in this Book, but a

mere *Charletan,* a *Persona Dramatis,* a *Mountebank,* a Counterfeit *Colley"* (15).

The Laureat feels that Cibber does not approach his writing task with the appropriate consciousness of his unworthiness to be an author. Unlike Betterton and Booth, Cibber has no humility: when Cibber does not divulge his patron's name, the anonymous author states ironically, "[t]his is very modestly said, and I honour the Laureat for this single and singular Instance of his Humility and Integrity" (5). Indeed, Cibber is insufferably vain about his writing: "He is in a Rapture that he, now as a Writer, can talk to himself and not be interrupted" (19). And *The Laureat* attacks Cibber in his class ambitions, just as Akerby attacked James Spiller: "[A]ll the World knows that thy *plain Heart* did always hang after People of *Figure* and *Rank* and Fortune" (8). When Cibber implies that a "noble person" may publish characters of his "Brother Actors . . . by Way of Supplement" to the *Apology,* the *Laureat* responds, "Thou dost not surely hope to make us believe, that any noble Person can be reduced so low, to become thy Scavenger" (77–8).

This author has little patience with hack authors or ambitious actors. He defines authors (though apparently not himself) as "*Word drawers* or *Syllable Spinners* . . . [who] are able to fill the unlearned World with Folio's without being guilty of Learning or Labour" (13). He asks how a "mere Actor" like Cibber could become a corrector of other writers' plays at Drury Lane: "[I]f it should be asked, how a common *Comedian,* without any Morals, without Humanity, or any kind of Literature, came to be intrusted with this Office; we shall be obliged to impute it to the Corruption of the Manners of the Time" (119). Whereas Cibber blamed the corruption of the audience and critics, like this one, *The Laureat* blames the corruption of theatrical authority, actor-managers like Cibber with insufficiently genteel taste. With some few exceptions, *The Laureat's* opinion of players' private characters is not high: "Whatever the Actors appear'd upon the Stage, they were most of them *Barbarians* off on't, few of them having had the Education, or whose Fortunes could admit them to the Conversation of Gentlemen" (44). Most actors were, like Spiller, out of their proper sphere when fraternizing with their betters. Neither Spiller nor Cibber possessed the requisites of "ancient" learning that would allow them to play the gentleman role more convincingly, like Betterton.

In contrast, the author of *T. . . C. . .* seems concerned that people don't think well enough of actors; he has Theophilus say, "Nor is the theatrical Profession as contemptible as some affect to think. . . . But notwithstanding all I said, . . . the Profession of Player still continues, as by [Cibber's] Memoirs I find it has always done, to be held by many Gentlemen and People of Quality in no great Esteem."[32] In general much less harsh against Cibber than *The Laureat,* this book provides additional information on the theaters after Cibber left off his narrative. Yet it also focuses on Cibber's pride; Cibber "has set so great a Value on *himself,* that after being so long known, he will not let anyone know what he really is, under a less Consideration than a *Guinea*" (2), the sizable sum charged for the folio edition of the *Apology.* It implies, too, that Cibber (and Theophilus) wrote mainly for money (80). Its primary concern, however, is not that Cibber has all of these faults, but that his son Theophilus has them too. For example, Theophilus exposes his pride: "After having wrote my play called the *Lover,* I began to think myself every Day of more and more Consequence" (85). Both father and son use their hackwork to get above themselves.

In its ironic structural imitation of the chapters of the *Apology,* *T. . . C. . .* discusses Theophilus's writing activity, particularly his ability to pen self-serving theater ads and bills. Theophilus's writing ability reflects, of course, on his father (and vice versa). This author seems worried that not only the bad character of Cibber will continue (and be amplified) in his son but so will the bad writing, and London will have an established dynasty of bad writers—a concern we address more thoroughly in the next chapter. In this, *T. . . C. . .* engages with a popular contemporary trope of authorship as fatherhood; indeed, one of the defenses of eighteenth-century copyright according to Richard G. Schwarz was that it gave a sound patrimony to the written "sons."[33] All three texts under examination here refer to Colley or Theophilus as the "Sires" of their writings or the writings as the "offspring." *T. . . C. . .* mocks not only Cibber's real son, Theophilus, but also his textual son, the *Apology,* by revealing the unattractive qualities of both. "Like father, like son" comparisons fill *T. . . C. . .,* which states, "As in our Tempers there is a peculiar Similitude, so there is in our Faculties in Writing" (21). Theophilus admits that audiences laughed at one of his epilogues, which his first wife, Jenny, tells him he was "a *Blockhead to write,* and that [he] was [his] *father's own Son*" (82). Cibber's *Apology* is just another dreadful son of a talentless father.

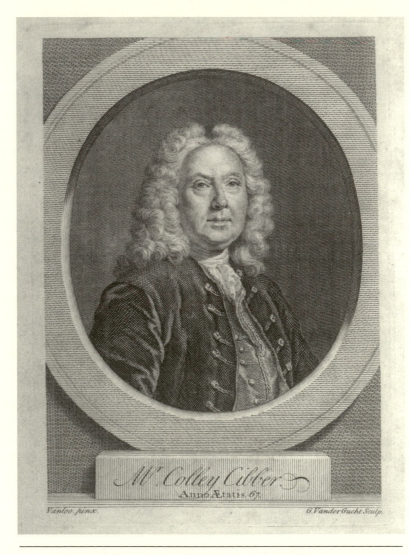

Fig. 8. Colley Cibber, frontispiece to his
Apology for the Life of Colley Cibber.
REPRODUCED WITH PERMISSION BY HORACE HOWARD FURNESS
MEMORIAL LIBRARY, ANNENBERG RARE BOOK AND MANUSCRIPT
LIBRARY, UNIVERSITY OF PENNSYLVANIA.

In both *T. . . C. . .* and *The Laureat,* Cibber appears as impertinent, bold, self-serving, and undignified, with a writing style to match. His imprecise style, absurd metaphors, disorganized digressions—all are interpreted not only as Cibber's inability to write but also as a warning of what happens when the wrong people put their written work before the public. But Cibber had anticipated many of his critics' complaints about his writing in the *Apology* itself: "[T]hat my Style is unequal, pert, and frothy, patch'd and party-coulour'd like the Coat of an *Harlequin*; low and pompous, cramm'd with Epithets, shrew'd [*sic*] with Scraps of second-hand *Latin* from common Quotations; frequently aiming at Wit, without ever hitting the Mark; a mere Ragoust, toss'd up from the Offals of other Authors: My Subject below all Pens but my own, which, whenever I keep to, is flatly dawb'd by one external [*sic*] Egotism" (29). He admits his style is "low," plagiarized, and a feeble attempt at wit. He also ostensibly (if ironically) agrees with a common opinion about the place of the theater in society when he states both of himself and of the theater: "My Subject is below all Pens but my own." Such an admission answers readers like Pope, who insist on an authorial dignity Cibber refuses to uphold (in fact, he creates a mock apology much in the way that Pope creates a mock epic). Cibber seems to say that if indeed he *is* the wrong type of person to write, at least he is not pretending to be otherwise.

It is significant that these detractors expended this much energy on Cibber's writerly crimes. Cibber did not present himself unassumingly, as befitted a man of his low literary stature, but brought his selfish foppery from the stage into the pages of his book. Indeed, the sheer physical luxuriousness of an early edition—a leather-bound quarto with a full-page frontispiece of Cibber—asserted a print presence as exaggerated as the narrative persona presiding within the covers. And Cibber will continue attempting to increase his authorial dignity in 1747 with the publication of *The Character and Conduct of Cicero.* Though Cibber's *Apology* may not be considered great prose, it must be seen as an attempt to establish the actor as an author with the ability (or effrontery) to assert a strong personality and his own version of events. Certainly the two responses to the *Apology* interpreted it thus and reacted by exposing strong cultural assumptions about actors-turned-authors.

CONCLUSION: CIBBER AND THEATER HISTORY

The author of *T. . . C. . .* is not convinced that print controversy helps the reputation or cause of the performers who engage in it: "I do not find that any of these epistolary Addresses to the Town from Theatric Performers have done them any Service, nor would I advise, on any Occasion, to have Recourse to such Expedients" (84). Nonetheless, Cibber's *Apology* emerges from its immersion in print controversy to become an important book for the later eighteenth century. In 1780 Thomas Davies proclaimed in *Memoirs of Garrick* that "[t]he *Apology* . . . is one of those original performances that scarcely ever was excelled, and will last as long as our language" (2:207) Even Johnson (who did not respect Cibber either as a man or as an artist) grudgingly admitted the book was "very entertaining" and "very well done."[34] The book's publication pointed new directions in performance criticism and theater history and, ironically in light of its literary embroilments, becomes itself a literary model from which other theatrical compilations will filch.

Whatever one might think about the vanity or the writing skill of the man who wrote the *Apology*, Cibber's impact on the course of all theatrical writing would be difficult to overestimate. As we've noted, Cibber's modern critics most value the *Apology* for its factual contributions to theater history, but the book even influenced the histories that immediately followed its publication in the eighteenth century. In these histories, we can notice a gradual expansion of options that parallel those opening up in thespian biographies. History and biography shared many features in the eighteenth century, as they still do. Like biographies, seventeenth- and early-eighteenth-century histories usually focused on great events and the lives of the great—royalty, nobility, powerful churchmen—a focus that is joined over the course of the century by histories of the press, of Freemasons, and even, using the term's broadest denotation, the history of comestibles such as wheat and malt. But while a new acceptance of unconventional historical subjects may have encouraged writers to chronicle the stage, precedent still urged them to write about the theatrical "great." And who, then, were the theatrical great? The question echoes my earlier inquiry into the redefinition of fame and the identification of the cultural hero that we considered with *The Beggar's Opera*. Answering this question

forced eighteenth-century writers to take positions on an unacknowledged struggle: who was more crucial to the stage, writers or actors?

Though this struggle preceded the *Apology,* Cibber's book served as a milestone in the development of theatrical history, as he exposed the fascinating characters and backstage machinations of the theaters of his lifetime, placing the actors at their center. Because drama-based histories (quite often simply playlists) sprang from the respectable literary realm of poetry, they dominated theatrical discourse long before other elements of the theater provoked interest.[35] Stage history and dramatic criticism solely based on dramatic texts were joined by history based on what happens in the theaters between performers, managers, and audiences. Thomas Davies gives us an example, as he appreciates the author-actor synthesis necessary to produce Garrick's Lear: "Who does not rejoice, when the creative hand of the poet, in the great actor, restores him [Lear] to the use of his faculties!"[36] This more inclusive history derives in part from preservation and dissemination of materials on which a broader theater history can be based, as writers learn to rely on other documents and data besides the printed dramatic text.

David C. Douglas has argued that after 1660, some areas of antiquarian scholarship became so large that specialization was necessary. Too much raw material in too many repositories caused those interested in history to pursue narrower topics.[37] These effects may be evident in the changing methods of establishing a theatrical past. Traces of the ancients and moderns controversy is also evident: as writers think more about the contemporary stage (both English and Continental) and modern history as opposed to classical stage history, necessarily constrained by rare and incomplete written records, alternative versions of the theatrical past emerge.

The controversy surrounding the *Apology* helped generate the publicity that spurs interest not only in historians (and readers) but in other writers whose motives may not be the most lofty. Cibber's book demonstrated that writers could gain income and also notoriety by penning theatrical memoirs. Not just the existence of this popular performer but his print manifestation helped generate a type of textual paparazzi who attempt to create a celebrity aura for themselves by latching onto performers in person and print. Cibber's focus on the character of the actor, his eccentric narrative

voice, his position at the center of print controversy—each of these choices inspired trends and imitators. From his own children to those who simply lifted sections of the *Apology* for inclusion in their own books, Cibber's descendents prove the indelible mark Cibber left on eighteenth-century writing.

CHAPTER 6

Inherited Authority?

IN THE SHADOW OF
COLLEY CIBBER

I know not but from my Father's Apology
some new Philosophers may arise, and
Posterity not give a proper Title to their Sect,
therefore I here mention that all who are of
our Opinion may distinguish themselves by
the name of CIBBERIANI.

An Apology for the Life of Mr. T . . . C . . . ,
Comedian (1740)

THE NUMBER of theatrical publications, especially biographies, increases dramatically in the second half of the eighteenth century, and though their authors may not have been exactly of the same "Opinion," many of them could be classified as "CIBBERIANI." Thespian autobiographers attempt to use their books as self-defense and acknowledge Cibber indirectly by entitling their books "apologies."[1] Among them are Theophilus Cibber, who publishes his

Serio-Comic Apology in 1748, mimicking his father's work like his sister; George Anne Bellamy (1785) and Mary Wrighten (1789), who create elaborate victim subject positions for their narrative voices in their *Apologies*; and Ann [Dancer Barry] Crawford (1759), who finds herself constructed in an *Apology* by a presumptuous author.[2] *T. . . C. . .*'s worst fears have been realized: Cibber has spawned a mob of progeny, a line of theatrical writers who explain and defend themselves vociferously, attempting to be as singular and eccentric as the original. Colley has fathered not only Theophilus and Charlotte but, textually, many others, and the prognosis for literary health—and literary authority—is not good.

T. . . C. . . jokingly makes Theophilus speak of being "my father's own Son," of owing "something to having *good Blood in my Veins*," and of the "Species of Ambition which by hereditary Happiness descends to me, call'd Vanity" (15, 4, 2). Yet in life, the close father-son relationship that *T. . . C. . .* ridicules and Theophilus affirms grew conflicted and frustrated. Prevented from taking over as Drury Lane manager in his father's place, Theophilus finds other ways of following in Colley's footsteps—composing his own *Apology*—and he looks to additional textual fathers. Examining closely Theophilus's life, autobiography, and his textual models will reveal the results of Theophilus's troubled relationship with the authority of the father.

Numerous autobiographers and biographers that followed Cibber's *Apology* in the next few decades also looked to other literary forebears besides Cibber. These texts borrow from outside of the theatrical tradition, and in doing so, they side with the defenders of literary authority against those who would claim authority for the performer. This continues the impulse we saw in the biographies following *The Beggar's Opera*: containing the rising prominence of the celebrity by deprecating the acting subject. They choose models from the world of fiction, seeming to follow the dictates of Roger North, who wrote biographies of his brothers in the late seventeenth century (which were not published until the 1740s): "The same ingredients that are usually brought to adorn fiction may come forward, and be as well applied to the setting forth of truths."[3] Yet they do not choose didactic or respectable fiction to set forth their biographical "truths." The models they select often have unusual narrative methods and voices, such as Lawrence Sterne's *Tristram Shandy* and Henry Fielding's *Tom Jones*. Such links echo the questions of paternity familiar from

Theophilus's struggles—after all, *Tristram Shandy* is primarily a book centered on the father-son relationship, as the child attempts to be born, and Tom's journey is a quest for his true genealogy. Furthermore, in relying on fiction, these books call into question the truth value of their own narratives, suggesting that this new type of person, the celebrity, is really as inconsequential as a character in a story—and thus not a threat. None of these writers turns to the historical, classical tradition that includes the legend of Roscius; they are looking for homegrown models who will be familiar and amusing to their readers (thus helping to sell more copies) and who will fit the outré, ambiguous status of the celebrity performer.

So the thespian biographies that follow Cibber's *Apology* are not only numerous, they suggest numerous authority struggles. The tendency for them to build on narratives of troubled paternity shows an uneasiness with one of the most basic authority structures of society. In this, they join the many plays and novels that center on intergenerational conflict, usually over marriage and money. Parental authority is never shaken in the eighteenth century but, as Lawrence Stone and others have made clear, we can see some shift in what is accepted as appropriate behavior between parents and children.[4] The CIBBERIANI express these shifts as yet another variation on the celebrity challenge to traditional authorities.

THEOPHILUS CIBBER AND HIS ANXIETY OF INFLUENCE

Theophilus was Colley Cibber's first son. He followed his father to the stage by age sixteen, when he left school to join the Drury Lane company, then under Colley's management. Though he had initial success on the stage and seems to have been an effective if inconsistent manager during his few seasons in charge, in the later part of his career, Theophilus often scrounged for security and acceptance, frustrated that he could not inherit his father's privileged status as well as his name. The *Biographical Dictionary* tells us that while Colley helped Theophilus to a decent position at Drury Lane, he also sold his share in the company to the businessman John Highmore instead of to Theophilus in 1733 for three thousand guineas.[5]

Theophilus publicly maintained the image of the respectful son. In *A Letter from Theophilus Cibber, Comedian, to John Highmore, Esq.,* Theophilus depicts Highmore and his cronies as opportunistic "Stock-jobbers"

who "eagerly pursued Mr. *Cibber,* Senior, and, with a large Sum, tempted him to sell, what any one who reads the first Articles of the Patent, would reasonably conclude was my Birthright."[6] The fury of this publication, as well as the way he refers to the patent, clearly indicates that he felt his father's slight deeply. More than a personal injury, it was a blow to primogeniture: Theophilus, Colley's first son, should inherit his "Birthright," and these businessmen had stolen it from him—with his father's approval.

After this affront and symbolic disinheritance by his father, Theophilus's life goes awry. Victor considers his removal a benefit to the theater, calling Theophilus someone "who wanted nothing but power to be as troublesome as any young Man living" (*History of the Theatres from the Year 1730,* 1:9). In his stage career, he "concentrated more and more on foppish and braggadocio roles, . . . and, like his father before him, tragic parts for which he was unsuited." He gambled himself into debt; he began absconding with the salary of his second wife, Susanna Maria; and he subsequently attempted to prostitute her in a scandal amply aired in cheap pamphlets. Colley was reported to have remarked that "he would never have believed that Theophilus was his son, but that he knew the mother of him was too proud to be a whore." [7] The relationship between the two fractured. Theophilus seemed torn between trying to be like his father (while knowing that he wasn't and knowing that his father did not want him to be) and trying to establish his own individual public identity.

Theophilus's extraordinary print output is one of the distinguishing differences between his methods and character and his father's. While the elder Cibber held his (print) tongue through most early attacks, answering his critics in one comprehensive blow, Theophilus littered the town with petulant open letters, petitions, pamphlets, essays, and "dissertations" from the beginning of his career. Speaking in *T. . . C. . .,* "Theophilus" reflects on his addiction to print controversy: "I have indeed sometimes been induc'd to give publick Answers, and publick Appeals; but I think, in my own Judgment, and by experimental Knowledge, that such a Proceeding is wrong" (15). The difference in the way the two Cibbers used the press primarily reflects their different social positions. Colley was materially comfortable enough to bide his time, but Theophilus felt the desperation of need. Plus, Theophilus did not possess the tact to publish his opinions only on theatrical matters. He addressed the town on very personal

140

topics as well, ignoring Cibber's cautious strategic muting of his private life. For example, after involving his wife in prostitution with William Sloper, Theophilus published an "Advertisement. Whereas Susannah Maria, the wife of Theophilus Cibber, not only been, long since, convicted of adultery, but did, on September the 7th, 1738, elope from her husband . . ." (1739).[8] Shrill defenses of his conduct fooled no one, and the juries to whom Theophilus turned with his legal complaints awarded him sums far below those he demanded. *T. . . C. . .* mocks Theophilus's marital problems, stating: "The Affair was of a *private* Nature, and therefore was thought a *publick* Audience had no Right to take it under their Cognizance" (though, the narrator continues, "[t]he Affair was this . . .") (62). Unlike his father, Theophilus did not protect the divide between public and private important to the defensive stance of a player in print; neither did he possess the aptitude for turning either scandal or criticism into publicity.

In 1740 Theophilus planned an *Apology* for his own life to capitalize on the family literary connection, perhaps as compensation for his theatrical disowning. He advertised for subscriptions, but the book never materialized, perhaps forestalled by the appearance of *T. . . C. . .*, a false textual son usurping his right to print an *Apology* like his father's.[9] However, in 1748, after providing his readers with bits and pieces of apologies throughout his print battles, Theophilus finally published his scrappy *A Serio-Comic Apology, for Part of the Life of Theophilus Cibber.* Its title reveals two debts to his father's work. First, of course, is its identification as an "apology"; Theophilus asks flippantly, "APOLOGIES are now become the Mode, and who would be out of it? So I plead Fashion for appearing abroad in this Manner."[10] Theophilus had committed quite a few acts that needed defending, and so while he may have been responding to fashion, itself market-driven in its thirst for the continuously new, he was also serving his own ends. The second debt is the title's—and the book's—tone, which indicate to us his method for defending those acts. The voice of Cibber's own *Apology* could easily be dubbed "seriocomic" because of its self-deprecatory good nature and backhanded criticisms. In trying to capitalize on the success of this voice, Theophilus announces it overtly but succeeds only in upsetting the delicate satiric balance his father's book established—and he certainly did not earn credit for originality. Ultimately, he could not sustain this tone. He could not imitate his father's *Apology* persona and laugh away

problems by playing the "butt": by keeping his incapacities and misbehavior in the public eye via this book and his other publications, Theophilus only ends up looking like an ass.[11]

The text of the *Serio-Comic Apology* itself does not compare well in size or method with the other *Apology*. It extends to only thirty-seven pages, and its London edition was appended to Theophilus's adaptation of *Romeo and Juliet*. In a loose chronology, the narrative provides little besides a rehash of old failures and scandals. The *Serio-Comic Apology* brims with recycled ephemera such as an old advertisement for performances at the Haymarket theater, a series of private letters concerning the formation of an acting academy, prologues and epilogues, a reprint of his own nine-year-old public letter about his wife and marital problems, and his own "Copy of Verses, entitled 'The Contrite Comedian's Confession.'" As he states—and practices—in his "Life of Booth" (1753), he uses "Books, Manuscripts, Traditions, or what my own Memory can furnish me with" to fill out his work.[12] Yet Theophilus castigates other writers for the same methods he employs. He justifies composing his own *Apology* by explaining how another might give the public "a long bead-Roll of various Parts, Tragic and Comic, in every one of which I appeared with Applause; and then have added, The Testimonies of Authors in praise of my extraordinary Merits, collected from ransacked Dedications, and Prefaces . . . or from *quondam* occasional Copies of Verses, the frequent Embellishments of Daily News-Papers, Weekly Journals and Monthly Magazines" (72). Appreciating irony was not one of Theophilus's strengths.

Slight as it is, the *Serio-Comic Apology* illustrates the most obvious lesson of the *Apology* for Cibber's literary heirs. The *Apology* was not interpreted as a work of self-expression or autobiographical coming-to-terms, as some modern scholars would like it to be, but instead as a polemical document. Theophilus presents his hard work and bad luck to gain sympathy and, as a result of that sympathy (he hopes), money. He describes his botched moneymaking plans: promoting his daughter's acting, attempting to provide entertainment at the Haymarket, opening a histrionic academy. His father never was forced to plead for charity in print, because he succeeded onstage and in management. While Cibber dedicated his *Apology* to "A Certain Gentleman," aiming at an upscale audience that could afford his first edition (or at least striking that pose), Theophilus attempts to insinuate himself with a broad audience to achieve his goals: John Rich (to

whom his *Romeo and Juliet* is dedicated), John Highmore, David Garrick, Thomas Sheridan, his second wife, "the Publick." He does not have the luxury of condemning his audiences, like his father. In the book he flatters "the Town": "I have my self upwards of Thirteen Years been endeavouring, with indefatigable Pains and Study, to make myself useful to the Company. And *the Indulgence I have met with from the Town has prompted me to proceed.—I never vainly received their Favours as my Due, but regarded em as the Effect of their Good-nature and Benevolence*" (1). Like his sister's, Theophilus's primary intended reader was Colley himself: he offers the dubious tribute of praising "*the celebrated Apologist*" who added "a Brilliancy to the Scenes wherein he appeared." Years later, Theophilus continues the public flattery of his father, in hopes, perhaps, of repairing the connection. Colley seldom reverts to such overt sycophancy—even the "Dedication" to the *Apology* is so overwrought that it reads ironically. Cibber aimed at a select audience; Theophilus needs *any* patronage. Very few other actor autobiographers express their prostitution so strongly.

In short, Theophilus's autobiographical effort is unsatisfying: short, scrappy, and, especially in comparison with his father's massive accomplishment, pitiful. Jean Marsden, one of the very few to discuss Theophilus's writing, has noted that the *Serio-Comic Apology* is "a rambling and unchronological series of anecdotes, letters, self praise, and congratulatory prologues" that "quotes extensively from his father's work," and that Theophilus "remains both the most aggressively public of the Cibber clan and the least successful in his attempt to construct a public image." She argues that the *Serio-Comic Apology* "is most interesting in its attempts to refigure Theophilus's character into the dual roles of good father and good son," a tactic his sister Charlotte also attempts—with the same lack of success.[13]

Theophilus's efforts do not achieve their intended aims—to follow his father's lead in self-defense or earn him a more stable cultural standing from which he could generate income. Theophilus's work might also be interpreted as I interpreted his sister's—as a failed gender performance, an inability to perform the role of the strong, seamless male in a society that, as Straub has shown and Theophilus's father had demonstrated, did not accord an actor full membership in masculinity. And, in part, we might attribute this to his problems refiguring his identity outside of the role of firstborn son that Colley had denied, generated from a debilitating anxiety

of influence. But Theophilus's *Serio-Comic Apology* is not a narrative with disruptions, like Charke's. It is a jumble of primarily preexistent texts, most of which he himself had previously published. Why should this be taken seriously (or even seriocomically) as a *biography*? Because by looking at the history of eighteenth-century biography, we can see that this method was quite common during the period, and that it served an important biographical function.

Its most famous—or infamous—proponent was Edmund Curll. Curll had conducted a long career in the book trade and sold many respectable as well as ignominious publications. Because, like Cibber, he appears unflatteringly in *The Dunciad,* Curll is remembered primarily for his rancorous feud with Pope.[14] Most eighteenth-century and modern commentators dismiss Curll's publications as low mercenary work. Curll's business tactics were frequently disreputable—Frank Arthur Mumby has labeled Curll's press "an ugly blot on the history of eighteenth-century bookselling"—and he trafficked in inflammatory political pamphlets and pseudoscholarly treatises on venereal disease and therapeutic flagellation.[15] Biography, however, seems to have held special fascination for him: Ralph Straus's bibliography of his press indicates that between 1706 and 1746, Curll produced almost 1,100 works, nearly 10 percent of which called themselves biographies. This is a greater percentage than offered by other houses, such as those of Dodsley or Tonson. One of Curll's critics remarks on this penchant: "His Love of Memoirs, and Secret History, the Things he has been so fond of since, began almost as early as the rest; for before he was twelve Years old, he compiled a History of the Life and Character of the Parson of the Parish."[16]

Curll was also noted for his love of the theater and attraction to its inhabitants: Thomas Amory says in *John Buncle:* "[H]e conducted me to the playhouses and gave me a judicious account of every actor. He understood those things very well. No man could talk better on theatrical subjects."[17] Curll published plays as well as biographies of playwrights and of two performers: "William Egerton" [Edmund Curll], *Faithful Memoirs of the Life, Amours, and Performances of . . . Mrs. Anne Oldfield* (1731) and *The Life of That Eminent Comedian Robert Wilks, Esq.* (1733). For these, as for his other biographies, Curll assembled unassimilated records—letters, poems, wills, play excerpts, prologues and epilogues—in a fairly random arrangement. Reactions to Curll's work indicate that his choices did not

accord with the biographical expectations his contemporaries would have derived from models such as Plutarch. In "Verses on the Death of Dr. Swift," Swift's narrator projects the dreadful muddle of material that will shape his image once Curll sets to work:

> Now *Curl* his Shop from Rubbish drains;
> Three genuine Tomes of *Swift's* remains.
> And then to make them pass the glibber,
> Revis'd by *Tibbalds, Moore, and Cibber.*
> He'll treat me as he does my Betters.
> Publish my Will, my Life, my Letters.[18]

The *Grub-street Journal* anticipated Swift's objections by printing its own satirical "ad" for Curll's *Life of Wilks* in 1733. After listing the book's miscellany of components, the ad states: "The reader, by casting his eye upon this table, will be surprized to see the *Life* of so great an actor, drawn within the narrow compass of 8 pages; for which he cannot grudge to pay 1s. 6d. having 4 pages of his last will and testament, and 66 of useful digressions into the bargain."[19] The *Grub-street Journal* reviewer implies that such a compilation does not qualify as a "*Life*" at all, however, and tells readers they are being cheated. Similarly, Curll's *Oldfield* assembles all kinds of information related to the actress and her associates: prologues and epilogues she delivered, excerpts from plays in which she starred, five letters supposedly from William Egerton to Oldfield defending drama and expounding on stage history and philosophy, a list of Oldfield's roles, capsule biographies of her lover Arthur Mainwaring and of William Wycherley, the last wills and testaments of all three.[20] J. Paul Hunter's statement that "[m]aterials for contemporary biographies nearly always came from the diaries and private papers of the biographees" is certainly not true in the case of Curll's many biographies.[21]

Because Curll relies mainly on printed, public sources of information without a strong narrative voice, his subjects are perceived as public figures, living in these multiple print manifestations. While this "method" elicited scornful comments, it is precisely its shoddiness that exposes for us (and presumably for eighteenth-century readers) some basic issues of biographical writing. Curll's method bares the underpinnings of *all* biography, inviting questions about legitimacy and interpretation of sources

and about the need for appropriate documentation. Curll's embryonic precursors of today's "documentary" biographies confront readers with the question of what does and does not constitute acceptable biographical material.

In addition, this documentary method foregrounds the very real difficulties of constructing a biography in the eighteenth century. Boswell used many sources in his *Life of Johnson,* but he relies most heavily on the conversation and company of the great man himself. If a biographer lacked this personal contact, where could one obtain materials for a *Life?* Without libraries, newspaper archives, or bibliographical and genealogical tools, finding enough relevant information with which to build a unified history of an individual would be an arduous task. Samuel Johnson himself complained of the problems in obtaining "authentick information" for biography.[22] Players would be particularly challenging assignments because, unlike royalty, nobility, statesmen, and authors, they did not leave extensive paper trails—until the eighteenth century. Even in 1801, Arthur Murphy deplores the fact that friends have not immortalized the great men and writers of England, especially his subject, David Garrick, and now "the Biographer must collect his facts from scattered fragments and oral tradition."[23] Curll's books illuminate how an author who was not a theatrical insider could now begin to piece together public resources to build the biography of a player.[24] John Nichols summarizes: "The memory of Edmund Curll has been transmitted to posterity with an obloquy he ill deserved. Whatever his demerits, they were amply atoned for by his indefatigable industry in preserving our national remains. Nor did he publish a single volume, but what, amidst a profusion of baser metal, contained some precious ore, some valuable reliques, which future collectors could no where else have found."[25] As these "future collectors," we gain some of our most valuable information about these players from Curll's *Lives* and his other theater-related publications, which are drawn on heavily by the authors of the *Biographical Dictionary.*[26]

This quick summary of Curll's contributions to biography and to thespian biography in particular helps us understand Theophilus's *Serio-Comic Apology* in two ways. First, we can see a generic precursor for his book, as he attempts to integrate Curll's methods with his father's legacy and his own autobiographical aims. I do not claim that Theophilus was intentionally imitating Curll; I suggest that he was following a well-known

biographical method that had compromising associations of which he must also have been aware. Second, Theophilus and his textual progeny inherited a dual patrimony. Note how often—in the works of Pope, of Swift—both Curll and Colley Cibber appear, though I have found no information that indicates they ever met each other. Instead, they are linked by their similar personalities and relations to the media. Pope and Swift consider both men as part of a cultural collaboration bent on challenging true literary authority through the opportunities of a commercial print marketplace. Cibber was the type of upstart hack whose work was encouraged by sordid tradesmen like Curll.[27] To find Theophilus adopting tactics from both of these "fathers" not only brings to fruition the dynasty of "bad" writers that *T. . . C. . .* dreaded but showed that anyone with audacity, a grudge, and a pair of scissors could piece together a printable artifact. What we also see—and what his father may have also already seen when he sold the patent to Highmore—is that Theophilus did not inherit the savvy public relations and business acumen of his "fathers," either in the print or theater world. Both Cibber and Curll, while they were castigated by the literati, managed to conduct successful, profitable careers as well as create powerful public personae that protected them. Theophilus—shrill, unfocused, and desperate—could not achieve this balance of being notorious while also being fascinating: he is an obvious failed celebrity.

While the actual products of Curll's and Theophilus's biographical efforts may no longer be appealing, the act of collecting and saving documents relevant to actors is an important innovation—John Roberts's brief biographical sketches of Shakespearean actors show the sad state of early theatrical history in 1729—as is the actor's effort to shape the version of events communicated by those documents. Though later thespian biographers will not follow Theophilus's unsuccessful lead, they will search for narrative parents. They will locate them in popular books that may be more entertaining, though perhaps not any more respected, than those Theophilus used.

FICTIONAL DEPENDENCY: THE USES OF NOVELS

Once the print controversy surrounding Colley Cibber's *Apology* articulated the literary battle, the relationship between thespian biography and other printed works begins to change. These texts did more than borrow,

Curll-style, from preexistent works, though that method remains common. They also incorporated new narrative techniques absent from the documentary biographies but suggested by Cibber's waggish narrator. Most of the new influences on thespian biography derive from the world of fiction: Straub has identified particular similarities to sentimental novels and "secret histories"; thespian biographies also reflect the popularity of Henry Fielding's *Tom Jones,* John Cleland's *Memoirs of a Woman of Pleasure,* and Laurence Sterne's *Tristram Shandy.*[28] The biographies use these novels most obviously to capitalize on their popularity. Yet the choice of these *particular* novels is significant. The biographers choose novels whose techniques involve parody, humor, and an arch distance from their subjects—not morally serious novelists such as Richardson—and novels with overt sexual content. They are chosen because of their unique, prominent, and theatrical narrators, as though the liveliness of the narrative voice could capture the oddity and excitement of these unconventional lives. These novels are also works that challenged eighteenth-century generic conventions of fiction; though the novel's generic conventions, like those of biography, were not solidified, readers still had expectations, which is one reason why public response to these three novels was so strong. To link the life story of a celebrity to a radical novel was to emphasize the challenge that the celebrity him- or herself posed for the culture.

Rosalind; or, An Apology for the History of a Theatrical Lady (1759) relates the story of Ann Dancer, who later became Ann (Spranger) Barry and then Ann (Thomas) Crawford, an actress who excelled in her role in *As You Like It*—hence the book's title.[29] Just as Lavinia Fenton was referred to as "Polly" throughout *Life of Fenton,* and Mary Robinson will be referred to as "Perdita" in her biography (1784), Dancer is always called "Rosalind" in her *Apology,* though unlike *Life of Fenton, Rosalind* employs pseudonyms for all of its characters. This technique fictionalizes the whole book and distances both narrator and reader from the characters, a distance that allows room to laugh at the characters' follies.

The fanciful approach to its characters marks a difference between *Rosalind* and what we might speculate to be its main model, Cibber's *Apology.* Rosalind's *Apology* differs from Cibber's in three ways. First, it covers only the actress's life, without the broad historical sweep of Cibber's book. (Actresses' biographies infrequently served as vehicles for theatrical history.) Second, it "apologizes" primarily for only one scandalous rumor

about its subject's life—indeed, the book was written on the occasion of that scandal. And third, an anonymous writer has assumed the task of "apologizing" for Dancer—she herself was apparently not the author or narrator. *Rosalind*'s relationship with this textual father is tenuous.

The narrator seems to enjoy his role as apologist for Dancer's conduct.[30] Far more than in any earlier player's biography (except for Cibber's), the narrator is a real presence, using the first-person pronoun frequently. All Dublin was gossiping about Dancer's rumored infidelity with a "Monsieur Coupée," and this author composed his book to lay before the public the circumstances of this event.[31] He presents himself as the servant of Truth: "I solemnly aver to act the faithful Historian, and not the enraged Satirist. . . . I am unbiassed; I am impartial; I am absolutely free from Malice or Revenge" (xvi–xvii). He refrains from judging Dancer overtly: "I pretend not to give my opinion, whether Rosalind is guilty of what the million lay to her charge or not" (110–1). Why then must he recount her whole life to determine the truth of one rumor? He explains that he "shall inform the Public of the whole of her Life's History . . . and shall make such Reflections on her whole Conduct, and in particular, relating to the latter Part of it as I conceive pertinent, and the Subject seems to require" (xvi). To uncover the truth behind the scandal he must pry into her earlier sexual conduct to find the "pertinent" detail. He states, "I have undertaken my present Office of enquiring into the Conduct of a celebrated Actress, whose *faux Pas* transacted on the *great Theatre* of the World, has rendered her much more remarkable and __famous than when acting on one of the lesser Theatres established in it" (xv). As usual, the actress's sexual conduct is more important than her acting abilities. Her present, as an actress, determines the shape of her past.

This narrator uses suggestive omission to titillate his readers. His extended description of Dancer's anatomy lingers over the beauty of her breasts and "——." His ambiguous phrasing allows double entendre: "[S]he had Publicly shewn herself and sat for her picture; not to a few virtuosos and limners, but more extensively kind, she has given pleasure and transports to multitudes" (28–9). He provides a long paragraph about how he will not describe the "transports" of her wedding night (61). He attempts to disavow licentious rumors about her arrangements with a gentleman who helped her and her husband out of distress by elaborately recounting those rumors (86). These stories about what she did not do

and what the narrator will not tell only serve to call attention to what she might have done and what he might have told, helping readers to interpret the Dublin scandal. So although Dancer's life seems riddled with moral lapses, many of them actually originate in the narrator.

That readers are intended to view Ann Dancer as guilty is reinforced by the narrator's invocation of John Cleland. He longingly regrets not being able to write like Cleland, whose publication of *Memoirs of the Life of a Woman of Pleasure* (1748) would still be fresh in the reading public's memory, "He could have drawn fine luscious descriptions of some amorous scenes, for the perusal of all the tender virgins and wanton widows of this metropolis" (110). Here his "negative" technique links his subject with pornography, insinuating a similarity of subject. In a Cibberian way, he admits his own writerly incapacities, which allow him to avoid charges of bad writing by blaming others, as well as shaming his readers' expectations. He also attempts to write like Henry Fielding; at the beginning of chapter 8 he announces: "A digression in imitation of my late friend mr. [*sic*] Fielding, shewing the difficulty of writing true history, and explaining a wonderful strong reason for my writing this history at all" (61). He refers to himself as a "great Man" in his position as a "true Biographer" (63), invoking his "brother authors" (61).

By substituting his own voice for Dancer's, and by ceding his narrative control to those of famous scandalous fictions, he reinforces patriarchal control over female identity, as we saw in *Life of Fenton*. But now the narrator/author is not alone in this construction; he has numerous male author-authorities to enforce it. The (at least) four male narrative voices that establish the intertextual space for Rosalind—Cibber, Cleland, Fielding, and the anonymous narrator himself—allow no arguing with the sexualization of Dancer. Rather than invoking literary authority to help "raise" the character of the actress, this text musters its male chorus to keep her in her place. As he states, "[T]hough the generality of writers are so condescending to follow their subject, I shall be so bold as to make my subject follow me" (31).

Almost all the mid-century actress biographies use masculinized intertexts to reinforce the femininity (typically, whorishness) of their actress subjects. Writers of actresses' biographies also used Lawrence Sterne's *Life and Opinions of Tristram Shandy* (1759–67), another fiction that many eighteenth-century readers considered obscene.[32] The melodramatic nar-

rator of *Memoirs of the Celebrated Mrs. W*ff**gt*n* (1760) is coyly unwilling to "represent the frail Girl sinking into the Arms of unbridled Lust," so when her neighbor, Bob, assaults her, the narrator resorts to typographical teasing: Bob "threw her on the ***"—then appear four lines filled with asterisks. The narrator then exclaims, "Oh happy BOB!" The narrator uses the same method when describing her later affair with Garrick: "Oh happy G*RR*K!"[33] While dashes and asterisks had always been popular among seventeenth- and eighteenth-century writers who wished to divulge identities without being prosecuted for libel, use of abrupt starts and stops and other playful typography became widespread as part of a narrative after *Shandy*.[34] It becomes common procedure for describing actresses' sex scenes, as it appears again in *Perdita*.

Straub has noted the power relationship of spectacle that Shandyisms construct in an actress's biography: "[T]he text genders the sexual spectacle as feminine and the ringmaster, as it were, as masculine, albeit in a qualified, nonmasterful sense."[35] Five years after *Woffington*, the title page of a biography of Ann Catley declared its literary influences: *Miss C——y's Cabinet of Curiosities; or, The Green-Room Broke Open*, by "Tristram Shandy" (1765).[36] The author of this book is much more concerned to prove himself a second Sterne than to discuss Catley, even though he exclaims "Oh, these Plaguy Imitators!" (4). At the beginning of chapter 3, we read, "NOT a Syllable of the *Green Room* yet!—'Tis, fine Work, indeed, if the Public is to be hummed—and choused [swindled]—and troubled—and bubbled—and bamboozled—with a Cock and a Bull Story.—'Sdeath! I wish I had my Six-pence half-penny again" (4). The author includes a paragraph of asterisks, follows digressions, and then lambastes the previously published Curllian *Memoirs of Miss C——y* as a collection of "Husks and Nutshells, of no value or Consequence . . . it was the vamped up Work of some mercenary Bookseller, or hungry Devil of an Author" (21)—even though his book provides even less information than a Curll production.[37]

The narrator indulges in witty Shandyisms at the expense of Catley's sexuality, though he never describes Catley's amours but revels instead in innuendo, like the author of *Rosalind*. Readers encounter predictable "cabinet" jokes: Catley "had been in Possession of it ever since her Birth—It was a mighty pretty one—fringed about with curling Ornaments, and precious Jewels—A Cabinet that the greatest Monarchs would have been delighted to have laid their Hands on, and which had been enjoyed by

Numbers of the greatest Personages in both Kingdoms" (15). Such a passage figures Catley's body as an object to be handled by the upper classes, again reinforcing the perception that actresses traded their only commodity for upward mobility, if they could.

Class distinctions seem to be this outlandish narrator's main concerns. Ironically, he states, "As to Authors and Actors they are Pests of Society—not fit to be patronised or esteemed by the Great—Rascals, Thieves, Pickpockets, &c. &c. &c." (13). Then he reestablishes "true" social value: actors "are not so witty, or well-bred, as eminent Citizens who sell Raisins, and Oil, and Leather. . . . Nor such useful Members of Society, as those that cure Cl——s, or that mend bad Soals, or that repair old Sauce Pans" (13). He uses his Shandean voice to ridicule those who would place themselves above actors and authors. After all, "[a]n Actor is frequently a more honest Man, ay, and a more merry Companion, than a Parson; And, by the Powers of VENUS! I would prefer the Company of a pretty Actress, for an odd Hour or so, to a fat Alderman's fat Lady" (38). He sides with Catley against those who do not respect both of their professions, but yet maintains that authorship is superior; his tone and his own debasement of Catley force us to read these defenses of players as ironic.

Randolph Trumbach has argued for the polarizing of two genders over the course of the eighteenth century—a trend that excludes other gender identities, such as that of the late-seventeenth-century male homosexual or, perhaps, of the energetic public woman, such as the actress.[38] Instead of creating textual roles that articulated the "abnormal" gender identity of actresses, the whore identity became calcified in biography. Perhaps this image endures for the reasons Laura J. Rosenthal detects in the Restoration years. In her view, class tension between the well-bred characters actresses performed on stage and their own lower social position generated the need to construct actresses as whores, who presumably could not marry into the upper classes. As she notes, "As long as the actress could not claim virtue, she could not parley her professionalized seductiveness into class mobility."[39] The surprising continuation—even hysterical escalation—of this tension throughout the later eighteenth century may be testimony to the real economic gains women could achieve through the stage. After all, the women treated as whores by their biographers were commercially successful in their acting careers.

Interestingly, no mid-eighteenth-century biography was published of

an actress who was *not* involved in sexual scandal. Kitty Clive, Hannah Pritchard, even Susannah Maria Cibber—who appeared in smutty pamphlets concerning Theophilus's lawsuits against Sloper—were not treated to biography (Susannah was spared perhaps because of public disgust with Theophilus). Biography contributes to the creation of celebrity for actresses by defining that social space as one of excessive sexuality even through the actresses who do *not* receive biographical treatment. They are constructed through silence.

In *An Apology for the Life and Conduct of Mrs. Mary Wrighten* (c. 1789), Mary Wrighten adopts Cibber's apology model as well as contributing to the hypersexualized gender role of the actress. What happens when a female apologist adopts this male precursor, casts her own story as that of a textual daughter? She can splinter, like Charke, or she can use the *Apology*'s example to create her own unified, internally consistent narrator. Wrighten does the second, presenting herself solely as a victim, just as George Anne Bellamy does in her 1785 *Apology*.[40] Wrighten justifies her conduct through a combination of pathos and rational argument, to cast her as the innocent and mistreated wife. According to Wrighten, she was married to an abusive spouse for many years. He abandoned his first wife and children to marry her (29), he "brought disease to her bed" (56), he jealously reproached her for the attention and earnings her stage successes brought (34), his temper was "boisterous and flinty" (7), he once even threw her out into the streets at midnight (35). She eventually left him and found refuge with another man: mistreatment will "wear out meek submission, and make the sufferer, like Mrs. Wrighten, give way to calamity; then seek relief at the expense of reputation, with all the ill founded surmises of a babbling world" (24). Her *Apology* is a narrative of her life written to hush that babbling. She concludes: "Should it be asked why Mrs. Wrighten came forward at all, it is because her patience was exhausted. She has borne much, and she was desirous of undeceiving the public as much as possible. When a woman leaves her husband, a thousand presumptions may be raised against her, and it may well be believed it is not on the score of his goodness to her" (73). Surprisingly, Wrighten follows the lead of male biographers of actresses and highlights little of her stage career, overshadowed as it was by the circumstances of her private life. Because she was an *actress,* she is forced to account for her private life, unlike Cibber's *Apology,* which addressed only public issues in his own strategy of self-

defense. It is in Wrighten's best interest to de-emphasize her active, public role as an actress, which might contradict her helplessness as a victim of marital unhappiness.

The other main differences between Wrighten's *Apology* and Cibber's are that she refers to herself in the third person, as if dissociated from herself or constructing textual identity as the uniformly gendered subject of actress biography that we have seen earlier. She is most interested in appealing to female readers through this role, another innovation mirrored in fiction, which increasingly aimed at this market segment. She is especially concerned in equating herself with these women, casting herself as one of them: "In regard to herself she has endeavoured to be candid, artless, and explicit, and whatever may be thought by the men, the best friends in general to the fair, to the women she makes her best curtsy, taking the liberty to whisper in their ears, that if they had been in her situation they would have felt and acted as she hath done" (77). More specifically, she reminds women that they should not condemn her, using both appeal and threat: "The present enquiry extends only to her own sex, who, like her, have been untimely married. She flatters herself that her readers will go along with her in this apology for her conduct, and in their judgment be mindful that they may be judged in their turn" (69). And she wants only to align herself with the "virtuous fair" (42). She pardons her own conduct by castigating those women who did not have as good an excuse: "Far be it from Mrs. Wrighten's intention to justify by the colour of language, vice and infamy, or the aberrations of any of her sex, who may have wantonly swerved from the paths of virtue and duty" (67). Such women, of course, include all actresses as they had been portrayed in the biographies Wrighten's readers may have known. Thus like most autobiographers—especially actress-autobiographers—Wrighten tactfully avoids "delicious romance" and "wanton amours." She swears to the propriety and truth of her account:

> Mrs. Wrighten has striven to make her apology palatable by giving it an agreeable flavour, and she saves to herself a right of enlarging it as occasion may require. To those, however, who pry into books for secrets, let it be known that if they search here for scenes of delicious romance, vicious intrigues, or wanton amours, they will be deceived. Nothing but truth in all

the nakedness of beauty is here to be seen. No fiction is called on to catch a greedy attention, or interest the reader in worthless discoveries. No character is convulsed in the drawing, nor no inflammatory tale is told to poison the passions, or lead them astray. (vi–viii)

Such a statement from an actress directly confronts expectations of an actress's biography. Wrighten inhabits the difficult position of having to defend her sexual conduct without actually referring to it. She rewrites the narrative of sexually driven upward mobility to prove that her suspect conduct is simply the struggle to be a successful domestic woman. The happy ending is her escape to America, where she can reshape her personal story.[41]

Wrighten's piggybacking on the apology genre popularized by Cibber thus allows the monolithic gendering of actress-as-whore to stand. By distinguishing herself from immoral women, she sides with all of the other male narrators of actress biographies. She avoids causing the tension Rosenthal notes by portraying herself as a devoted (if abused) wife, and thus not attempting to raise herself by an advantageous marriage. She also eases any literary alarm an actress-author might cause by downplaying her role as a *writer*. She is not trying to raise herself by authorial achievements, either, but simply writing to earn enough money to provide for herself and her children. Thus in her *Apology* we see the struggle for authority between actors and authors subsumed in a larger gender struggle. Since both professions are public ones, Wrighten had to emphasize her private conduct to gain sympathy.

One male apologist repudiated novelistic techniques to throw his own taste into relief. George Stayley was an Irish actor-author who published *The Life and Opinions of an Actor: A Real History, in Two Real Volumes* (1762); the "Life and Opinions" of his title alludes ironically to Sterne's book.[42] Stayley closes his first volume with "A digressive chapter, with a remark, Proper to be bound with *Tristram Shandy*; a work which every body reads and nobody understands" and "Commentary Remarks on *Tristram Shandy*." Stayley offers critical analysis of Sterne's narrative techniques, using those techniques to ridicule them. He calls *Tristram Shandy* "an heap of unprofitable, incoherent vanity! A perfect dunghil of filth and rubbish! . . . surely we have a very good right to expect something more than trash from a man who has seemingly swallowed so much of the seeds

of learning" (1:213). Stayley parodies *Shandy* by blackening two pages to represent night, adding stars and moon (1:208–9)—his main character has gone to bed; on the next two pages a sun rises as morning breaks (1:210–1). Stayley disparages Sterne to prove himself a sober literary critic, unimpressed by upstart mass-appeal novels.

He is particularly incensed by the novel's "filth": "[A] more indecent performance than *Tristram Shandy,* I think I never read in my life" (1:214). Stayley's account of his own life carefully avoids such material: "I must apprize the reader of one thing, that he may either stop where he is, or not blame me, if, on procedure, he meet with disappointment: which is, that he must not look for any amorous adventures, or midnight excursions, in the composition of my life" (1:28). While others were out carousing, he was in—writing. Such a statement indicates that readers of players' biographies expected amorous content. Like other autobiographers, Stayley chooses not to incriminate himself sexually, and by condemning Sterne he shows his moral uprightness.

Stayley's criticism of Sterne supports his self-presentation in his *Life and Opinions,* since he wants readers to consider him as an author instead of as an actor. He frequently discusses his own dramatic productions; in 1753 he becomes "poet *Laureat* to the company" (1:24). But he would prefer that his readers regard him as a talented nondramatic writer. He includes over 130 pages of his own works in poetry and prose in his 215-page first volume. Their titles show his literary aspirations: "Stolen Waters Are Sweet: A Moral Tale," "Robin and Simon: A Dialogue Pastoral," "The Author's Note-book; or, Religious, Moral, and Critical Observations on Men and Things," and so on. "The Storm; or, Cibber's Epitaph," eulogizes Theophilus Cibber after he was drowned in a shipwreck and was "intended to rescue his memory, from the defamation of an inhuman scribbler" (1:39). The last employs predictable eulogistic topoi, complete with a weeping comic muse. In his second volume, he prints a series of lectures on social, literary, and theatrical topics. Stayley held conservative and respectable literary aspirations, which he bolsters by condemning Shandean high jinks and obscenity.

Other male writers created their own hybrid genres, such as George Alexander Stevens in his *The Dramatic History of Master Edward, Miss Ann, and Others* (1763).[43] This "history" is a Shandean narrative in dramatic form—complete with a list of dramatis personae—supposedly put together

by an editor for a "Mr. Zaphaniel" to relate the romance between the actor Edward "Ned" Shuter and the dancer Nancy "Ann" Dawson. It opens with a dialogue between the editor, Zaphaniel, and a dancing master who has brought the two together: "Mr. Zaphaniel has got some very curious stories relating to a particular player; but he wants to have them put into a proper stile" (2). They decide on the "drole stile," and the editor explains, "The MSS. I took home with me, and, being promised ready money, began to digest the materials immediately" (4). At the beginning of what is entitled a "metaphysical scene," the narrator states: "The authors of *Joseph Andrews* and *Tristram Shandy* wrote themselves into reputation, and I believe got money by what they did; and really deserved it.—Ever since I have engaged in this work, I have endeavoured to copy one or both of their stiles, manners, or maxims; but I cannot fancy myself quite so clever" (126).

Yet attempts at "cleverness" fill this *History*. Like *Tristram Shandy,* the narrative starts before the birth of the hero, Master Ned, giving us a lengthy history of his mother's amours, of her "longings" while pregnant, and of his parents' courtship. This description of parentage only serves to ridicule Ned's low origins, much as readers of *Tristram Shandy* would have been amused by the antics of Walter and Uncle Toby. Ned is finally born on page 126, and soon after, the narrative shifts to the "History of Miss Ann." The book contains a love poem complete with scholarly explication, a "History of the human Mind," an essay on "The Originality of Ghosts; and Anatomy of Phantoms," and so on.

Stevens not only uses Sterne's example, but he turns to his own previous works. His taste in comic pastiche is shown in the earlier, never-performed *Distress upon Distress; or, Tragedy in True Taste. A Heroi-Comi-Parodi-Tragedi-Farcical Burlesque in Two Acts* (1752), and his tendency toward satire and contemporary commentary is seen in his humorous lectures and his early novels. *The Dramatic History* preceded by one year the first performance of Stevens's most famous work, the *Lecture on Heads* (1764).[44] Gerald Kahan has noted the influence of *Tristram Shandy* on Stevens's *Lecture on Heads,* but its impact on the earlier *Dramatic History* is unmistakable.[45] Stevens himself influenced other thespian writers: Charke notes in her dedication to her *Narrative* that she and Stevens "are, without Exception, two of *the greatest Curiosities* that ever were the Incentives to the most *profound Astonishment*" (vi).

Like *Lecture on Heads* and the early volumes of its other literary model,

Tristram Shandy, The Dramatic History is primarily a satire. Stevens and Shuter had once worked closely together but had then fallen out. *The Dramatic History* accuses Shuter of ingratitude when Miss Ann asks Master Edward, "There was, *what's his name,* who wrote the droll for you, . . . and several comic songs, which have been of such service to you in your benefits both in the town and the country, how did your [*sic*] serve him? did'nt you expose him falsely, and scandalously; and strove, by what you said of him publickly, in some of the infamous bawdy-houses, that you frequent, to render him contemptible? And he had never done any thing, to my knowledge, to merit such treatment" (145–6). The *Biographical Dictionary* identifies *"what's his name"* as Stevens. Insinuations about the bawdy houses Shuter "frequents" give this jovial book a sarcastic edge. Its satire is not palliated by other information: omitting comment on its characters as actors and actresses contributes to its ultimate characterization of performers as irresponsible and insignificant. We see Shuter as an infant and then as a suitor to Miss Ann, but not as an applauded comedian. We encounter Dawson as a scheming woman out to "tickle" Ned for whatever he is worth, not as a popular dancer. *The Dramatic History* thus uses its textual gimmicks to keep its subjects in their proper places, submissive to writers like Stevens who supplied them with their dramatic material. By claiming his right to compose their biographical as well as stage roles, Stevens uses the new literary self-consciousness of thespian biography to restrain the narrative of social mobility for actors and actresses.

In the narratives that imitated Sterne, Fielding, and Cleland, these thespian lives probably did not emerge as a separate category for readers. Instead of being read as biographies that experimented in novelistic technique, they may have been read more as novels that happened to have theatrical protagonists and that capitalized on theatrical subjects. Certainly the many other imitators of Fielding, Cleland, and Sterne could have encouraged readers of these biographies to have perceived them as just more of the same. In this way, the subjects of these books recede even further into the background, behind the narrative methods used to describe them. These players become fictionalized, their cultural power thus dismissed as negligible. That many of them were Irish, or at least spent significant time in Ireland, also contributes to the overpowering presence of their English-inspired narrators: these texts become another method of colonization, through their narrative voices.

These biographies are not the only ones published in the decades after Cibber's *Apology;* we will consider others in the next chapter. Yet in this trend to bring the acting life under the control of a powerful narrator, we see the author's need to contain these creatures whose growing power threatens a writer's ability to fix the words actors must speak. The popular press allows players more varied articulation than earlier in the century, when the play was the main printed medium available to represent the player. With so many representations of players available, the techniques of all genres are used to establish the boundaries of their conduct and character. Some of these followers of Cibber actually use Cibber's techniques to *undermine* one of his main goals: they strive to *dis*empower the player.

CONCLUSION: BEYOND CIBBER

These later books do not show the conflicted relationship with paternal authority that Theophilus's does. Many of them do "honor" Cibber the father and precursor model by following his example in writing "apologies" and by creating eccentric narrators. Yet even those critics who may find calling Cibber the "father" of thespian biography in the later eighteenth century far-fetched can notice how these books continue to establish the author-narrator as the controlling voice, the authority, the parent. Thus while they may in some ways follow Cibber the writer, they militate against Cibber the actor. The subjects of the books—the performers—are infantilized and restrained, even sometimes when the performer him- or herself is the author-narrator. Mary Wrighten keeps herself in her place by acceding to her own victim status, stating that she tried to defer to male authority but was repulsed; George Stayley denigrates his life and companions while an actor in favor of his career as a writer. Even the novels on which they often lean—those that show difficult or disruptive parental relationships—are books that reinscribe patriarchal heredity: the unfortunate Tristram *is* eventually born to follow his father, and Tom finally discovers his true parents, knowledge that allows him inherit his uncle's estate. *Rosalind*'s idealized, benevolent father dies when she is young, and the narrator analyzes the conduct of the actress's neglectful mother. If she "divests herself of her natural authority over her children, and Forces them whether they will or no, to despise her, is it the child that is in fault for

rejecting a sway not founded in equity, but merely an arbitrary custom. No certainly: The parent is answerable for these miscarriages and errors, naturally and Consequentially resulting, from their own cruel and inhuman conduct" (34–5). If the wrong people (like unsupervised mothers) are left in authority, they will misuse it; and thus important social relations, such as that between parent and child, will disintegrate. According to many of these biographies, too, if actors are granted authority, the same sort of social destruction will result.

After mid-century, biographies and autobiographies grow even longer than Cibber's healthy girth: both biographies of David Garrick run to two quarto volumes, Stayley's *Life* and lengthy opinions run to two as well; and George Anne Bellamy believes that her story is not properly communicated unless she uses six octavo volumes. The number of short pamphlet biographies like Thomas's *Life of Hayns,* Victor's *Life of Booth,* or the *Beggar's Opera* biographies dwindles, but the lengthy biographies are joined by more histories, criticism, journalism, spouting manuals, and ephemera such as a "theatrical time-piece" listing the approximate lengths of acts of plays, so that spectators could enter late and get ticket discounts.

These works were of varying use and quality, and they perhaps were more influential in their collective rather than individual impact. This increase in publication did not go unremarked. Colley Cibber's critics noted it, as did *Rosalind's* narrator. *Rosalind's* narrator also complains: "There are always multitudes of buzzing insects of Parnassus, who, knowing how to make lines jingle to each other, fancy themselves poets, and call their motley-medley productions, poetical essays, &c. 'though there is not a single ingredient to entitle them to that name. The sacred fire of the bard, the whirl of imagination, and the high reach of thought, are but in the power of a few, and those who possess them not, should at least, be so discreet, as to exterminate their Cacoethes scribendi, and apply their talents on subjects they are more capable of" (91–2). Those writers who are not high-minded, inspired poets should find "lower" topics, like the theater. This narrator doesn't condemn theatrical writers (after all, he is one), but he implies a hierarchy of topics and expects all writers to operate at their proper social and intellectual levels. Hacks cannot give birth to works with a "high reach of thought." Giving thespian biographies fictional fathers reinforces this assumption of patrilineage.

As he abuses his actress-subject, the narrator of *Rosalind* simultaneous-

ly maintains that "this is an Age that interests itself remarkably in every Scene relative to the Dramatic World" (vi). The reader of many of these biographies might indeed wonder with the authors of the *British Magazine and Monthly Repository* about the "favourable treatment [players] meet with from the very persons who affect to look upon them as the pests of society."[46] A stark contrast exists between the proliferation of interest and the degradation that occurs within the pages of many of these biographies. What exactly did readers value in all of this theatrical publication? The next chapter treats the question of players' value as shown by their material circumstances and communicated in their biographies.

CHAPTER 7

Parable of the Talent(s)

THE ECONOMICS OF ACTING
AUTHORITY

The Members of the Stage have generally
engrossed the Attention of the learned and
the polite. Their Follies, Caprices, Merits,
and Defects, have ever afforded
Opportunities to consider their intrinsic
Utility with Respect to Society, as well as
furnished Matter for the Consideration of
the Literati, whether they are essentially
requisite to it.

*Rosalind; or, An Apology for the History of a
Theatrical Lady* (1759)

IMPLICIT in the biographers'
work lies the assumption of the
inherent worth of their subjects:
that stories of players' lives and the
history of their art merit reading, that
readers will gain instruction or entertainment from reading them, and that
they deserve the investment of capital
and materials that printing requires.
By the mid-eighteenth century, pref-

aces and dedications to thespian biographies that ask readers to excuse the frivolity of their subjects have all but disappeared.

But once one raises the concept of worth, a question follows immediately: How *much* are these subjects worth? Only by trying to answer this question could authors and printers know what kind of book to produce, if they would produce one at all. The question of any player's value was a hotly contested one, linked to questions of the social value of their jobs and their personal popularity. The economic contributions of acting are difficult to perceive when compared with other services and manufactures that produce tangible results. And, of course, no unchallenged answer to this question arises, then or now, but the need to prove actors valuable, to justify their popularity, could explain the increase in biographies after mid-century, especially those of enormous length, such as George Anne Bellamy's *Apology,* and the flourishing of theatrical criticism. Writers seem to want to make sure they are valuing these performers correctly, at least relative to each other, and it is in part the uncertainty about the overall and then relative value of these performers that causes the public discussions that produce more fame and create celebrities.

In one famous anecdote, reported by Thomas Davies in his *Memoirs of the Life of David Garrick* (1780), Garrick, Charles Macklin, and other actors walk out of Fleetwood's Drury Lane in 1743 because of underpayment and mistreatment. The duke of Grafton, then Lord Chamberlain, reviewed their request for a license to perform elsewhere, and "coldly" remarked that they were getting paid too much for "merely playing," and that an officer in the army, who risks his own life for his country, does not get nearly so much (1:74).[1] We can make the same comparison still today: is the work of a Tom Hanks or Julia Roberts (leading film actors in 2003) more valuable than that of a sergeant in the Marines? Are players overpaid or are officers underpaid, or does the function of being a cultural icon whose effects are not so overt and direct equal the immediate function of offering one's life for one's country? If there is a disparity, why does it exist? Marx notes that "[s]ince money does not reveal what has been transformed into it, everything, commodity or not, is convertible into money. Everything becomes saleable and purchasable. Circulation becomes the great social retort into which everything is thrown, to come out again as the money crystal."[2] Grafton's response rests on this phenomenon, that the work of an officer and the work of an actor are converted into the same

thing, money, which is assumed, then, to be a measure of social value. People in the eighteenth century, as today, grapple with the mechanisms of how this conversion occurs and the justice of the results.

Questions of value have crucial bearing on those of authority. Value's manifestation as money—rather than as name, or as land, more traditional methods of indicating a person's value—increasingly becomes a signifier of cultural standing. Money confers and reflects status and authority. Yet the source of one's money is also of great importance. Many plays and novels of the century are centered around the genealogy of money and the type of worth it grants. As the merchant Mr. Sealand rebukes Sir John Bevil in *The Conscious Lovers,* "[W]e merchants are a species of gentry, that have grown into the world this last century, and are as honourable, and almost as useful, as you landed folks, that have always thought yourselves so much above us."[3] These plots primarily consider the struggle between "old" aristocratically derived money and "new" or mercantile money. Colin Nicholson states that "[t]he emergence of classes whose property consisted not of lands or goods or even bullion, but of paper promises to repay in an undefined future, was seen as entailing the emergence of new types of personality, unprecedentedly dangerous and unstable."[4] Successful performers were undoubtedly categorized within these "new types of personality," and though they are neither merchants nor aristocrats, they receive their money through their theater management from both groups and all others: apprentices, servants, other artists, foreigners, Jews, Papists. This indiscriminate payment connects them with prostitution and authorship—other professions that take their income from whoever will pay for their product.

Actors' nontraditional source of money is troubling, especially since the particularly successful make a lot of it. Players can trade on their prospects and popularity—Bellamy, for example, is able to secure sums to pay her large debts just because she is well known. Players' association with money helps shore up their authority, but it also makes them easy targets of suspicion—a dynamic very clear in many of the thespian biographies, as it is in Grafton's comments. Are these the "right people" to possess all of this money and the social potential that goes along with it? Biographers often feel compelled to explain what players *do* with all of their money. Are they usefully employing their acting talent as well as their monetary "talents"? Just as proper sources of income are status-laden, so

is evidence of the proper distribution of funds. The biographical subject's relation to money indicates where the biographer was placing the subject in the social hierarchy, and if the biographer was supporting or questioning that hierarchy.

As many scholars have shown, the state of currency itself caused concern to political economists and other writers of the eighteenth century. P. G. M. Dickson has described the "financial revolution" of the late seventeenth and eighteenth centuries, when England struggled to manage its national debt and established values of currency, lotteries, and public credit, especially after the disaster of the South Sea Bubble in 1720. Throughout this period, questions about the government's uncertain ability to meet its financial obligations occasioned distrust and consternation. Dickson summarizes the reactions to financial change between the Glorious Revolution and the mid-eighteenth century: "They were essentially ones of alarm and disapproval. They were based on fear of dislocation of the social order by the rise of new economic interests, and dislike of commercial and financial manipulation of all kinds, and had roots going back into the Middle Ages. They were to be much in evidence again during the early stages of industrialism, which also seemed to threaten 'traditional' society."[5]

Critics such as Swift voiced hostile opinions about the effects of these changes on traditional authority: "So that *Power,* which according to the old Maxim, was used to follow *Land,* is now gone over to *Money.*"[6] Because of the way actors' uncertain value mimicked that of currency and threatened social order, the hostility was often similar. Money could "act," or pretend to be worth more than it was, just as actors could be something other than they were, both on stage and in daily life. James Thompson has traced the changes in theories of currency in the eighteenth century in his discussion of money and the eighteenth-century novel. He describes "the early modern reconceptualization of money from treasure to capital and the consequent refiguration of money from specie to paper. This historical event or transformation was in the eighteenth century represented or thematized as a crisis in the notion of value—that is, where is value or worth to be located—in silver or paper, thing or name?"[7]

Theater historians queried where the value lay in the theater—in players or dramatists or managers, in spectacle or seriousness—and the developing genre of acting criticism asked where value lay in the performance—in oratory or expression, in pleasing the mind or the heart.

Biographers asked whether performers were to be valued for their ability to play roles on stage or for their characters as private citizens, or both. Thompson writes of courtship novels, but we can also apply his words to the cultural formation of the celebrity: "As in economic theory, these are crucial questions of what or who authorizes an individual subject's social value and in what does this value consist." Celebrities are figures developed by crisis in social value and authority, but they are also figures who fundamentally question both. Thompson reports, "[A] cash economy threatens social revolution, for it is the cash nexus that can make a Peter Pounce in *Joseph Andrews,* can transform the master into a servant and the servant into a master," as in *The Beggar's Opera.* "[P]aper credit exacerbates all of the dangerously changeable, movable, fluid qualities of money, as opposed to the stability and constancy represented by land, the hereditary estate, a metonym for genealogical and possessive continuity."[8] The public must be able to trust the authority and legitimacy of the currency and of the government's financial planning, as the shift to a commerce economy erodes the traditional forms of value. The development of the celebrity is a concomitant shift of valuation and thus authority.

As we have already discussed other related forms of valuation such as literary merit, this chapter explores the relationships among players, value, and money. Beginning by examining some data about players' income, we can then look at some thespian biographies of the mid-eighteenth century and their methods of evaluation. In conflicted ways, these biographies help teach readers how to value players.

THE VALUE OF PLAYERS

Monetary amounts present the easiest way to begin measuring perceived value. Other expressions of esteem (or its opposite) then explain, justify, revise, and add to these mere numbers. As I have stated elsewhere, salaries for performers rose gradually over the century; however, the most noticeable change over the period was the amount that a star performer could command.[9] Actors hired by performance and those on the lower end of the salary scale earned about the same pittance at the end of the century as they did at the beginning: Ned Ward in 1697 says an actor earned about £22 per season; an 1822 contract for Elizabeth Edwards gives her salary as £36 a season. Though these amounts were not high, they did allow players

to survive, and most provincial strollers' lives were more financially desperate. At mid-century, £40 per year could just support a rural family of four, though at the end of the century, as Edward Copeland has shown, this amount is the poverty level.[10] Comfort does depend on expectations, but in Copeland's estimates, £200 seems to be a minimum for a genteel though quiet life. Star performers such as Ann Oldfield could earn a salary of £420 in the 1728–9 season; James Quin could earn £500 in the 1749–50 season; and the popular (but not stellar) performer Samuel Reddish could earn £300 in the 1777–8 season.[11] By the end of the century, a superstar like Sarah Siddons could demand £31 10s. per night (though management had trouble paying this on time).[12] Salary could be lower or higher depending on terms of a contract, nights performed, unforeseen success in a role, and/or addition or removal of rival players from the company. In addition, discrepancies often occurred between *reported* and *paid* salaries for numerous reasons.[13]

For the popular performers, however, salary is just part of the story. With their benefit performances, such performers could more than double their annual salary in a single evening: Oldfield, for example, probably received £500 at her 1729 benefit (and she had been receiving as much for numerous years), thus bringing her income for her last year of performing to at least £750. Quin received £188 in 1728 (minus house charges of £40), as he was on his way up the popularity ladder, and one can only assume that this amount rose with his ensuing fame. Siddons could command £618 at a benefit (from which would have been subtracted £211 for house charges). [14] Unfortunately, Reddish became afflicted with mental illness, and thus the *Biographical Dictionary* reports that his last benefit was well attended—by spectators who wanted to abuse him for his irregularities on stage.[15] Benefit performances were also accompanied by gifts beyond the asking price of the ticket itself. In addition, these annual sums would be augmented for some top male players by their income deriving from shares in the theater companies or theater buildings. Thus performers with steady appointments at one of the London theaters could expect a comfortable income, though the most favored of them could make much more.

Within a company, these gradations via salary were accompanied and reinforced by other signifiers of value. The timing of a benefit performance denoted one's value within a company and was a contentious issue.

Scheduling a performer's benefit earlier in the spring enabled most of the gentry to attend, and they would not yet have been molested by too many requests to attend benefits. Performers of less regard were scheduled in late May and June, after many wealthy spectators had left town for the summer. Benefit dates carried prestige or lack of it as well as the opportunity for higher returns. Oldfield was distinguished by having the first benefit of the season, as befitted her station as the top actress in her company, and later in the century Bellamy testifies to "the credit of having the *first* benefit in the season."[16] *Memoirs of That Celebrated Comedian . . . Thomas Weston* (1776) reports that Weston, insulted, did not condescend to appear at his one of his own benefits because it was scheduled too late in the season. Popular players could also merit "clear" benefits—that is, the managers did not deduct the usual operating costs from the overall box office take—and could enjoy individual benefits, rather than, as occurred with lesser players, sharing a benefit night with others. In his lecture "Benefits; or, The Actor's Bane" in *Life and Opinions,* George Stayley complains that benefits are only useful to the big stars, who scarcely need them (2:153). We should note that the audience also gains cultural capital, a return on their benefit investment, by being seen at the most fashionable players' benefits, thus affirming their good taste, and by assuring the regard and deference of a popular performer. Bourdieu states, "Consumption is . . . a stage in the process of communication, that is, an act of deciphering, decoding, which presupposes practical or explicit mastery of a cipher or code."[17] The benefit structure is part of this "code" of taste.[18]

The earliest biographies—those of Coppinger, Hayns, Betterton, Keene—do not include much information about salaries, benefits, or other payments. But at the end of the century, while information could still be spotty and sporadic, numbers of some sort were hardly ever omitted. For example, in *The Life of James Quin, Comedian* (1766), readers learn that Quin joined Fleetwood's company in 1733–4, when Fleetwood was accepting company members under "the general conditions . . . [of] two hundred pounds a year to each managing actor, and a clear benefit." Quin was offered "still more advantageous terms, and such, indeed, as no hired actor ever had before."[19] This information gives readers a quantitative index of Quin's quality, thus helping solidify their regard for him and justifying their purchase and reading of the biography.

Why hadn't financial data been included earlier? The most obvious

answer is that it simply was not available. Its inclusion may also possibly reflect the maturation of the biographical genre, the gradual turn from stories of a type of person—the adventurous rogue, the esteemed gentleman, the amorous harlot—to the emphasis on particulars (if not facts) that characterizes Curll's productions, to the reportage of Thomas Davies or James Boswell. (A similar process occurs with dates in these biographies. The earlier texts do not even mention years—sometimes not even the birth year of their subject—but, over time, dating becomes much more meticulous.) Public opinion seems also to have become more sensitive to players' remuneration. In 1733 the anonymous author of *The Players: A Satire* points out that some actors are just "sordid, mean spirited Fellows, who have no Notions above that of a large Sallary, and a good benefit-night," stressing their economic unproductivity by stating they desire "a fine lazy sort of Life." The salary scale within the company often corrupts the performances themselves: first a king appears on stage, and then

> Swift a Prime Minister of stately Port,
> Enters, and struts in Presence of the Court.
> The Monarch wisely whispers in his Ear,
> Your distance keep, and let the King appear:
> Peace, Animal! he answers in a Rage,
> My Salary must sure command the Stage!
> The King, too conscious of his scanty pay,
> Behind his own Attendants slinks away.[20]

Knowledge of wealth and payment can help a spectating and reading public, gaining in critical skills, to understand that what happens on stage may be more a product of material than aesthetic conditions.

Inclusion of financial data suggests a need to ascertain the biographical subject's true value, as a clue to his or her identity. Numbers become important, as society moved from valuing people in traditional ways, through property or proximity to gentility—the focus of *Betterton*—to an economy that understood value more in terms of what that property or proximity translated to: money. Certainly this mechanism was already at work in the comedy and fiction of the time, in which the first question asked about an unmarried person was usually, "How much is he or she worth?"

Without citing sums, readers (especially those outside of London) may not as easily discern the social worth of the player, but as soon as a sum is noted, readers can place the person, comparing him or her to their own positions and inciting inquiry into self-worth. When readers track Old-field's salary increases from £100 to £500 over the course of her *Authentick Memoirs*, they have a shorthand estimate of her upward trajectory, one that causes the mixed response of admiration and envy that we see in the biographies and in most celebrity discourse.

Citing figures also legitimizes the biography in which they appear, since one can base the value of the book somewhat on the value of its subject. The mere existence of these biographies was an admission of the value of these performers. The performers whose lives were memorialized in print were usually those who commanded the best value in the theaters as well, though, as we have noted, popularity did not necessarily guarantee the appearance of a biography. Biographies report the salaries made, the acclaim garnered, the lovers seduced, and the scandal generated, all in order to raise the value (if not the propriety) of their subjects and thus the value of their textual productions.

The books themselves had lengths, prices, and physical characteristics that signaled the value of their subjects. For example, *Life of Hayns*, at about nineteen thousand words, was advertised as costing one shilling, and the price for *Life of Betterton*, approximately three times as long, was 3s. 6d. stitched and bound. The anonymous *Authentick Memoirs of . . . Oldfield*, at approximately four thousand words, cost one shilling, but William Egerton's (that is, Curll's) biography of the same actress, at sixty-two thousand words, went for three shillings stitched and 3s. 6d. stitched and bound. (Of course, Curll took and used large quantities of words wherever he found them!) *Life of Spiller* (1729), at eleven thousand words, cost one shilling; Victor's *Life of Booth* (1733), of approximately eight thousand words, cost 1s. 6d.; but *Rosalind* (1759), at twenty-two thousand words, states its price as "One British shilling." The two-volume octavo edition of Thomas Davies's *Life of Garrick* was advertised in the *Monthly Review* of August 1780 as ten shillings. So one shilling seems to have been the usual cost for an actor's biography over the course of the century, unless the book was especially lengthy or bound, or its subject was especially popular—or both. An actual ticket to the boxes in the theater would cost a spectator four shillings in 1660–1700 and five shillings in 1776, while

a gallery ticket would cost in 1660–1700 about 1s. 6d. Victor maintains that "From the Beginning of *Cibber's* History to the End, the Prices at the Theatres were constantly Four Shillings, Two Shillings and Six-pence, Eighteen-pence, and One Shilling" (*History of the Theatres from the Year 1730*, 1:43–6). These biographies were priced well within the range of a middle-class spectator, and the less well off would only have to miss one or two nights of theater to afford one of them.

Actor-authors try to increase their own market value, to create their own "buzz." Yet as we have noted earlier, Cibber's narrative persona often tries to devalue himself in his *Apology* by admitting, ironically, his faults and foibles. Some of the biographies' jocular or contemptuous narrators were using the time-honored scheme of trying to engage the reader on the narrator's superior side against the biographical subject—ridiculing the subject to flatter the reader. They reassure readers that the traditional social hierarchy is still intact, and that it can absorb these fascinating celebrity creatures without disruption. As modern "unauthorized" biographies prove, one need only take a snide or uncomplimentary slant toward one's biographical subject for one's work to receive more attention than it might otherwise. Devaluing one's biographical subject can be a way of making one's commodity, the biography, more valuable.

Salaries, benefits, and book prices were thus a code for readers roughly to ascertain a player's worth, since theater manager and printers could not price their products above what the market would bear. Equally important was the source of this money and how it was later spent. Players take money from all of their spectators, and we will shortly discuss how the public attention confers value. But the public often demanded much for its money; both players and management found difficulty in trying to please the various constituencies in their audiences. They often encountered hostility and the attitude voiced by Charles Churchill in *The Apology* (1761, a sequel to *The Rosciad*): "Ne'er will I flatter, cringe or bend the knee / To those who, Slaves to ALL, are Slaves to ME."[21]

The biographies do not approve of just anyone's approval. As theatrical and acting criticism developed, biographers identified exactly *whose* approval the performer received. So, though Spiller may have been the toast of the butchers of London, informing readers of that fact did not secure him any wider acclaim. In fact, as I mentioned in the *Beggar's Opera* chapter, this is a point of ridicule for his biographer. Like a streetwalker as

opposed to a courtesan, it is important for the player who can please all to please the genteel connoisseur: "the judicious," not "the Mob." Identifying who was in which category, however, proved less simple. In its satirical abuse of Ann Dancer's husband, *Rosalind* states in disgust, "[S]o that he could set the Galleries in a roar and make the greasy rogues grin applause; he cared not for that of the judicious; nor would he use his endeavours to corrects his errors, by conversing with men of sense and judgment" (59). In their periodical the *Prompter,* William Popple and Aaron Hill suggest the establishment of "Commissioners of Taste"—gentlemen like themselves who would judge from moral value rather than being "*Mercenary Undertakers*" who have "no purpose but gain."[22] Such a call echoes Gildon's earlier suggestion that "some Men of good Sense" should lay down rules for young players, since the current management of the theater is incapable of doing so. George Stayley cautions, "[T]here cannot be a greater Error in Nature, perhaps, that to estimate a Player's Merit by his Success; for a Man may be what we call a fashionable Actor, and yet not a good Player," and "Public Applause is undoubtedly the Sun-shine of an Actor; but then unlike the Sun of heaven I say, it shines not equally on all; and what is worse, beams strongest sometimes on the least deserving (2:52, 2:55)." Evaluative instruments such as Churchill's *Rosciad* (1761) showed how one of these gentlemen took matters into his own hands—and thereby raised a storm in the presses. Earlier, *The Players: A Satire* had cast Shakespeare as a judge of acting, pointing out that true judgment comes from the "discerning" within the audience, not the arbitrary clapping of the unlearned. Both of these poems, however, focused on stage acting; the biographies consider the subject's life on- and offstage, raising the issue, to which we will soon turn, of the relationship of a player's private life to his or her public value.

Public support provides the money that undergirds status and authority for actors. Also important is what the performers do with that wealth. (This is especially important since many writers seemed to assume that players had too much money—though few then stopped underwriting players' wealth by boycotting the theaters.) How do the biographies treat the deployment of money? And what is implied by this treatment? Answering such questions will show how the biographies help establish or undermine the authority players gained through their income.

PROFLIGACY, GENEROSITY, AND GREED

The biographies show three common ways that players handle the money they receive. The first, profligate dissipation, is a common accusation. To illuminate it, we'll look at *Memoirs of That Celebrated Comedian and Very Singular Genius, Thomas Weston* (1776). The other side of the "profligate" coin, however, is generosity. Thomas Davies writes that players are always the readiest to assist other people in times of distress, perhaps because many of them came from impoverished roots (1:278). The anonymous biographer of *Sketch of the Theatrical Life of Mr. John Palmer* (1798) asserts, "[N]o profession is more ready, on all occasions, to step forward to the relief of the distressed, than the theatrical one."[23] Actress biographies in particular stress the generosity of their subjects. Finally, some players will not spend their money at all: some, like David Garrick, were accused of hoarding. These three relationships with money become indices of the player's value, but they can also help indicate larger problems of the theater: in the *Prompter* (1734–6), Popple and Hill boldly state, "[T]he true root of decay in our theatrical establishments, was not from the bad taste of the public, but that bad taste from the players' gross ignorance in their art and the too-sordid motive whereby they are governed and conduct-ed."[24] Spectators' knowledge of the source of players' money encouraged the urge to police their use of that money:

> If then they receive our Wages, they are accountable to us for their Con-duct; and not only that Part of it, which relates to their immediately acting in the Province assigned them by us, for our Service and Amusement, but in their *private* Behaviour when our Business has been transacted. Good Servants of any Kind, whether Butlers, Stewards, or Foot-men, House-maids, Chambermaids or Cooks, have no Right to withdraw themselves from their respective Masters, and act in an unbecoming Manner when their Masters Business is finished; nor has an Actor a Right, on his quitting the *small* Stage for the Entertainment of his Master, to act on the *great one* with Indiscretion, Folly or Vice; for in both Respects their Masters are injured, and themselves receive no Service, but rather lasting Opprobrium, and justly merited Dishonour. (*Rosalind*, xiii–xv)

For eighteenth-century observers, knowing how players used their money

connected to the need to oversee and control both players and the theater.

Thomas Weston was a popular comedian during the second half of the eighteenth century. He specialized in low comic roles, though in *Memoirs of Weston*, a sixty-page book, he states that he always pined to play tragedy, for which he was not suited. But this book focuses more on his financial escapades than on his acting. It is an unflattering portrait of a player who, no matter how high his salary, could not live within his means. As the narrator says, he was "no œconomist," and can't live on the pittance he earns in one of his first appointments, a strolling company.[25]

Weston's relations with money are merely an extension of his other qualities. Before he went on the stage—and even later in his life—he would stay in bed all day, "to repair the rest which he lost by setting up all night, frequently getting into quarrels and disputes, which sometimes ended in being sent to the watchhouse" (6). Though his father tries to discipline Weston's "vicious behaviour . . . his pleasures had taken such deep possession of his soul, that nothing could change his purpose" (6). Since "for business he was no ways fit" (6), he is placed as a sailor, but leaves that employment when he sees his shipboard accommodations and comprehends the confinement of his employment on board; "He thought his genius cramped" (9). Escaping from the navy, he heads to London where, after he "gave a full range to his passions . . . he found his wardrobe decrease apace, his cash was soon gone, and he had begun to borrow on his clothes for present subsistance" (10). He realizes that he needs income, so "he looked round him for some eligible means of subsistance, and, after a few moments thinking, concluded on the stage" (11).

In other words, the theater is the refuge of those who don't want to work hard and who can't find work elsewhere. While this characterization is familiar to us from the rogue biographies like *Hayns* and *Spiller,* it is noticeably different in Weston because of its grimness and its unremitting stress on Weston's bad disposition. He is not portrayed as a charming Haynsian wag. The stage becomes the refuge of scoundrels by accepting a negligent, reckless person like Weston. Indeed, even in his stage career, he is dismissed, reinstated, chastised, and forgiven again and again. His salary is held to pay his debts, he is dunned continually, outside subscriptions are raised for him to allay his expenses. A troublesome burden like Richard Savage, Weston does not even hold an imaginary claim to illustrious birth to legitimate his extravagance and irresponsibility. While such conduct

might be excused in the offspring of good family—a Charles Surface, per-haps—in a low actor, they are signs of his profession's inability to know or learn the value of money. Perhaps he believes his popularity with audi-ences substitutes for birth.

Profligacy is the key to his character: once he gets money, he does not know how to manage it properly. At one desperate early moment in his career, he resolves to return to his father, ask forgiveness, and try to make a new start, but then he meets an old schoolfellow who "lent, or rather gave" Weston five guineas; this immediately makes him feel rich and thus "changed his thoughts from going home" (16). He responds to this small sum inappropriately, not realizing how little it is worth. When first engaged at Drury Lane, he has some success and thus receives £3 per week, "and so began to consider his appointments larger than they were; though a good scholar, he was no great arithmetician; he could easily *tell* his receipts, but he could not *count* his expenses" (23). After separating from his wife—ironically, "she complained of his brutality, and he of her *extrav-agance* and disobedience" (my emphasis, 22)—he takes up with several young ladies, settling on a streetwalker with whom he then resides (25). His salary at Drury Lane "was pawned to the managers for money advanced to his creditors. . . . he therefore did not receive above half, on which he and his demoiselle were obliged to subsist" (26). The narrator archly points to Weston's inability to value the right type of woman.

Dismissed from his company, he finds himself deeply in debt, with "no money for present subsistence," and supporting "a young mistress . . . who was no greater œconomist than himself" (27). In addition, he has pressing medical concerns, "a scorbutic complaint, which not only affected his face by breaking out in blotches in a very disagreeable manner, but also his legs, one of which had a hole in it that discharged a very great quantity of matter, that was not only offensive to himself, but to everyone about him" (27). The narrator couples Weston's constant outflowing of funds with the same actions of his body. Both his attitude toward money and his body's effluence make him "offensive."

As Weston's health worsens, his narrator links his financial irresponsi-bility to his body's lack of discipline. The narrator states that at one point, "he had not patience to wait for a perfect cure, but going out one Saturday night, gave a loose to his inclinations, . . . and forgetting all that had been

said to him, plunged deeply into excess, and by one drunken bout, had nigh shortened his life some years" (40). He neglects his body's health and his financial health, and the circulation of funds through him is as loose and as unregulated as the circulation of fluids into and out of his body. Thus like the actress who is negligent with the "currency" of her body, the actor can be as guilty of mismanagement. The actor's lack of control over monetary spending is linked to other uncontrollable processes, thus making an actor's fiscal irresponsibility seem as "natural" as a foul disease.

Yet *Memoirs of Weston* does not argue that Weston represents all actors; indeed, it supports the opposite. This text upholds the theater's professionalism by showing that people like Weston are a strain on the theater management and a constant source of uncertainty for the audience—will he show up to perform, or won't he? The other performers who appear in this biography are not profligate and lazy but are victims of this bad behavior.

This biography and its foregrounding of the financial return us to questions of value. Unlike Weston, the rest of the players are not unworthy of the applause they receive. Weston is not a representative player but an anomaly, and thus *Memoirs of Weston* warns the reading audience that they may be mistaken in indiscriminate applause for all the players who entertain them. The biography asks its readers to consider whether a person deserves the acclaim of public life when she or he is a vicious and unappealing private person. It indirectly raises the question of whether performers should be expected to become "role models" because of the responsibility of being the center of such attention. The question echoes for posterity, as well: modern readers would probably find difficulty in appreciating Weston as a person or performer with only this biography to recommend him.

A clue to another way of expressing a player's common relationship with money occurs late in *Memoirs of Weston*. In the book's closing estimation of this actor, the narrator states that after his death he was "universally regretted as an actor, and as a man, within the small circle of his acquaintance, all of whom have reason to deplore his loss, for he was good-natured even to a fault, and would share with an acquaintance the last shilling he had" (47). The narrator attempts to show the positive side of Weston's inability to manage his money as generosity. Unlike other

performers praised for this quality, however, Weston seems not to distinguish fitting objects for charity. He values inappropriately, which raises suspicion of his own value.

In other biographies, readers see more fitting deployments of the money they have invested in these performers. Stressing the subject's generosity is a standard biographical trope of the period; however, it seems to take on more urgency in thespian biographies, and often large portions of already short biographies are devoted to enumerating charitable acts. For example, Daniel O'Bryan lists several of Robert Wilks's good deeds, adding, "To mention the generous and charitable Actions of Mr. *Wilks*, would be an endless Task."[26] Interestingly, the generosity trope is most common in the actress biographies—*Memoirs of the Life of Eleanor Gwinn* (1752) and *Authentick Memoirs of Oldfield,* for instance. The women who are generous with their physical currency also are generous with their monetary resources. Gwinn, for example, "possessed Good-nature and social Benevolence in the most eminent Degree. She could never suffer any one to want, whose Merit entitled them to Relief; and, in Point of Generosity, there were few Ladies then at Court, who had any Pretensions to be compared with her. Her Fault was a predominant Love of Pleasure, a Desire of shining in a conspicuous Sphere; but in recompense for Want of Chastity, she united as many private Virtues as any Character in her Time."[27] Then follows an anecdote of how she exerted herself for Dryden's interest. But her generosity hinges on the merit of the object—unlike Weston, she is selective in the dispersion of funds. After she became mistress to Charles II, a position that allowed her to bestow charity more widely, she worked to help Samuel Butler, author of *Hudibras.* "No sooner had she rose to this high Station, but her Heart, naturally benevolent, overflowed in Acts of Kindness to distressed Merit."[28] In some ways, she is trained by her circumstances to do this, just as she must find the most politic use for her body. She can discern the best objects of charity using the same judgment of value that allows her to choose the next, and next highest, recipient of her physical favors. As this passage makes clear, the connection between her generosity and her "Want of Chastity" is a close one. Like Weston, whose bodily fluids ran in uncontrolled spending, Nell's determined control of her sexuality is linked to her ability to "spend" wisely and admirably in charity. The usual condemnation of the upwardly

mobile woman becomes linked to admiration for market smarts and com-passion.

George Anne Bellamy's six-volume *Apology* walks an uncertain line between profligacy and generosity. Like *Memoirs of Weston,* this text is primarily a recital (often inaccurate) of debts, betrayals, borrowings, and business deals, especially in the later volumes. Bellamy consistently shows her ability to make money—and her inability to manage it. She tries to use her wealth wisely, but her inattention to detail, her bad luck, her persecu-tion by heartless creditors, and her desertion(s) by unfaithful and improv-ident male protectors leave her more and more desperate. She claims that many of her debts arise from good deeds for, as she rhapsodizes, "To light up the face of distress into gladness, and to pour the balm of comfort into the wounded mind, is the truest felicity the human heart is capable of feel-ing." She also admits that the company she kept urges her to spend unwisely: "I had now contracted a taste for expence; and without consid-ering that I was not intitled to gratify it equally with the persons of fashion with whom I was intimate, could not think of curbing this propensity." She relies on common tropes of genteel femininity: generosity, frivolity, and a distaste for money talk—"pecuniary subjects were ever . . . discor-dant to my soul."[29] She attempts to increase her own value for her readers by translating her mismanagement of money into the generosity expected of actresses (and all women), as shown in the other biographies.

A key to the dispersal of a player's money is what happens after the player dies. The biographies begin consistently to detail the contents of performers' wills, if not to print them. Oldfield bequeaths her wealth to her two sons. The narrator of *Authentick Memoirs of Oldfield* approves, chastising other women who "marry second Husbands, and thoughtless of your first Brood, suffer your Spouses, for the sake of a Bedfellow, to waste your Childrens Patrimony, and bring them to the Parish."[30] For the sake of their uncontrolled sexuality, women would cheat their own children—but not Oldfield. Weston's appended will is an extended joke, as he leaves his contemporaries qualities he thinks they need: "I leave to Mr. Reddish a grain of honesty" (55); "I leave to the ladies in general, on the stage, . . . the appearance of modesty" (57–8); and to Garrick, "I . . . bequeath him all the money I die possessed of, as there is nothing on earth he is so very fond of" (54). The last is a nasty parting shot, considering that Weston was

continually broke and continually being forgiven and reengaged by Garrick for Drury Lane—evidence of a generous spirit.

But generosity can also be interpreted as protecting one's own interest: perhaps Garrick was trying to retain a popular player merely for his own selfish commercial ends. He and others were accused of greed, of stopping the healthy flow of money. Bellamy (no friend to Garrick) accuses him of "meanness" proceeding from vanity, and he is imagined as snubbed and ridiculed by Shakespeare after his death, according to *Garrick in the Shades; or, A Peep into Elyzium* (1779). Shakespeare says that Garrick staged his Jubilee only for his own profit, not to honor Shakespeare. However, just as much evidence exists to support Garrick's largesse. The "Old Comedian" notes Garrick's charity, and Garrick's modern biographers, Stone and Kahrl, have listed his generosity to numerous friends: Thomas Davies, Churchill, Foote, Hogarth, Macklin, and Hannah More, among others. Samuel Johnson shrewdly analyzed Garrick's relation to money and publicity:

> I know that Garrick has given away more money than any man in England that I am acquainted with, and that not from ostentatious views. Garrick was very poor when he began life; so when he came to have money, he probably was very unskilful in giving away, and saved when he should not. But Garrick began to be liberal as soon as he could; and I am of opinion, the reputation of avarice that he has had, has been very lucky for him, and prevented his having many enemies. You despise a man for avarice, but do not hate him. Garrick might have been much better attacked for living with more splendour than is suitable to a player: if they had had the wit to have assaulted him in that quarter, they might have galled him more. But they have kept clamouring about his avarice, which has rescued him from much obloquy and envy. [31]

Management of money becomes entangled with public relations and what is expected of a player's living arrangements. Of course, most managers, acting and nonacting, are accused of greed—Betterton, Cibber, John and Christopher Rich. Since they decided what plays would or would not be produced at their theaters, they had the unenviable duty of informing writers of their negative decisions, thus offending those with the positions and ability to publicize. Assuring the popularity of a play could be inter-

preted as assuring the profitability of acting shares, often owned by actor-managers. However, accusations of greed are often leveled at those who make a lot of money, and so such statements are also evidence of social presence.

Thespian biographies seem to testify that those whose wealth derives from the general public have a responsibility to use that wealth in an approved manner. The authority that the player derives from his or her income can depend on how the money is used. Neither indiscriminate spending nor shameless hoarding is applauded. The first strategy undermines social hierarchies by showing disrespect toward the people who granted them their income and by distributing it according to their own wishes. The second, greed, shows too much self-absorption and attempts to enrich and raise oneself at the expense of others. Only by a tempered generosity could performers show that they knew the true value of money and the reasons it was bestowed on them. Generosity marks a genteel character possessed of the sensibility so admired in the second half of the century. That this quality was often stressed in actress biographies is not inconsequential. It is linked to other configurations of value, to which we now turn.

GENDER AND CURRENCY

Public opinion of the right kind was thus a major factor determining a player's value, which could then be communicated back to the public via biography, constructing a circle that could help regulate players' value. If the performer portrayed a character to the taste of the town, the player's metaphorical "stock" went up, and then so would his or her actual income. If a particular play did well, the players involved were more highly valued. Then the performer's own attitudes toward and dispersion of money, combined with the other information of the biography, could help assure audiences they were valuing the player correctly and thus should continue to patronize their performances. For male and female performers, however, the process of valuation within the theaters and biographies could be very different.

For example, Lavinia Fenton was much more "valuable" as a commodity after her performance as Polly in *The Beggar's Opera* than before. Her success as part of this play increased her value so much that she attracted

the attentions of the duke of Bolton. Alternatively, one might also say that the play allowed her inherent value to be presented to an audience who would have dismissed a woman of her humble and compromised origins. Successful actresses become too valuable as *women* for their positions on stage, and thus they are taken from the stage by their benefactors—not only Fenton, but Nell Gwyn, Eva Maria Garrick, George Anne Bellamy, and Mary Robinson. Like a precious object or rare coin, the actress is removed from circulation. Her value as a circulating marketplace object is replaced by her value as treasure—she passes from a commodity wealth system, which the acting profession represents, to a traditional specie system. The ex-actress does not lose value that she gained on the stage when she leaves the stage, as long as she enjoys the care and good will of her keeper. If she loses this care, she must reenter the marketplace and reestablish her earlier value, sometimes increased but often tarnished by her previous kept status (and more advanced age).

In *Life of Gwynn*, this actress's value is determined by who has possession of her at that moment: she is obviously much more valuable when she is the king's mistress, rather than that of "Earl Wilmot" (Rochester) or the "Duke of Beau." The adventures of an actress's sexuality resemble those mid-eighteenth-century novels narrated by inanimate objects—bank notes, guineas—except that these objects are gendered male. As Deidre Lynch has remarked, "The piece of current money or the circulating commodity resembles the woman of the town whose tale he relates, in that her relations with others are, like his, entirely commercial. At the same time, however, no moral opprobrium attaches to his wanderings across the social order."[32] Women embody different relations to money than men—if they circulate as currency, possessed by more than one owner, most women lose value. But the case of the celebrity is different, especially one like Gwyn, who doesn't wander *across* the social order but moves *up*. As Nell circulates—and as her biographer tries to laugh at her for doing so—her value increases, both as an actress who is kept by increasingly wealthy and powerful men and as a subject for a biography. Only the actress auto-biographies describe the pain of devaluation that occurs when the actress separates from her keeper, a tactic of survival rhetoric to gain sympathy and perhaps monetary support.

The tension between increasing and diminishing value is echoed in *Authentick Memoirs of Oldfield*. In this generally positive—indeed, lauda-

tory—biography, the subject's value is quite often signaled by how much she would bring in a market. For example, the narrator observes how any male spectator would trade a king's ransom to be playing opposite her, thus implying a high value. The biography reports her love affair with Arthur Mainwaring, a prominent Whig gentleman and friend of Sarah Churchill. The narrator states that Oldfield's relationship with Mainwaring proves her to be of the highest value: that a respected gentleman of wit and reputation who could choose from all of the available ladies in London picked Oldfield as his intimate companion. The writer of this biography must prove that Oldfield is worthwhile as a private woman before her claim as a spectacularly talented actress and a worthy biographical subject will be credited. Indeed, Curll's rival *Memoirs of the Life of Mrs. Oldfield* even ascribes Oldfield's total value as an actress to this relationship: "It was doubtless owing, in a great Measure, to his Instructions, that Mrs. OLD-FIELD became so admirable a *Player*."[33]

Not surprisingly, no actor biography demonstrates the value of its male subject by showing how the actor won the confidence and hand of a high-placed, noble woman, though some are congratulated on choosing sober, modest mates. More likely, a woman is ridiculed for stooping to a lowly player. While she also was lambasted for her other affairs, Barbara Palmer, the Duchess of Cleveland, was viciously maligned for taking up with the actor Cardell Goodman, who had earlier been prosecuted for theft. The anonymous "Satire on Bent[in]g" (1689) calls her "Goodman's whore," and attacks her for mistreating her children to favor him:

> Who can to such a spendthrift grant relief
> That gives her children's birthright to a thief?
> The vaunting vagabond lives high, looks great.
> Whilst she not plays, but begs gold at basset.
>
> . . . .
>
> In Goodman's grave may fate her carcass lay,
> And every man avoid that foul highway.[34]

Again, the conjunction between money and lasciviousness shows that, unlike Oldfield, she plays an unnatural role by cheating her children of their inheritance as she continues her deviant sexual role. She adopts an attitude toward money that more resembles Weston's, one based on the

masculine model of spending indiscriminately. Cleveland fails to fade into the background after being Charles II's paramour: "So mean her spirits now are grown / Stoop to a dunghill from a Throne."[35] Cleveland betrays her class by bedding down with a mere player, as the *Night Walker* (1696) states: "It was a mighty downfall from being the darling of a M[onar]ch to become the Mistress of a Com[edia]n."[36] That the actor could satisfy her as well as the king reflects poorly on Charles as well, by implicitly paralleling king and player. After this highest value had been assigned to Cleveland as a sexual object, she devalues herself by insisting on *her* possession of her own sexuality, acting as a sexual agent.

Socially prominent and sexualized women like Cleveland and all actresses have a further connection with other, more ambiguous manifestations of money—credit, "stockjobbing," and speculation—that proliferate over the eighteenth century. While the word "speculate" in its financial sense was not current until the third quarter of the eighteenth century, both *spectate* and *speculate* derive from the same Latin root—to observe closely, to spy. Both are associated with gain: one gains instruction and amusement from a performance as one profits from financial changes. In their insistence on the preeminence of the eyes, both words focus attention on the play between surface appearances and the possibilities of inherent worth. While the men on stage are spectacle, they do not have the close metaphorical connection with speculation that women do, especially actresses whose worth fluctuates so extremely, as in the cases of Fenton or Gwyn. Erin Mackie has pointed out the gendered identity of credit: "[T]hose men engaged in speculation are in danger of losing their reason and themselves to the passionate seduction of this fickle femme fatale. Predictably, the financial market underwritten by credit also was figured as feminine, with all of the connotations of fantasy, instability, and danger that attend that assignation."[37] Men who "speculate" or spectate at plays, at actresses, are similarly in danger of being taken advantage of by those avaricious creatures, who are looking to remedy their compromised value through affairs with more prestigious men. But though the male spectator was vulnerable to the actress femme fatale, he also held the power of conferring the worth on her, through his approval in the theaters and his extracurricular attentions. He himself may not gain any value through his attentions to her, but at least he does not lose any.

Connections between gender and value are confused because a player's

gender is confused. "Unfeminine" actresses support themselves and are accepted into society after numerous very public affairs, and "emasculated" actors prostitute themselves as spectacle nightly. Where the gender of the subject is in question or "unnatural," processes of valuation become problematic.

For example, Hill and Popple in the *Prompter* are disgusted by the favor shown to foreign opera singers, especially to Farinelli. This disgust is triggered both by their dislike of opera's lack of moral aim and the dubious gender identity of the castrato. Their words echo those of the Lord Chamberlain:

> The *Daily Advertiser* . . . makes the profit of Senor Carlo Broschi Farinelli amount to upwards of two thousand pounds, to which if we add fifteen hundred pounds salary, and casual presents, we may compute his annual income at near four thousand pounds a year.
>
> The highest offices in His Majesty's Household, executed by men of the first quality in England, have no salaries annexed to them that come near this sum. . . . Gentlemen who have served their country ten, fifteen, twenty years, think themselves amply rewarded if they can procure a son a place of four or five hundred pounds a year. [Then they give the examples of a lawyer and an officer.] Whilst a fellow who is only fit to enervate the youth of Great Britain by the pernicious influence of his unnatural voice . . . shall be recompensed, for the mischiefs he does, beyond the first nobleman in England, for his services.[38]

They admit that Farinelli sings beautifully, "but by what argument in nature can he be proved to deserve more than any actor, that can express with grace, and beautify with action, a noble or a tender sentiment, that inspires with virtue or warms with becoming passion the understanding or compassionate auditor?"[39] In Hill and Popple's view, the stage performance cannot possibly be enjoyed without remembering the invisible physical characteristic, and the question of appropriate monetary value depends on one's physical identity as a man or woman. Someone so privately "lacking" is not fit for public applause nor the bestowal of public funds.

Allowing these castrati to perform only causes faulty valuation to continue, which especially affects female audience members. Ladies who, like Lady Fidget in *The Country Wife,* should be appalled at the thought of a

man so physically compromised, must always have the thought of his physicality in mind when they see him, and thus should shun him. But Popple and Hill are amazed that women actually seek him out to reward him even more: "A woman of the first quality in England fearing lest the Senor should be affronted at receiving a bank note of 50 £. for *one* ticket, . . . purchase[d] a gold snuff-box of thirty guineas value, in which having enclosed the note, she ventured, with fear and trembling, to make her offering at the eunuch's shrine."[40] The writers are unwilling to entertain the possibility that the emotional pitch of the men's voices combined with their minimized physical threat made castrati appealing to women. They condemn a system of valuation that is not based on clear, traditional, and patriarchal gender identities, a new system established by female fans. Such condemnation continues to this day, when genres and celebrities valued primarily by women are dismissed as romance, escapism, "chick flicks," or artistic sellouts.

Like the long hair of early male rock musicians, which similarly produced gender-based moral outrage, whatever allure the castrati have for women points to the depravity and confusion of gender hierarchy of British society, according to the *Prompter*. Nationalism coincides with gender confusion in these performers. The castrati are foreign rarities, a status that can increase value with some of the audience but decrease it with others; witness the numerous riots, such as at Garrick's Chinese Festival, that occurred simply because French performers appeared onstage at a time of tense Anglo-Gallic relations. Castrati epitomize the effeminacy and artificiality of the Catholic countries, which are often contrasted with the masculine bluntness of England. Like other developing theatrical criticism of the mid-eighteenth century, the *Prompter's* pieces attempt to educate readers into valuing the correct objects for the country and its moral health.

CONCLUSION: PURCHASING VALUE

The first thespian subject of a biography, Matthew Coppinger, was hanged for his thievery: illegal appropriation of valuable items. One other piece of evidence we have about Coppinger sheds more light on how much players' relations to money changes from the late seventeenth to the late eighteenth century. Tom Brown identifies "Coppinger, formerly a strowling Player,

executed at Tyburn" as "an Impenitent Clipper." He prints an anecdote of how Coppinger clipped some shillings, which, Coppinger claims, will have the same value both before and after the clipping: "I only par'd off their Superfluities. They would have bought but Twelve Penn'oth of Beef and Turnips at first, and they'll buy Twelve Penn'oth of Beef and Turnips still." The prison ordinary convinces him that the action of clipping is that of making an object more round, which is actually the same as circumcision: "And who, under the Evangelical Dispensation dares practice Circumcision, but one that has actually renounc'd the Christian Religion, and is a *Jew*, a most obstinate perverse *Jew* in his Heart?" This argument convinces Coppinger of his crime—that his illegal handling of money and manipulation of its value is actually a key to his own character: "Upon this, the poor Clipper threw himself at his Feet, own'd the Heinousness of his Sin, confess'd, That Sabbath-breaking had brought him to't, and wept like a Church spout."[41] By linking Coppinger to Jews, reviled in seventeenth- and eighteenth-century Britain for their perceived preoccupation with money and their sexualized religious practices, the ordinary is able to gain a confession and return Coppinger, the threatening criminal-actor, to the sanctioned Christian hierarchy of society. Correct value is restored.

Biographies and criticism help regulate the value of players. Biographies in particular reflect the broader scope that readers were beginning to use to evaluate their public figures. These were not simply performers operating in the limited world of the theater, whose stage action and delivery of lines could be weighed and judged, they were also private people who made and spent large sums of money, and who thus had important economic impact—or were perceived as such. Both their real and metaphoric relations to money came under increasing scrutiny.

Money is "dross" but also the goal of many endeavors. Its possession can indicate greedy hoarding or a designation of merit. Its movement can signal contemptible looseness or admirable generosity. Part of its power comes from its many significations. Money has a multivalency and exists in a social nexus of contradictory qualities, similar to the celebrity.

The readers of these biographies also can affect their *own* value. By being "in the know" about these new cultural icons, readers can increase their own cultural capital via the biography's information and by possessing the physical book itself. Whereas access to cultural power used to be restricted to those who could rub elbows with the great and had court

connections, now one can purchase familiarity with greatness. The multi-valency persists: it is this ability to be bought by anyone that simultaneously increases and decreases the celebrity's value; everything is reducible to money. Bellamy enjoys the popularity the marketplace affords her, yet she strains under its rules:

> I never before viewed that profession I had embraced in so humiliating a light as I now did through Medlicote's aspersions. That every fool who happened to be possessed of a fortune, should think himself licensed to take liberties with me; or even that my own footman, upon any dislike, should be able to go for a shilling into the theatre, and insult me; was what I could not bear to think of.[42]

The same commercial system that allows her to upset the social order and earn unprecedented income also allow those she considers below her in this order to purchase a supremacy over her.

After a while, admiring the same old celebrity loses its appeal and the cultural value of the information decreases as everyone begins to possess it (supply and demand), and so the next new sensation is sought anxiously. The drive for continually new celebrities increases velocity toward Warhol's fifteen minutes of fame.

One eighteenth-century celebrity with phenomenal staying power was Garrick. Bellamy credits this in part to opportunities beyond his acting ability: if he "had not had the *management of himself,* the choice of his characters, and the timing of the representations, he would not have retained the estimation he so justly deserved, and carried with him to the grave."[43] She identifies him as his own *manager,* in our modern sense of the word, as someone who not only performs but who shapes a performing career by smart professional choices. Yet by looking at the biographies of Garrick, we can understand how his formidable talent, his fortuitous timing, and his regulation of his image during his lifetime allow many of the disruptions in thespian discourse I have discussed in this book to be harmonized. With Garrick, a high and nearly undisputed standard of value for at least some actors is established. The jostling for cultural authority does not disappear, but Garrick's biographical representations show that the opportunity for a performer's cultural prominence does exist at the end of the eighteenth century. At least for the exceptional player, the new category of the celebrity is firmly entrenched.

CHAPTER 8

The Authority of the Celebrity

DAVID GARRICK

[B]ehold that little, elevated Cit—observe
him well—Believes he not himself, think
you, a *Roscius*—a *Wilks*—a *Betterton*?—Else
whence that Stiffness, however aukward,
however unbecoming?—View his
ungoverned Pride—That young Gentleman,
Sir, said *Mr. Williams,* seems to be greatly
agitated by that almost universal Passion,
Love of Fame—As yet an Infant only in the
Theatre—Playing a few Parts well—he
persuades his sweet self, he can accomplish
all . . . the aspiring Boy, scarce two years a
Subject, grasps at the *Theatrical Sceptre.*

---

*Theatrical Correspondence in Death: An
Epistle from Mrs. Oldfield, in the Shades, to
Mrs. Br——ceg——dle, upon Earth* (1743)

A FTER learning the history of
thespian biography, a reader
encountering the biographies
of David Garrick by Thomas Davies
and Arthur Murphy may be surprised

at the lack of conflict in them. Both narrators are respectful, candid, willing to identify their subject's flaws yet also willing to defend him against unjust accusations. There are no discordant speeches on oratory, no gruesome descriptions of dissection, and no preoccupations with crime, debt, or sex. No popular novelists and historians are imitated or mentioned as inspirations. Readers find lengthy chronologies of Garrick's involvement with the stage and a biographical method much closer to a modern style. These texts seem not to be struggling against literary, class, professional, or any other sort of authority. After the end of Garrick's prosperous life, his value and the authority that value confers are *assumed* by these biographers, and they have no need to prove the value of their subject.

This does not mean that Garrick did not have vocal detractors over the course of his life. George Winchester Stone Jr. has located more than five hundred items of critical commentary printed during Garrick's lifetime.[1] Early in Garrick's career, the writer of *Theatrical Correspondence in Death*, above, points to Garrick's ambitious quest for fame and his desire to control a theater company. *D——ry-L——ne P——yh——se Broke Open. In a Letter to Mr. G——* (1748) snarls, "The Press swarms with Pamphlets address'd to you; and, how the Authors or Printers can find it worth their while to publish 'em, is a Matter of some Wonder. I cou'd wish my Countrymen had something of more Importance to show their Concern about."[2] Even as this writer contributes to the problem he describes, the question he raises echoes the issues of value we reviewed in the previous chapter: why was Garrick important enough to provoke this swarming press? Yet by the time of Garrick's death, this question did not seem to be one worth asking.

Garrick's power at Drury Lane theater was indisputable. As an actor, he could move a theater audience to tears or applause; as a manager, he could make or break dramatists' and actors' careers; as a society figure, he could intercede with important people for favors. His power was not traditional political, aristocratic, or religious authority, but Garrick had very real control over many people's lives. Overall, Garrick's range, ability, and position resembled those of Thomas Betterton. The primary difference between the two actors' careers lies in Garrick's fortuitous timing, the nearly eighty years that separated the two men's first appearances on the stage. Joseph Roach explains that Garrick "lived at the decisive moment in the development of theatrical theory" when the sciences first examined actors' emo-

tion from outside assumptions of classical rhetoric. In contrast to the theory of acting espoused by Betterton's biographer Gildon, "Garrick, entering at the right historical moment, renovated theatrical semiotics, founding his vocabulary of expressive gesture on a new order of understanding, a revised concept of what nature is and means."[3] More important than Garrick's place in this possible paradigm shift, however, is his place in reference to the change in the publicity opportunities available to the two actors. This is the difference that enables Garrick's particular form of authority, one that is less actual power and more the perception of power and the acceptance of an actor as a person worthy of holding power. Garrick's celebrity (and that of others of the time) depends on media, and the print industry simply was not as active and widespread in Betterton's time as in Garrick's. Just as Garrick's opportunity to become manager of Drury Lane in 1747 was facilitated by Charles Fleetwood's financial ruin and the ensuing chaos, so his opportunity to become a theatrical legend was made possible by an expanding London publishing trade and the increasing amount of attention the previous generation of performers had received in print. By the time of his debut, the print pump was primed. By the time of his death in 1779, no performer had been so discussed in papers and pamphlets—or biography.

What the biographies published after Garrick's death try to do is to explain this new type of authority to their readers. The first, *The Life and Death of David Garrick, Esq.*, supposedly written by an "Old Comedian," uses the familiar Curllian compilation method, including a breakdown of Garrick's power through his figure, face, voice, and education. These categories recapitulate the two types of authority discussed earlier, the gentleman/rogue, ancient/modern distinctions, in a way that integrates rather than divides the sources of authority. Garrick's authority arises from both, in his energized native acting talent and his obvious disciplined learning. The Old Comedian also links Garrick's status to a long lineage of English actors by providing a short biography of Edward Alleyn: "[I]t is incontestably evident that Mr. Alleyn could be little less than the Garrick of his time."[4]

But the two major biographies of Garrick are more subtle and complex. Like the Old Comedian book, each of the others engages with many of the issues this study has already raised—of the source and use of talent, of concepts of fame, of gender stability, of control over the body and one's

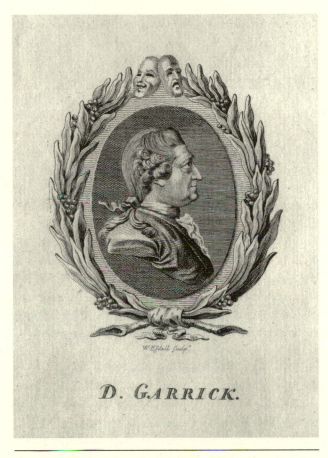

Fig. 9. David Garrick, from Davies's
Memoirs of the Life of David Garrick.
REPRODUCED WITH PERMISSION BY HORACE HOWARD FURNESS
MEMORIAL LIBRARY, ANNENBERG RARE BOOK AND
MANUSCRIPT LIBRARY, UNIVERSITY
OF PENNSYLVANIA.

powers of imposture, and of literary authority. Both Davies and Murphy knew and worked with Garrick, and both were involved with the theater and Garrick's circle. They both wrote lengthy two-volume biographies with "slants" that derived from this experience. Though they both felt Garrick's power, they expressed it in different ways. From a unique cache of memory and print material, both establish Garrick as a cultural arbiter. By the end of the eighteenth century, the mechanisms of celebrity had developed to a point at which the biographers of mere actors could claim their subjects' positions as cultural authorities.

THE THEATRICAL LIFE: THOMAS DAVIES'S
Memoirs of the Life of David Garrick

When Thomas Davies began writing his *Memoirs of the Life of David Garrick, Esq.* (1780), discussion of Garrick had saturated the presses for forty years.[5] Facing such an amount of material and, even if the individual pieces were not immediately available, facing the composite image of Garrick in the public mind must have been daunting. However, it seems as though Davies had little choice. As Boswell recounts, Davies's bookselling business was foundering in the late 1770s. After Garrick's death, Johnson suggested that Davies write the actor's biography. Indeed, Johnson provided the first resounding sentences: "All excellence has a right to be recorded. I shall therefore think it superfluous to apologize for writing the life of a man who, by an uncommon assemblage of private virtues, adorned the highest eminence in a public profession" (1:1).[6] Davies's work is the longest, most thorough, and most balanced biography of an actor to this date. The publication of this biography lands thespian subjects directly in the biographical mainstream of the time, claiming social acceptance for this talented, fortunate actor.

Having begun his theatrical life in Henry Fielding's Haymarket company, Davies turned to bookselling after the Licensing Act of 1737 shut Fielding down. Eight years later, he returned to acting at Covent Garden, provincial theaters, and then in Garrick's Drury Lane; he went back to bookselling full time in 1762, which he practiced until his death in 1785. As a bookseller, Davies was ideally positioned for accessing printed material about Garrick, for knowing what readers wanted from biography, and for being able to provide the commercial support his venture required. Stone and Kahrl have

described Davies's often touchy relationship with Garrick: his reported ingratitude after Garrick had lent him money, his decision to leave Drury Lane because of Garrick's domineering control, his oversensitivity to criticism (according to Garrick).[7] The chilly relations between them seem never to have thawed, despite their mutual acquaintances such as Johnson and Boswell. Boswell met Johnson for the first time in Davies's shop in 1763.[8]

Given this situation, Davies might not be expected to produce a favorable and balanced biography of Garrick. Yet favorable it is. Davies's description of Garrick's first appearance on stage gives us an idea of the volumes' tone, employing the illumination imagery often used to praise Garrick's acting: "Mr. Garrick shone forth like a theatrical Newton; he threw new light on elocution and action; he banished ranting, bombast, and grimace; and restored nature, ease, simplicity, and genuine humour" (1:49). Davies also addresses accusations of Garrick's avarice and vanity, opinions with which he might have concurred at certain junctures in their relationship. He acknowledges some of Garrick's managerial mistakes, as when he disdains his friends' advice and will not hire the singer Miss Brent (2:64), or, with Robert Dodsley's *Cleone*: "[H]is conduct in the whole dispute was unjustifiable; and . . . he treated a worthy man, and an old acquaintance, with severity and unkindness" (1:225). But these are presented as minor blemishes in a theatrical genius. If Davies's contemporary readers—Boswell, Johnson, Murphy, and other writers who knew Garrick well—had found the *Memoirs* intrusive or offensive, some outraged response would certainly have been recorded, and we have none. Unlike the reception of Cibber's self-promoting *Apology*, no chorus of disgust greeted this somewhat hagiographic treatment. Davies maintains an even portrait of a man who seemed to have superhuman acting powers—as well as some human foibles.[9]

In publishing this biography, Davies had a lot at stake—his business. So after the death of the great man, he would have little to gain from a biography full of scandalous accusation, much to gain through an extended eulogy. All of the biographical elements of Davies's book supports Garrick's superiority to other actors and managers—and thus his natural claim to authority. For example, he provides us with minibiographies of peripheral figures such as Charles Fleetwood, manager of Drury Lane in the early forties. Fleetwood was "irregular and expensive" (1:68) with a

passion for gambling and "low diversion" who eventually "entertained the public with sights of tall monsters and contemptible rope-dancers" on the Drury Lane stage (1:69). According to Davies, "Such a conductor of a theatre was unequal to the task of displaying to advantage the talents of a Garrick, or the humour of a Clive; or, indeed, of furnishing any rational entertainment for an enlightened public" (1:69–70). Not only does such a portrait cause readers to sympathize with the actors who rebel from Fleetwood's control, it also prepares readers for the rational and enlightened management of Garrick himself, and impresses upon them the important cultural work a theater manager does for his community and his country.

The idea that a life cannot be understood properly without the context of its times and descriptions of those with whom the subject interacted is not revolutionary, though it does imply a large amount of raw material not often available to thespian biographers. Colley Cibber implemented this "life and times" approach for his *Apology* because of his personal reminiscence of three decades in the theater, similar to what Davies was able to draw upon. The anonymous author of *Life of Quin* (1766) tells us that the "Histories of the Stage, the Annals of the Theatre, scarce mention him [Quin] either as an actor or a man," but claims that Quin's life cannot be understood without a review of contemporary theatrical history.[10] Likewise, Davies's title page not only claims the book as a *Life* but also tells us that it is "Interspersed with Characters and Anecdotes of His Theatrical Contemporaries, The Whole Forming A History of the Stage, which includes a Period of Thirty-Six Years." He also writes: "In a narrative of Mr. Garrick's life will unavoidably be included many theatrical anecdotes, and a variety of observations upon several comedians of both sexes, who distinguished themselves by superiority in their profession. Their merits I shall endeavour to display, and their characters I intend to delineate with truth and candour" (1:2). He gives details about the players active at the beginning of Garrick's career, plus those with whom Garrick worked, devoting two chapters to short descriptions and anecdotes of Quin, Ryan, Walker, Pritchard, and Abington, among many others, and diffusing biographical information on others, for example, Susannah Maria Cibber, throughout the volumes. Davies seems to believe that if people were involved in the theater during Garrick's career, they were part of Garrick's life.

⚭

The effect is to provide a background against which Garrick can shine. While many of these other actors are praised—Thomas Walker, for example, is commended for his rendition of the Bastard in King John, which not even Garrick or Sheridan can touch (1:307)—the capsule biographies or descriptions included usually serve as enhancements of or foils to Garrick. Garrick's prestige is increased when he performs across from talented actresses, such as Susannah Maria Cibber, who "was not the mere actress; her accomplishments rendered her dear to persons of the first quality of her own sex" (2:112). Such a consort reflects well upon the ability and gentility of Garrick. The chapter Davies devotes to Samuel Foote serves to enhance Garrick's reputation in the opposite manner. Foote's acting attempts are described, with the conclusion that "Foote was a despicable player in almost all parts but those which he wrote for himself" (1:200). In choosing plays as a part manager, Foote is also contrasted unfavorably to Garrick. Foote mimics his intimate acquaintance "Mr. A——" (Apreece) on stage as Mr. Cadwallader in *The Author*. Friendship is no bar: even though Mr. A—— was "greatly respected for his good-nature, and readiness to do acts of kindness . . . as long as Foote got money by exposing him, it was hopeless to think of prevailing upon him to stop the abuse. When gain was in view, humanity was out of the question" (1:202–4). Mr. A—— becomes upset and applies to Garrick. Garrick "heard his complaints with politeness," but when Mr. A—— threatens Garrick with a duel to give him satisfaction, Garrick merely smiles and gently explains his disadvantages. However, since Garrick "really felt for Mr. A——, he advised him to apply to the lord chamberlain, a nobleman who, he was sure, had too much humanity to suffer any gentleman to be hurt by personal representation" (1:204–5). So while satisfying the ostensible aim of providing a history of the theaters, Davies, through his descriptions of other theatrical personnel, allows Garrick to emerge as a better actor, a more compassionate manager, and a gentleman with important connections in a genteel world.

All of Davies's biographical choices support this characterization of Garrick as well bred and behaved, especially in the theatrical world of rivalry and jealousy. Garrick's conduct often shows him as an exception rather than the common person of the theater. In this, Davies helps readers understand and approve of the acclaim that Garrick achieved: Garrick deserves his celebrity because of his measured behavior in a setting that

does not foster such values. Davies shows Garrick as the consummate theatrical professional in a time when acting itself was not completely acknowledged as a profession. Davies's Garrick is a public man; readers do not encounter Johnson's biographical ideal of *Rambler,* no. 60 (13 October 1750): "[T]he business of the biographer is to pass slightly over those performances and incidents which produce vulgar greatness, to lead the thoughts into domestic privacies, and display the minute details of daily life, where exterior appendages are cast aside, and men excel each other only by prudence and by virtue." Few of Garrick's "domestic privacies" emerge from Davies's book. Readers hear how Garrick handled malicious authors, peevish actresses, and affronted actors, but they never see the daily theatrical Garrick—practicing his lines, attending rehearsals, supervising stagehands—nor do they encounter Garrick at home among his friends and family. Where did he live? How many children did he sire? How did he relax after his exertions on the stage? Neither these details nor the conversation, argument, and attention to the ephemeral performances of daily life that will animate Boswell's characterization of Johnson appear here, even though Davies claims that "[t]he true character of a man is always more accurately known to his neighbors than to the world at large; to those who live with him, near him, and round about him, than to persons at a distance. Go, then, you, who still entertain a doubt of Mr. Garrick's bounty and benevolence, go to Hampton, and learn what every inhabitant of that village will say of him" (2:398–9).

This statement indirectly defends his primary source of information—his own personal knowledge of Garrick. As he writes in the preface to the biography's third edition, he is indebted to Samuel Johnson for information on Garrick's early life and for "several diverting anecdotes." But then he states that "[a] long acquaintance with the stage, and an earnest inclination to excel in the profession of acting, to which I was for many years attached, afforded me an opportunity to know much of plays and theatrical history. I can truly say, that I have no where willingly misrepresented either fact or character. Mistakes I may have fallen into; but I shall not incur the charge of falshood, for that implies an intention to deceive" (1:A4r). Though he seems to argue that the best portrait of Garrick would be one that exposes his private life to the public, he also believes that he is doing this, that Garrick's behind-the-scenes machinations at Drury Lane, or his performances in his roles, or the information on these other theatri-

cal characters would be information that his readers would not have all in one place. Just as the discussion of the domestic arrangements of a great general would be out of place in a biography, so are they left unsaid and undesired in biographical treatments of Garrick. Richard Sennett might explain this phenomenon as the society's different understanding of private and public—that the public persona was not necessarily seen as a forced and fake role distinct from the private person.

Others have claimed that Garrick had no private life to offer. Garrick's acquaintances commented on his tendency to remain "in character" even when not on stage. Samuel Johnson declared that Garrick kept others at a distance and had "friends but no friend"—and Goldsmith seems peevishly to have agreed: "On the stage he was natural, simple, affecting, / 'Twas only that, when he was off, he was acting."[11] In his private writings, Sir Joshua Reynolds left a brief character sketch of Garrick in which he emphasized the practiced nature of Garrick's supposedly natural action: "Great as Garrick was on the stage, he was at least equal if not still superior at the table, and here he had too much the same habit of preparing himself, as if he was to act a principal part." His ability to be a good friend was prevented by his position as a great actor: "Being used to exhibit himself at a theater or a large table, he did not consider an individual as worth powder and shot. . . . The habit of seeking fame in this manner left his mind unfit for the cultivation of private friendship."[12] Such admissions reveal a distrust of the successful star actor, because he or she points out the uncomfortable possibility of a lack of human essence and the performative nature of human interaction. Davies (and Murphy), who knew Garrick personally, must answer the late-century desire for biography that exposes private life by writing about a subject who seems always to be cultivating a public image. Even Garrick's own writing leaves little information on the private man—his letters are evasive, and his published writings are composed in character or are anonymous.[13]

For Davies, if a part of Garrick's life does not have direct relation to the theater, it does not appear in his biography. Davies could have presented his account of the Garricks' two-year hiatus on the Continent in many ways; he chooses to present two chapters on "The State of the Stage during Mr. Garrick's Absence on His Tour to the Continent"—an indication that the London stage is perhaps the true protagonist in this *Life* (though Davies does briefly report on Garrick's trips to foreign theaters and his

encounters with Continental players). Of course, the sources of Davies's information may have determined such imbalance and omission: neither Johnson nor Davies himself would have known much about Garrick's European tour. Davies was not a Garrick intimate, so while he was a theatrical "insider," able both to sketch portraits of contemporary players and to recount the various stage controversies of Garrick's day, he had little access to personal information. Unlike Boswell, he does not mention any attempts to interrogate Garrick's friends, relations, or servants.

So Davies's biography is a contributing factor to sustaining Garrick's self-image of the public, professional man. Most telling is the way Davies handles Garrick's intimate affairs. His treatment of two women in Garrick's life, Peg Woffington and Eva Maria Veigel (Mrs. Garrick), is particularly telling. Woffington and Garrick had been lovers in the early forties, had considered marriage, and had even cohabitated (Boswell tells us how Johnson went to visit them), but then broke off for an unspecified reason. But the reader of Davies's *Memoirs of Garrick* will look in vain for information about this affair. Davies acknowledges his readers' curiosity about her, but not the love affair, by prefacing his Woffington chapter with the words, "A short sketch of an actress so celebrated for beauty of countenance and elegance of form, as well as merit in her profession, . . . will be expected by the reader of this narrative" (1:312). He relies on the reader's prior knowledge to fill in the details and to understand why he chose to set Mrs. Woffington apart in a chapter of her own—and thus seems to be writing with a specific contemporary readership in mind.[14] Davies only mentions Garrick's "acquaintance" with Woffington. His biography is very chaste—no hint of immoral conduct on Garrick's part either before or after his marriage—and the differences between this treatment of the Garrick/Woffington liaison with the bawdy, snide account in the *Memoirs of the Celebrated Mrs. W*ff**gt*n* ([1760]) only further emphasize for us how differently actors and actresses were commodified.[15] Davies may have avoided intimate subjects out of sympathy for or fear of Garrick's still socially influential widow or because of anticipated censure from Johnson and other powerful friends of Garrick (considerations hardly ever taken for the survivors in actresses' families).

In contrast to the treatment of Woffington, Davies summarizes Garrick's courtship and marriage in one sentence: "In July 1749 Mr. Garrick was married to Mademoiselle Violetti [Veigel], a young lady, who to great

elegance of form, and many polite accomplishments, joined the more amiable virtues of the mind" (1:171). Mrs. Garrick receives general approval throughout the *Memoirs,* but she never appears as a personality or as the professional dancer Garrick wooed (she gave up her career after marriage).[16] These strategic omissions serve to emphasize Garrick's public-ness. It is as if, like a great general, his service to his country cannot be sullied by such small concerns. Certainly, sexual questions arose during his career. He appears in the Woffington biography; he frolics with several ladies in Edward Kimber's *Juvenile Adventures of David Ranger;* William Kendrick attaches Garrick's name to Isaac Bickerstaff, a popular playwright who wrote for Garrick and who fled to the Continent when he was accused of propositioning a man. Straub notes how Garrick is portrayed as uniformly masculine in comparison to the compromised Cibber in public discourse.[17] Davies's Garrick is not subject to the feminizing amours and sentiments of actress biography. His unified gender performance denies sexuality, as though a man in his lofty position, with his serious concerns, would not trifle with such indignity, unless to take on a socially respectable bride. Garrick provided a perfect vehicle for consolidating all of the perceived antisocial, immoral, and suspect tendencies of the celebrity into a gentlemanly image.

Garrick is in the public eye, but the public itself plays a small role in Davies's text, except, once again, as a foil to Garrick, an adversary in Garrick's efforts to give the town good, improving entertainment. Audiences are most often pictured as factions and gangs in various theatrical controversies. For example, when audiences were upset over foreign performers in the Chinese Festival, Davies shows how the vulgar can take over and destroy the best efforts of a careful manager. Garrick invites Monsieur Noverre to Drury Lane in 1754, "to compose such dances as would surprize and captivate all ranks of people" (1:187). However, "the uninformed part of the people, stimulated by others, whose envy of superior merit and good fortune is ever disguised with the specious shew of public spirit, denounced vengeance against the managers, and particularly Mr. Garrick, for employing such a large number of Frenchmen in an English theater, at a time of open war with their countrymen" (1:188). The uproar began first with "the plebeian part of the audience" (1:190), which incensed the people of fashion in the boxes; those in the pit took offense and joined forces with the galleries against the boxes; and all of them "demolished the scenes,

tore up the benches, broke the lustres and girandoles," causing the theater to be unusable for several days (1:191). Davies continues that Garrick may be blamed for persisting in his plan to present this entertainment, but he is more apt to "condemn that public which could reject an entertainment, merely because a few helpless foreigners, who had a just claim to their protection, from their being invited to the service, were employed in it" (1:192). As we saw previously, this biography helps to educate the public by condemning its excesses and explaining how good managers make wise choices for everyone's benefit.

The same attitude is apparent in James Boaden's accounts of the 1809 Old Price riots in his *Memoirs of the Life of John Philip Kemble* (1825) and *Memoirs of Mrs. Siddons* (1827). If spectators knew true value, they would not judge aesthetic productions on the basis of social criteria, such as the composition of the company. Greater publicity can, disastrously, allow an audience to know who is performing and to judge the merit of their performances on criteria that have nothing to do with the performance itself. Davies tries to give even more information to counteract this trend: by showing that Garrick was only thinking of the good of the audience and by stressing the innocence of the performers (whom, he maintains, were *Swiss* and not French), audiences can have the correct "background" information to allow them to derive correct decisions about the stage.

But the challenge to Garrick's authority as a manager does not always come from the "vulgar" public of the galleries. Davies also shows how supposed gentlemen cause Garrick problems. The "half-price riots" of 1763 were waged over Garrick's announcement that spectators were not to be allowed in for half price after the third act when a new play was being performed. A "conspiracy," according to Davies, headed by Thomas Fitzpatrick, demanded that this be the rule only when a new pantomime was being performed, and they destroyed the theaters and demanded that a player who talked back to them and refused to go to his knees and ask pardon not be allowed onstage. Davies reproaches the supposedly well-bred men who whipped up the frenzy, and suggests that their conduct toward players reflects their own moral standing: "[D]egrading the actor must tend to lessen the pleasure of the spectator. What just notions of propriety of behaviour, what knowledge of elegance in manners, or representation of what is grand or graceful, humourous or gay, can an audience expect from a wretch who is driven to a degree of meanness unworthy of a man?"

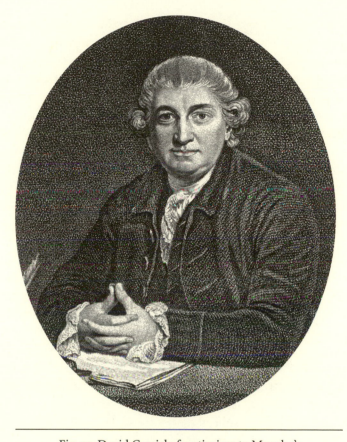

Fig. 10. David Garrick, frontispiece to Murphy's
The Life of David Garrick.
REPRODUCED WITH PERMISSION BY HORACE HOWARD FURNESS
MEMORIAL LIBRARY, ANNENBERG RARE BOOK AND
MANUSCRIPT LIBRARY, UNIVERSITY
OF PENNSYLVANIA.

(2:10). Ill treatment of actors will only undermine the noble purposes of the theater. Davies tells readers that "they owed this great prerogative [of getting to see two acts of a play for half price] to the private resentment of a splenetick man, not to publick spirit or patriotick principle" (2:15). He continues, explaining why Fitzpatrick and Garrick clashed privately and in print, and condemning its public resolution in threat and violence.

Davies does not have to argue for Garrick's talent as an actor in this biography. As a matter of fact, since he has "promised to give a review of his principal characters in another place" (1:61–2)—his forthcoming *Dramatic Miscellanies*—Davies does not even comment on Garrick's Shakespearean roles except for Hamlet in the *Life*. But after years of managerial squabbling, Garrick had need of a biographer who would champion the decisions he had made for the theater against other actors, writers, and outsiders—like the audiences, to whom he often had to apologize. Davies did not have to build authority for the acting profession—to fight against overt denunciations of the profession or against attempts to keep actors submissive—as so many of the other biographies do. His job was to describe the proper use of theatrical authority through the character of this singular figure. Davies creates the consummate manager, the man destined to uphold the dignity of the English stage in face of challenges from puerile pantomime, ignorant audiences, scabrous critics, and arrogant society men.

THE LITERARY LIFE: ARTHUR MURPHY'S
The Life of David Garrick

By the time Arthur Murphy published his *Life of Garrick* in 1801, he had lived a long life, involved nearly continuously in theatrical projects. He had acted for several seasons, but his main theatrical tie was as an important dramatist. Howard Hunter Dunbar has echoed Johnson's estimate of Murphy, saying that although he may not have been a dramatist of the very first rate, his standing among writers active during the later part of the century was certainly "superiour": "Murphy's contemporary claim to the post of leading dramatist is not an empty one."[18] He had seen twenty-one comedies, tragedies, and farces through production; some, such as *The Grecian Daughter* (1772), were major hits. He also practiced law and printed verses, journalism, satire, and criticism, including considerations

of Garrick's acting in the *Gray's Inn Journal* and elsewhere. Given this career, we should not be surprised to find that his *Life of Garrick* differs from Davies's account in its decidedly literary inclination. While Murphy certainly does not ignore Garrick's theatrical embroilments—his ties to other players, his staging of productions, his clashes with hostile audiences—Murphy's portrayal of Garrick emphasizes Garrick's contributions to and shaping of England's national dramatic heritage, establishing Garrick as a literary authority.

Structurally, Murphy's biography resembles Davies's account quite closely, recapitulating almost all of the same incidents, though Murphy never admits having read Davies's book. Murphy vigorously trims many descriptions of theatrical background and reduces the number of capsule biographies that Davies had provided, maintaining the focus on Garrick—and on Murphy himself. When Davies introduced a character, he often gave a short account of the life and works and followed the subject to his or her death. Not so Murphy: he picks up and drops characters as he needs them, stating, "the lives and characters of the authors would have drawn me into a length foreign to the work in hand. Such digressions would have made a motley mixture" (2:154). Davies's two minibiographies occasioned by the deaths of Mrs. Cibber and Quin late in Garrick's career are nowhere in Murphy's *Life:* although "two events happened in the course of the year 1766, which ought not to be passed by in silence" (2:34), he merely notes the two deaths, places of burial, and Garrick's brief reactions, stating, "We return from this digression to the business of the stage" (2:36). Murphy's near-contemporary Jesse Foot notes early nineteenth-century reaction to this quality of Murphy's biography: "He most undoubtedly has not gone fully into the life of the great actor, nor into the dramatic occurrences of the time of Mr. Garrick's life; but be it remembered, that those who agreed in that, no otherwise object to the life, but that there is not enough of it: that, of what is done, the specimen is so good, the facts are so produced, the judgment so displayed, and the manner, style, and experience, discover so many touches of this venerable Master of the Drama, that it is to be lamented he had given us no more on the same entertaining and interesting subject."[19] Foot's comments celebrate Murphy's style, reinforcing public appreciation of Murphy's literary ability.

Murphy seems much more self-consciously deliberate about his method and aims than Davies. Except for the opening line he received

from Johnson, Davies made no pretensions to the noble ideals of the genre in which he was writing. In contrast, Murphy declares:

> Biography, or a true account of the lives of men, who were eminent in their time, has been always considered as a pleasing, and most useful branch of polite Literature. It traces the man into his closest retirement; views his conduct in all the relations of life; discloses his principles, his passions, and, in short, lays the whole character open to our view. History does not afford so instructive a lesson; it does not descend from its dignity, to enter into the scenes of private life; it shews us the person in his public conduct, either acting with integrity, or serving the sinister views of his own ambition. But the entire character is not displayed. Biography supplies this defect. (1:1–2)

This passage echoes Johnson's *Rambler,* no. 60, with its higher estimation of biography than history, though Murphy still does not provide any of the private information that Davies omitted—a repudiation, perhaps, of the Boswellian example, which had provoked much public outcry. Like Davies, Murphy tries to capitalize on his privileged "insider's" ability for writing a biography of Garrick: he "was acquainted with Mr. Garrick so early as the latter end of 1752, and from that time lived in great intimacy with him to the hour of his death" (1:4). Murphy overstates the case in describing his often prickly relationship with Garrick as "great intimacy." But relations between them never seem to have disintegrated as completely as those between Davies and Garrick. After his life has become quiet, Murphy has leisure to "pay his tribute of friendship, and, at the same time, of strict justice, to the memory of David Garrick, in a fair, a just, and true account of his conduct in life, with all the lights and shades of the picture, touched with a firm, and impartial hand" (1:5).[20]

This biography emphasizes the gravity and dignity of literature; Murphy understands his subject's life through a literary lens. Murphy attributes the same loftiness of purpose to Garrick as he did for himself; for example, Murphy describes the season of 1747–8, in which Garrick bought the Drury Lane patent: "We enter now upon a new æra in the history of the English stage; the greatest and most splendid that the drama of this country has ever known. . . . To revive dramatic poetry in all its lustre was [Garrick's] ardent wish" (1:131, 136). While this may or may not have been Garrick's wish, it certainly reflected the way in which Murphy, at the end

of his own life, interpreted his own goals. Murphy attributes his own motivations to Garrick, conveniently finding the most glorious age of the English stage during the period in which he himself was writing plays.

Like some dramatic historians, Murphy considers the plays and their literary quality the heart of the dramatic enterprise, rather than management or acting, the daily grind of the theater. He summarizes and comments on plays; his brief description of Garrick attaining the Drury Lane patent, for example, quickly moves into an extended discussion of Otway's *Venice Preserv'd*. His opinions of the quality of certain plays color his memories of their theatrical fortunes; for example, though both biographers admit that Elizabeth Griffith's *The Platonic Wife* (1765) was not a success, Murphy's version differs quite substantially from Davies's. Davies's account explains that the actors Holland and Powell "had not been used to the noise of catcalls, hisses, groans, and horse laughs, the most powerful instruments in the exploding of a play, were so much intimidated, and so forgetful of their duty, as to thrust their heads on stage from behind the curtain, and to entreat these merciful gentlemen, . . . to put an end to the play that very night, that they might be no longer exposed to such terrible mortifications. But the absurd counsel of these actors did not prevail. . . . Against the next representation it was altered, to the general satisfaction of the publick, and the author had the good fortune to obtain two benefits" (2:89–90). Murphy's account lingers on his scorn for the play and playwright, then briefly tells how Powell and Holland "laboured through groans and hisses, to which they had not been accustomed, till they obtained a second benefit for Mrs. Griffiths, and then laid down their arms" (2:11). Davies accuses the actors of irresponsibility, thus once again stressing Garrick's equanimity and tact by contrast; Murphy interprets their actions as justifiable when forced to perform in such a bad play.

Murphy uses his literary authority to chastise many of his contemporaries, such as Mrs. Griffith. Wycherley's *The Plain Dealer,* approved by Dryden, was adapted by Isaac Bickerstaff. Murphy comments, "The judgement of so eminent a man [Dryden] ought to have made Bickerstaff pause, and, indeed, desist from his attempt. . . . [but] he was guilty of bold and rash presumption" (2:26). Murphy contends that Garrick had it "in his power to rise to eminence in the line of dramatic poetry. . . . He is, however, to be considered as an occasional adventurer, and yet his quick and lively genius contributed largely to give variety to the public entertain-

ment" (2:189). While Garrick always received praise for his prologues and epilogues—"What ease in the versification! what quick and lively strokes of wit! what variety of invention!" (2:191)—he was not immune from Murphy's censure when issues of dramatic composition were at stake. Michael Dobson has discussed how Murphy chided Garrick for his adaptation of *Hamlet* while Garrick was alive;[21] in the biography, Murphy scolds the actor for his adaptation of *The Country-Wife* to *The Country Girl* (1766): "That Garrick should forget his veneration for the best writers of the last century, is not a little surprising. Could he imagine that such an author as Wycherley ought to be superseded, and that his best plays were to be consigned to oblivion? The attempt does no honour to his memory" (2:37).

Perhaps Murphy's irritation arises from having had Garrick as a dramatic rival, since Garrick not only wrote and adapted many plays himself, he had the power to refuse Murphy's plays. In the biography, Murphy is surprisingly quiet on critical assessment of his own plays. He usually attributes their success, modestly, to the efforts of the actors: for example, he explains of *The Grecian Daughter* (1772): if "the play had uncommon success, he ["the writer," that is, Murphy himself] desires to have it understood, that he ascribes it to the merit of such admirable performers" (2:92), Spranger and Ann Barry.

When he and Garrick quarreled over one of Murphy's plays, however, Murphy's account expands. He spends twelve pages on the "first, and, indeed, the last, disagreeable controversy, this writer ever had with Mr. Garrick" (1:330)—his memory mistakes him here—over the refusal and eventual acceptance of his *Orphan of China*. He states: "Of the play itself, the author, as becomes him, chuses to remain in strict silence; but as it encountered a number of difficulties, it will not be improper to state the particulars, especially as a very lame and imperfect account has been published by different writers, who do not seem to have had authentic information" (1:330). Davies's version is fairly balanced and probably not one of these "lame" accounts to which Murphy replies. Though Davies claims that "no manager was better qualified to serve an author in the correcting, pruning, or enlarging of a dramatic piece . . . [i]t was his misfortune sometimes to err egregiously" (1:221). One error was *Orphan of China*, of which Davies provides "a history of an author's and manager's manœuvres in evading each other's schemes" (1:227); ultimately, Davies seems to admit that Garrick quibbled too much with Murphy's script. Murphy himself

describes the "paper-war" he started against Garrick, admitting, "perhaps he [Murphy] swelled with too much pride" (1:331). He concludes by praising the production and Garrick's performance in it, saying that Garrick "never appeared in any character (if we except *King Lear*) with such a brilliant lustre" (1:338), and by acknowledging, "the author is sensible that he has run into too much prolixity about things chiefly relating to himself" (1:340).

The force of Murphy's opinions and his personal appearances throughout this biography give the impression that Garrick is sharing the stage of his own *Life* with his biographer. In addition to the accounts of his own plays, Murphy throughout refers to himself often as "this writer" (Davies only used an infrequent "I"), and he includes anecdotes in which he is a character, such as a stroll with Samuel Foote during Garrick's Stratford Jubilee. Murphy also makes his presence felt through heavy metaphorical and literary language. Davies's version of Garrick's leaving for the Continent begins, "Mr. Garrick had long meditated a journey to the continent" (2:66), while Murphy rhapsodizes: "The season, on which we are now to enter, presents a gloomy prospect. The mind of the writer, instead of being invited to proceed with alacrity, feels its powers depressed, and almost recoils from the subject. The theatrical hemisphere is overcast; the vivifying rays, that enlivened and adorned the landscape, are for a time withdrawn, and the voice, that made the grove harmonious, is heard no more. To say all in a word, Garrick has abdicated" (2:1–2). The focus on the emotions of the writer—Murphy—and the Gothic imagery remind the reader of Murphy's status as a noted writer and his book's status as a work of a noted writer. The passage continues the illumination imagery of theatrical stardom, which appears elsewhere, especially when he romanticizes the past: "The theatre still went on with considerable profit, but the public wished for nothing so much as Garrick's return. The general voice was, that he staid too long. . . . They thought that his presence, like the spring, would give new life to every thing; make the days more pleasant, and lend new lustre to the sun" (2:12).

The tone of Murphy's *Life* is conscious of the biography as a literary artifact, often pompous and ornate. Even the physical characteristics of Murphy's two volumes distinguish them from Davies's: its frontispiece engraving from a Reynolds portrait shows Garrick sitting at his desk pausing from writing a prologue, whereas Davies's frontispiece reprints a fashionable,

elegant profile by Sherwin—neither, significantly, picture Garrick as a theatrical character, as do the multiple prints collected in the Old Comedian's biography. The pages of Murphy's *Life* are laid out with plenty of white space, and many of its chapters end with engraved ornaments, in contrast to the plain, cramped pages of the Davies biography.[22] Murphy seems to be trying to establish thespian biography as a respectable literary genre, just as he attempted to establish Garrick and himself as literary arbiters.

Even with Murphy's literary emphasis, Garrick remains the suave professional, always in his public role. We hear a bit more about the Woffington/Garrick relationship, that they nearly did marry. But once again, Garrick's courtship and marriage are accomplished in a paragraph. Murphy's last chapter, "Garrick in Private Life," does not attempt to explore such intimate issues further but focuses on Garrick's generosity and benevolence in an attempt to deny legends of Garrick's avarice. Like Davies, Murphy draws a favorable portrait of Garrick and understands Garrick's shortcomings only as they related to his own dealings with the manager; otherwise, his heavy praise of his subject throughout the book easily swallows any of Garrick's faults.

Although Murphy in 1801 had not written a play for three years (and that one, *Arminius,* was not produced), ten of his plays had been produced in the 1790s and four of these had appeared in the 1799–1800 season. He clearly saw himself as an important dramatic writer, and many of his contemporaries would probably have agreed. He was a genuine theatrical insider and prominent man of letters whose name would have been recognized by far more people than would have recognized Davies's—a celebrity writing about a celebrity. He testifies to the inadequacy of words in describing Garrick's acting: "To form an adequate idea of such a genius, it is necessary that he should be seen, heard, and felt" (2:174). Murphy's biographical efforts avoid the troubling difficulty of communicating superb acting by placing his subject in the tradition of dramatic authors and viewing him as the "reformer of the stage."

Murphy creates Garrick as a literary authority out of his respect for Garrick's managerial accomplishments but also to retain his own value as a literary man with substantial success in the drama. Instead of denigrating the actor's literary taste, as earlier thespian biographers would have done, Murphy links his success to Garrick's so they become mutually supporting: Garrick helped Murphy's fame by producing and acting in his plays,

and Murphy contributes to extending the ephemeral fame of the actor by resuscitating him in print twenty years after his death. Murphy's resounding finale reiterates the conception of Garrick that readers should take away from the text. "The conclusion from the whole is, that our English Roscius was an ornament of the age in which he lived, the restorer of dramatic literature, and the great reformer of the public taste. In his time, the theater engrossed the minds of men to such a degree, that it may now be said, that there existed in England a *fourth estate,* King, Lords, and Commons, and *Drury-Lane play-house*" (2:201). According to Murphy, Garrick's most enduring claim to fame was his contribution to dramatic literature; indeed, Murphy's chapter considering Garrick as a manager stresses what Garrick did for the *drama,* not for the theater. His fame raised him to a level equaling high political authority—he had that large an influence. Murphy attempts to change the type of fame Garrick received—the quick-fading kind linked to his acting and social accomplishments—to a most lasting contribution to national drama and thus to the country. In effect, Murphy works to reensconce the actor's evanescent celebrity as that of a classical hero.

CONCLUSION: GARRICK, BIOGRAPHY, AND CELEBRITY

Murphy's biography of Garrick concludes with a summary character sketch, as do most other biographies of the period. But he feels compelled to divide his sketch into "Garrick Considered As Manager of the Theatre," "Garrick Considered As an Actor," "Garrick Considered As an Author," and "Garrick in Private Life." Garrick's modern biographers George M. Kahrl and George Winchester Stone structure their 771-page book in a similar manner. Garrick's immense public presence seems more manageable when split into separate "roles." Even in his acting, Garrick was praised most often for his variety. The anonymous author of the *Life of James Quin* notes Garrick's "universality" and states that "there never existed any one performer, that came near his excellence in so great a variety of opposite characters."[23] *Theatrical Biography* (1772) differentiates Garrick from Burbage, Betterton, Booth, Wilks, and Cibber: "Thus we see each of those great names attached to their particular limits, till the eccentric genius of a Garrick united the *universality* of acting in one person." The same writer asserts, "As an actor, to describe the peculiar excellencies

in the great variety of characters he sustains, would render it a task too arduous, as well as too extensive, for the limits of this work; besides, it would be at present unnecessary, as where is the theatrical writer that has not one time or other paused upon this subject?"[24]

Garrick was known to entertain companions by discussing the "delineation of the passions," demonstrating them by "alternately throwing his features into the representations of Love, Hatred, Terror, Pity, Jealousy, Desire, Joy in so rapid and striking a manner as astounded" his viewers.[25] Even within one particular role, observers marveled at the range and combinations of "passions" he could express; in *The Actor* (1750), John Hill claims Garrick perfects "ductility," or the ability "to subject the soul to succeeding passions" in his portrayal of Archer in the *Beaux Stratagem*: "till this excellent performer play'd this part, we never knew what beauties it was capable of, in the sudden transitions from passion to passion."[26] From the earliest evaluations of his abilities in the *Gentleman's Magazine* of 1742 and 1743 to the panegyrics published on the occasion of his death, writers stressed this quality. An anonymous reviewer of Davies's biography comments:

> Mr. Garrick, in the opinion of many, who knew him not intimately, was a versatile character, formed by nature on a plan similar to Dryden's Zimri:
>
> > A man so various, that he seem'd to be
> > Not *one* but all mankind's epitome—
> > But this is not the precise idea . . .

The precise idea can be obtained only by the biographer who knew Garrick well, maintains this writer.[27] Like the actor who must assemble a conception of a character from a sequence of "passions" and lines, the late-eighteenth-century biographer must create a central character from a wide-ranging and often contradictory life. The biographer's job is to give order, somehow, to amazing variety. Davies and Murphy harnessed Garrick's variety to establish a professional theater man and important literary critic-patron, both versions of cultural authority.

As we have seen, one of the characteristics of the celebrity phenomenon is the existence of multiple versions of the person celebrated. This is not a fractured self-presentation, as in Charke's narrative, but a comprehensive

yoking of the notorious with the admired, the rogue with the gentleman, the whore with the fine lady: in Schickel's words, quoted in the introduction of this study, it is a "larger and more compelling drama . . . of the star's life and career." In his life, Garrick balanced the morally suspect acting life, which he had led early in his career during his liaison with Peg Woffington, and the "just like you and me" attributes of middle-class values and lifestyle. Dobson notes the example of Garrick's faithful marriage to Eva Maria Garrick, who was patronized by nobility and who respectably retired from her dancing career after marriage. He explains that Garrick's rise depended on the growing cult of Shakespeare as well as the middle-class values of domesticity, decency, morality, and respect for property that Garrick embraced and publicly promoted.[28] But Garrick also grafted these values onto a profession with which such values were not customarily associated—during a time when media mechanisms were in place to publicize his efforts. The life of this respectable public icon contained just enough scandal and lubricity to provide a frisson for biography readers.

Two later complementary but contrasting cases are important to note here. They are of late-eighteenth-century actresses—as we have already seen, frisson automatically accompanies that job title. First is Sarah Siddons, whose career spanned the years 1782 to 1812. As with Garrick, much was published about her throughout her active stage years, mostly positive although, like Garrick, she was also occasionally criticized for her parsimoniousness. Sexual scandal hardly touched her, as she became more known for her maternal responsibility and professional dignity. Her main biographer, James Boaden, controls her celebrity image by omitting unflattering and possibly disreputable reflections on her character. Recent studies of her visual presentations emphasize the multiplicity of those images, which gradually solidify under the general character of tragic, noble dignity. Very little evidence survives to show that she herself directed this public image, except through the roles she chose and the ways in which she allowed portraitists to portray her. As we have seen, if the public presses had wanted to complicate or degrade this image, they could have done so substantially.

Mary Robinson attempted to perform a public role like Garrick and Siddons, but because her character had been compromised by her early affair with the Prince of Wales, she could salvage it only so much. Judith Pascoe has shown the various roles Robinson played, especially in her later

incarnation as a critic and poet, from the Romantic Della Cruscan poet to Marie Antoinette conceived as a tragic heroine.[29] Her biographer, the anonymous author of *Memoirs of Perdita* (published in 1784, though Robinson lived until 1800), provides readers with the usual salacious narrative. The narrator explains that his slant derives from reader demand: "[H]owever the eccentricity of her conduct may excite our imagination, still the heart is never so much interested as in the history of such whose actions have been more immediately under the influences of the softer passions."[30] The narrator stresses her artful cunning, her ability to play the role of the innocent, which lures in the prince.

Robinson herself attempts self-fashioning in her *Memoirs of the Late Mrs Robinson, Written by Herself* (published posthumously in 1801). Although she succeeds better than Charke, consistently portraying herself as a weak yet well-meaning victim of circumstances, she must physically stop writing and disrupt her narrative when she reaches the point of her affair with the prince. While many agree that she did indeed write some of the next sections, the shame of admitting this dalliance publicly is too great; her textual identity cannot contain it. The numerous other performances Pascoe identifies assure Robinson of attention, but her self-presentation in her autobiography (unlike that of George Anne Bellamy) evinces an inability to sustain her textual role of misguided youth and ignorance.

The composite image of the celebrity, distilled in these biographies as well as in the growing amount of print and visual depictions, reflects a developing type of fame. This is not the fame of classical heroes, successful politicians, or glorified warriors, but a fame arising from success in such an affective employment as acting and then spread by being discussed publicly, by being well known, by the illusion of familiarity. It is a extension of "reputation," and its power is testified to by the increasing anxiety of many people to appear in the right way in public print—from "fallen" women like Robinson to desperate bullies like Theophilus Cibber. People spoke more frequently about figures with whom they had little or no contact, as newspapers and magazines worked to fill their pages, stoking and feeding readers' growing desire for information about their contemporaries. As the Old Comedian says of Garrick,

he belonged to a profession, the members of which feast upon their own fame more than those of any other; and feast upon it while their taste and

relish are yet alive—he acquired more fame in that profession than perhaps any of his predecessors in any country, he enjoyed every morsel of it, he was rewarded with something more substantial than even that fame. . . . he heared [*sic*] his whole country, a country of Englishmen, agree for once, in one opinion of his excellence; he saw that whole country mourn, when he took a final leave of its stage—and he died, at last, in the fulness of days, prosperities, and honours.[31]

This coexistence with one's own fame brings delight—and apprehension.

Garrick was more conscious of this new phenomenon than many, and more sensitive to it, probably because he understood its inherent implications for power. Garrick's biographers show how Garrick responded to his own position. Sometimes self-consciously insouciant, often nervous, Garrick sculpted his own public image through his publications, addresses to his audiences, and subtle control of newspapers and magazines. He pursued "that almost universal Passion, *Love of Fame*," and then he feared the corruption and diminution of his fame. Davies regretfully mentions that "Mr. Garrick, who, as an actor, scarce ever had a competitor, and perhaps will never have an equal, was weak enough to be alarmed at every shadow of a rival" (2:391). Davies also describes how Garrick went to Europe in part to makes audiences realize how much they missed him—even his absences from the theater were performative. Murphy tells us: "The love of fame was Garrick's ruling passion, even to anxiety" (2:13) and later reiterates, "One passion he had, which gained an entire ascendant over him, and that was an eager anxiety about his fame. It has been said by this writer in a former work, that he lived in a *whispering gallery*" (2:196–7). Murphy had indeed previously mentioned Garrick's tendency to listen to rumor—in accounting for the reasons why Garrick did not approve of Murphy's own *Orphan of China*. And in denying accusations of Garrick's other faults, Murphy notes that the only "avarice" Garrick possessed was "*avarice of fame*" (2:197). Bellamy further says he couldn't bear "*even a sister* near the throne."[32] Garrick does not worry about fame and heroism in the older sense—that his heroic actions will not be properly celebrated. He leaves for Europe not to perform great deeds, but to be able to create a larger public effect when he returns. He worries about being underappreciated, undernoticed, and inaccurately evaluated. Garrick's most consuming role was that of his life as a celebrity.

Preserving an appropriate public reputation allowed him to attain and preserve a social position in a still traditional society that was gradually beginning to value other types of people besides those blessed with birth and inherited wealth. In turn, the social position reinforced his public recognition. As many have noted, Garrick's enduring reputation also relies on what he achieved for the acting profession. Reynolds admits Garrick's ability to transgress class boundaries when he has Samuel Johnson say in an imaginary dialogue, "No man, however high in rank or literature, but was proud to know Garrick and was glad to have him at his table. No man ever considered or treated Garrick as a player. He may be said to have stepped out of his own rank into a higher, and by raising himself he raised the rank of his profession."[33]

Dobson evaluates Garrick's achievement in this way: "In the long term, his greatest professional achievements may have been not aesthetic but social, in his promotion of acting to the status of a reputable vocation."[34] Though he may have raised his profession, few who followed him enjoyed his success and popularity. Those lucky individuals who did were part of a new orientation of the London theaters, the organization of companies around individual stars. We have seen how other biographers chastised their performer subjects for getting above themselves. Even though Garrick's early career as a vintner was occasionally a topic of ridicule, the same accusations did not stick to him. Garrick, and those who memorialized him, helped establish a new space of cultural authority for the exceptional player.

CONCLUSION

Fortunately for the memory of deceased
merit, that spirit of contumely which
consigned to oblivion the lives of the Roman
actors, no longer extends its injurious
influence over the supporters of the British
stage. In the present age of liberal
refinement, the promoters of the arts may
find objects for their exertion as well upon
the stage as in the field; and the children of
the histrionic muse, equally with the patriot
or the hero, may claim a niche in the
proud structure of fame.

Review of the Theatrical Powers of the Late
Mr. John Palmer (1798)

T HE STRUGGLES for authority addressed in the biographies presented here assume
concrete, tangible life in the physical
disturbances that occurred regularly in
the London theaters throughout the
eighteenth century. We have already
looked at how Davies describes the
quarrel about Garrick's Chinese Festival, and in his *History of the Theatres*

of London and Dublin from the Year 1730 to the Present Time (1761), Benjamin Victor records another anecdote that clearly emphasizes the battles over theatrical control. It happened in 1738, soon after the passage of the Licensing Act, which limited the number of theaters in London to two and forced all plays to be read by a government censor. (The two-theater restriction remained in force until the 1843 Theatre Regulation Act, and centralized censorship was not eliminated until the 1968 Theatres Act.) The Licensing Act affected the acting climate of the rest of the eighteenth century, with actors arrested as vagrants even late in the century, like several in John Palmer's company in 1787.[1] Victor is still concerned about it thirty and forty years later.

The Licensing Act closed the Goodman's Fields theater, one of the unlicensed theaters operating in London—"effectually destroyed" it, throwing many actors out of work. Yet shortly afterward, it was announced that a company of French actors would perform at that theater: "The French Advertisement appeared with these Words at the Top, By AUTHORITY! But they soon found, by the Public Clamours, that something more than the *Sound* of Authority would be necessary to support them" (1:53). Victor refers here to the uproar that ensued among audience members. One of two "*Westminster* Justices" who attended that performance declared to the crowd, "That he was come here as a Magistrate to maintain the *King's* Authority . . . that it was at the KING's COMMAND the Play should be acted; and that obstructing it was opposing the KING's AUTHORITY" (1:55). He backs up his threats by stating that the guards outside would maintain order, if the audience forced him to read the Riot Act. The audience understands his speech as "arbitrary Threatenings, [and] Abuse of his MAJESTY's Name . . . That the Audience had a legal Right to shew their Dislike to any Play or Actor; that the common Laws of the Land were nothing but common Custom, and the antient Usuage of the People; that the Judicature of the Pit had been acknowledged and acquiesced to, Time immemorial; and as the present Set of Actors were to take their fate from the Public, they were free to receive them as they pleased" (1:55–6).

Victor notes the arrival then in the boxes of foreign ambassadors and their ladies, as well as English nobles and governmental officials. When the curtain rises, the actors are standing "between two Files of Grenadiers, with their Bayonets fixed, and resting on their Firelocks. There was a Sight! Enough to animate the coldest Briton" (1:56). The pit stands and demands

that the soldiers leave. Once they do, the pit uses catcalls and instruments to drown out the actors' voices, and peas are cast on stage to disrupt the dancing. The justice proposes that, if the audience allows the performance to continue, he will lay their concerns before the king. The pit responds, "NO TREATIES! NO TREATIES!" and the justice is prevailed on not to deploy the soldiers only by consideration of the violence and injury that would follow. The actors are again silenced; they leave the stage. Victor comments that "at no Battle gained over the French by the immortal MARLBOROUGH, the Shoutings could be more joyous on this Occasion" (1:60). The immediate engagement is settled in favor of the pit, though the Licensing Act continues to assert governmental authority over the larger theater system.

This physical manifestation of the tensions over theatrical authority embodies those we have traced through thespian biography. Like the textual struggle over the physical facts of Booth's body, this theater uproar points to the claims of different groups to authority over the theaters and the uses to which the theatrical can be put. This anecdote first shows the formal control of the king and the justices. The latter stand in for the king himself; in the theater, they play his role. By representing monarchical and martial power, the justices and guards assert the presence in the theaters of traditional hierarchy and assumptions about the sources of power. Victor's opinion of this type of authority over the stage is moderate yet clear. He admits that for actors, "the Honour of being his Majesty's Servants is no more," but he also supports the Lord Chamberlain's governance of the actors and audiences for better management of the theaters (1:49). He does not approve of inexperienced gentlemen-managers controlling theaters; he compares them to men who have never been to sea, but who nevertheless arrogantly take command of great ships. And, in a telling analogy, he aligns such a manager, Charles Fleetwood, with larger hierarchies of control: "This new Theatrical Monarch began his Reign with all that Dignity that attends a Man of great Fortune and Fashion" (1:26). This comparison suggests that the king as well as other forms of arbitrary, hereditary power may be inappropriate for the business of running theaters.

In this anecdote, authority is ensured physically, through the threat of the guards and soldiers, instead of through a Foucauldian "disciplining" or a gaze negotiated between players and spectators. These are strong-arm tactics, symbolizing traditional order, hierarchy, and control. This type of

power reminds us of many other instances of the "top-down" imposition of power: of university governors, who controlled access to received and classical knowledge; of the Royal College of Physicians, which licensed approved medical professionals to distinguish them from quacks; of classically trained writers, using their cultural capital and social standing to oppose hacks; of the father, as master of family and household through legal and religious dictate; and of patriarchy, maintaining control over women and constructs of gender. As we have seen, actors and their biographers both support and question these authority structures.

Against the historical claim of the throne to monitor theatrical events, Victor places the audience's claims. But not just any part of the audience: it is the pit, in opposition to the boxes from which the aristocracy watch the play. These (mostly) men in the pit assert their right to regulate the theater, stating that from "Time immemorial" this has been their privilege. We have seen how Cibber bridles against audience control, and Garrick and others must endure nightly humbling to satisfy the whims of the pit critics. Often, their control is manifested as physical force, as spectators rip up benches, tear down fixtures, and smash the orchestra when they are displeased. However, in Victor's telling, those in the pit counter the justices and soldiers with their voices, musical instruments, dried peas, and solidarity, and the threat of violence comes only from the impending actions of the soldiers. These spectators are depicted as the ones paying the theater bills through ticket prices, and so they represent the will of the consumer, of the market. Of course, this type of control is not completely distinct from the other, as Victor's account implies: as we have previously seen, the pit can stand as a symbol for the way spectators and the market project and control constructions of gender, as in the biography of Lavinia Fenton. And certainly the men in the pit were not arguing that they would share their "right" with their social subordinates up in the galleries. Market power derives from traditional power, building on and developing from it. What changes over the course of the century is the balance between the two: the market begins controlling more elements of the arts, and celebrities, as we have noted, are part of this emerging commercial control.

The anonymous French performers get lost in the mêlée. They do not interest Victor, because they are both foreign and unjustly privileged (foreign performers caused this sort of reaction at other times during the cen-

tury as well). They perform in a theater closed to English actors, thus rifling the pockets of the native performers. Of course, aristocrats are probably present in the pit, but Victor describes the fracas as a nationalistic victory of the patriots in the pit against their own upper classes and government which, for their own capricious pleasure, are willing to side with the French. His use of battle imagery, mention of treaties, and invocation of Marlborough cast this as a cultural war in which the French performers are supported by traditional, overbearing hierarchy, and the absent English performers are supported by popular approval and the marketplace. Both Victor and the spectators want to assert control over praise, condemnation, and success on stage and page through their attention and, if that is disallowed, they will express their frustrations through interrupting the performance or, in biography, presenting unattractive portraits. In other words, in both the theaters and in texts, spectators press their populist claim to create celebrities.

Victor's introduction to this anecdote in his brief discussion of the Licensing Act is also significant. Victor claims that contemporaries worried more that plays would have to be read and approved by a censor than that London actors would lose jobs because of the two-theater limit. The public "did not complain of the LORD CHAMBERLAIN'S POWER over the PLAYERS, but over the AUTHORS who wrote for the Stage . . . it was much feared that an Attack upon the Liberty of the Press would follow" (1: 49). Thus he notes that the Licensing Act was interpreted primarily as an attack on the rights and authority of authors, not performers, even though he understands and shows the problems for players. In the eighteenth century, the rights of authors and players are both conjoined and opposed in all writing about the stage. At least in Victor's version (always entertaining and suggestive, though not always reliable), it seems as though fear over the suppression of the press boils over into anger in the theaters themselves. The two are fundamentally connected in the public mind.

In thespian biography, as we have seen, the struggle for relative authority between actors and authors continues throughout the century, though an expansive public presence like Garrick's can allow the two to coexist peacefully for a while. The eighteenth century, like our own, operates under the assumption that fame itself is a commodity that must be of limited supply. If the supply is too great—too many celebrities in the public

eye—their fame (and fame in general) will not be worth much. If actors have too much fame, less will be available for deserving authors; if actors take credit for a successful production or theater company, neither play-wrights nor managers nor the traditional authority structures they represent will be appropriately valued. Yet fame may be one thing that does respond in this way to supply and demand, since, as Cowen explains, "fame supply is elastic."[2] As more people become literate or are able to attend the theater, and as more activities gain prominence through the expanding press, more territories of human life are available in which to gain fame. True, the celebrities in these areas may not have the large, uni-fied recognition expected of a hero—but then, neither did the Roman or Greek heroes supposedly admired by the eighteenth century. These were heroes only to the educated males who knew of them through their classi-cal training—or to those anxious to join or be mistaken for members of that educated, elite group.

Fame will devalue only if we consider one type of "hero" or invest in one type of hierarchical, traditional power. In writing about contemporary celebrity culture, Cowen agrees:

> Rather than centralizing fame rewards in an absolutist state or repressing fame-seeking impulses, commercialization decentralizes fame into market-based niches. In highly commercial societies, fame-seekers can achieve renown in science, sports, entertainment, and many other fields. These famous individuals cannot start wars, sway elections, or exercise coercive control over the lives of other people. Contemporary stars are impotent but well-paid puppets.[3]

As the above epigraph from *Review of . . . John Palmer* happily notes, by the end of the eighteenth century, performers inhabit one of these market-based niches. Thespian biography has both reflected the existence of this niche and helped create it. Yet while a star's fans will not necessarily do what the star tells them to do, many modern and eighteenth-century read-ers would disagree that prominent people are "impotent" and cannot "exercise coercive control"—they do by the very fact of their getting so much attention, which causes others to imitate them so they can be rich and famous, too. If leveraged properly, their wealth can buy them political

access and corporate influence. Commercial empires built around their names—Martha Stewart, for a recent example—can rise or fall depending on the celebrity's actions, affecting thousands of people. As Victor's anecdote shows, the celebrities rely on those who give them attention, since that attention can be converted into various forms of power. Often that attention exists as a commercial product itself—a published book, a theater ticket, memorabilia.

Victor's interpretation of the Licensing Act and Goodman's Fields confrontation ultimately points to the inevitable power of the market to decide quality and the distribution of fame. Members of the public want freedom of the press because it serves their information needs and lets them decide what is worthy of purchasing, and the spectators in the pit want control over the theaters because they are the purchasers who need to be pleased. Although this occurs in the late 1730s, Victor's anecdote symbolizes what happens to the theatrical: it becomes controlled primarily by the commercial market as opposed to the forms of traditional authority we have surveyed throughout this book. This is clear from descriptions of theatrical disturbances into the nineteenth century as well. The famous "Old Price" riots of 1809 at Covent Garden can essentially be interpreted as a struggle between two forms of market control of the theaters. Marc Baer and Elaine Hadley argue that the supporters of the old prices represent the status quo of tradition, while the managers of the theater imposing the new prices represented the less visible transactions of a more advanced capital market—in Baer's view, a traditional "moral economy" against the more modern market-driven "political economy."[4] Though Baer shows that audience members stood for the ideology of the past against newer, more private financial arrangements, in the eventual capitulation of management to the "OPers," management did not yield to an old ideology, it yielded to commercial pressures: it could not conduct business in the face of such vocal public disapproval, no matter what that disapproval actually stood for. No matter how it is sold, the power here is commercial.

The commercialization is also evident simply from the vast proliferation of thespian publications of all kinds by the end of the century. As we've noted, many writers would exclaim with *Theatrical Biography* (1772), "In the whole catalogue of public professions, none have engaged general curiosity so much as the theater: ministers of state, have indeed long been

a favourite topic with many, but then this is confined to a certain set, whilst the stage, like a game of chance, engages the attention of all."[5] Everyone wants to know what happens in the theater and with its people, especially those who have triumphed there. Attention is offered in biographies, newspaper accounts, and pictures, and players vie for that attention, as *Theatrical Biography* also states: "[T]here are several performers, who may think themselves aggrieved by not holding a rank in these memoirs, and will produce vouchers for this neglect, their *salaries,* and the parts they are in *possession of.*" [6] By the end of the century, players know the value of public print attention and how it contributes to their own continuing currency, and they try to prove they are worthy of it, blaming those whom they believe bar them from it.

Performers continued to be reminded of the contradictions of their social status: that they are in positions of wide fame, yet they are dependent on the fickle marketplace for that fame. In their challenge to the Licensing Act, members of John Palmer's Royalty Theatre Company could still be prosecuted as "rogues, vagabonds, and sturdy beggars" in 1787. Writers pointed to and exploited this incongruous reputation, as noted by a letter to *British Magazine and Monthly Repository* (1767), which asks whether "there is no contradiction in human affairs more glaring and most difficult to be accounted for, than the infamy annexed to the profession of a player in all countries, when we consider the favourable treatment they meet with from the very persons who affect to look upon them as the pests of society?"[7]

Then, as today, performers could behave badly. Palmer mistreats his wife, though that is completely whitewashed in the biographical *Sketch of John Palmer* and *Review of . . . John Palmer* (both 1798). George Frederick Cooke, like Thomas Weston, was a known alcoholic, as attested by his biographer, William Dunlap. But the *British Magazine* author correctly identifies that the dilemma resides in the spectators and readers who court players' company while condemning their profession. Celebrities are not role models, and those who expect them to be decorous and respectable ask them to be something incongruous with their profession. And, since every human being has faults, the vigilant and busy press will unearth shameful details. The more one looks, the more one will find—as twenty-first-century political candidates are well aware. Earlier heroes were not confronted with this need to begin managing their public image. Thespian

biographies grow more self-conscious, their authors admitting that they are part of the image-making process. They seem to realize that, if these people are the culture's new heroes—if we're stuck with them, through our own prurient interest—we must try to shape them, to make them into something as close to role models as possible, or to warn unwary readers about assuming them to be figures for emulation.

And so, into the nineteenth century, thespian biographies continue to flourish. Generic experimentation subsides as players' ambiguous social position becomes in itself a recognizable social position. Biographies will continue to track performers' amazing ascents to fame, tussles with debt, tumultuous love lives. But the main struggles are finished. Though the attention to players will continue to be lamented by some and seen as evidence of a decaying civilization, its existence no longer surprises. Through struggles in the theaters and in these texts, for better or for worse, the position of the celebrity stands assured.

NOTES

❧

INTRODUCTION

1. Benjamin Victor, *The History of the Theatres of London and Dublin, from the Year 1760 to the Present Time* (London: T. Becket, 1771), 83.

2. Indeed, calling some of these texts *biographies* and *autobiographies* approaches the ahistorical, since the authors themselves didn't use the terms, which would not be current until later in the eighteenth century. However, to refer to them consistently by their contemporary title, *Lives* (or *Accounts* or *Memoirs*), introduces unnecessary confusion.

3. The most complete list of all of these biographies and autobiographies is James Fullerton Arnott and John William Robinson, *English Theatrical Literature, 1559–1900: A Bibliography* (London: Society for Theatre Research, 1970).

4. Dustin Griffin, *Literary Patronage in England, 1650–1800* (Cambridge: Cambridge University Press, 1996); Julie Stone Peters, *Congreve, the Drama, and the Printed Word* (Stanford: Stanford University Press, 1990) and *Theatre of the Book, 1480–1880* (Oxford University Press, 2000); Alvin Kernan, *Print-*

❧

ing Technology, Letters, and Samuel Johnson (Princeton: Princeton University Press, 1987).

5. See J. H. Plumb, *The Commercialization of Leisure in Eighteenth-Century England* (Reading, England: University of Reading, 1973).

6. Francesco Alberoni, "The Powerless 'Elite': Theory and Sociological Research on the Phenomenon of the Stars," in *Sociology of Mass Communications,* ed. Denis McQuail (Harmondsworth, England: Penguin, 1972), 96.

7. Daniel Boorstin, *The Image: A Guide to Pseudo-Events in America* (New York: Atheneum, 1961), 57.

8. Pierre Bourdieu, *Distinction: A Social Critique of the Judgement of Taste* (Cambridge: Harvard University Press, 1984), 231.

9. Tyler Cowen, *What Price Fame?* (Cambridge: Harvard University Press, 2000), 14.

10. Richard Schickel, *Intimate Strangers: The Culture of Celebrity* (New York: Fromm International, 1986), 31.

11. Alexandra Halasz, "'So beloved that men use his picture for his signs': Richard Tarleton and the Uses of Sixteenth-Century Celebrity," in *Shakespeare Studies,* ed. Leeds Barroll (Madison: Fairleigh Dickinson University Press, 1995), 19–38; Peter M. Briggs, "Laurence Sterne and Literary Celebrity in 1760," *Age of Johnson* 4 (1991): 251–80; Judith Milhous, "Vestris-Mania and the Construction of Celebrity: Auguste Vestris in London, 1780–81," *Harvard Library Bulletin* 5 (1994–95): 30–64.

12. The *OED* cites Samuel Johnson's use of the word *celebrity* in the *Rambler* (1751) to mean "the condition of being much extolled or talked about"; however, it is not applied to a person until the early nineteenth century. The word *star* in reference to a popular performer is an older usage than "celebrity." Though the *OED* says that it was first used to describe Garrick in 1779, Edmund Curll described Anne Oldfield as a "star" in his 1731 biography of that actress.

13. Leo Braudy, *The Frenzy of Renown: Fame and Its History* (New York: Oxford University Press, 1986).

14. David Chaney, "The Spectacle of Honour: The Changing Dramatization of Status," *Theory, Culture, and Society* 12 (1995): 163. Chaney is quoting Mike Featherstone, "The Heroic Life and Everyday Life," *Theory, Culture, and Society* 9 (1992): 177.

15. Cowen, *Fame,* 65.

16. Alberoni, "Powerless 'Elite,'" 75, italics removed.

17. George Winchester Stone Jr. and George M. Kahrl, *David Garrick: A Critical Biography* (Carbondale: Southern Illinois University Press, 1979), chap. 14.

18. Charles Churchill, *The Apology,* in *The Poetical Works of Charles Churchill,* ed. Douglas Grant (Oxford: Clarendon, 1956), 44.

19. See Nancy Klein Maguire, *Regicide and Restoration: English Tragicomedy, 1660–1671* (Cambridge: Cambridge University Press, 1992); Paula R. Backscheider, *Spec-*

tacular Politics: Theatrical Power and Mass Culture in Early Modern England (Baltimore: Johns Hopkins University Press, 1993).

20. Geoffrey Holmes, *Augustan England: Professions, State, and Society, 1680–1730* (London: George Allen and Unwin, 1982).

21. James Boswell, *Life of Samuel Johnson,* ed. R. W. Chapman (London: Oxford University Press, 1953), 925.

22. Martha Walling Howard, *The Influence of Plutarch in the Major European Literatures of the Eighteenth Century* (Chapel Hill: University of North Carolina Press, 1970).

23. Thomas Sprat, *An Account of the Life and Writings of Mr Abraham Cowley,* in *Abraham Cowley: Poetry and Prose,* ed. L. C. Martin (Oxford: Clarendon, 1959), xxx.

24. Dryden (1683), quoted in Vivian de la Sola Pinto, *English Biography in the Seventeenth Century* (London: George Harrap, 1951), 202.

25. Hal Gladfelder, *Criminality and Narrative in Eighteenth-Century England: Beyond the Law* (Baltimore: Johns Hopkins University Press, 2001), 6.

26. Donald A. Stauffer quotes Fuller in *English Biography before 1700* (Cambridge: Harvard University Press, 1930), 239; Roger North, *General Preface,* ed. Peter Millard, in *General Preface and Life of Dr. John North* (Toronto: University of Toronto Press, 1984), 80.

27. Tate Wilkinson, *The Wandering Patentee,* 4 vols. (York: for the author, 1795), 1:233–35.

28. Mary Wrighten, *An Apology for the Life and Conduct of Mrs. Mary Wrighten, Late a Favorite Actress and Singer, of Drury-Lane and Vauxhall Gardens* (London: [Ridgeway], c. 1789), 3. I will include future page references parenthetically.

29. For more on audiences' and readers' control of actors and actresses, see Kristina Straub's *Sexual Suspects: Eighteenth-Century Players and Sexual Ideology* (Princeton: Princeton University Press, 1992), one of the few scholarly books to examine these biographies and autobiographies in depth.

30. Wilkinson, *Wandering Patentee,* 2:32–34.

31. Sir George Etherege, *The Dramatic Works,* 2 vols., ed. H. F. B. Brett-Smith (Oxford: Blackwell, 1927), 2:223.

32. Straub, *Sexual Suspects,* 26.

33. Gladfelder, *Criminality and Narrative,* 7.

34. Richard Sennett, *The Fall of Public Man* (New York: Alfred A. Knopf, 1977), 27.

35. Cowen, *Fame,* 3.

36. Schickel, *Intimate Strangers,* 48.

37. Alberoni, "Powerless 'Elite,'" 85.

38. "Biographical Memoirs of Mr. Kemble, Brother to Mrs. Siddons," *Gentleman's Magazine* (April 1783): 309–10.

39. Sennett, *Fall of Public Man;* Jürgen Habermas, *The Structural Transformation of the Public Sphere* (Cambridge: MIT Press, 1991).

40. Joseph M. Levine, *Between the Ancients and the Moderns: Baroque Culture in Restoration England* (New Haven: Yale University Press, 1999).

41. *Town and Country Magazine* (March 1779): 147.

42. Schickel, *Intimate Strangers,* 345.

1. ROGUES AND GENTLEMEN

1. For discussion of the profession of player in the earlier seventeenth century, see M. C. Bradbrook, *The Rise of the Common Player* (Cambridge: Harvard University Press, 1962) and Gerald Eades Bentley, *The Profession of Player in Shakespeare's Time, 1590–1642* (Princeton: Princeton University Press, 1984). The best information about post-Restoration players comes from *A Biographical Dictionary of Actors, Actresses, . . . and Other Stage Personnel in London,* 16 vols., ed. Philip H. Highfill Jr., Kalman A. Burnim, and Edward A. Langhans (Carbondale: Southern Illinois University Press, 1973–93); also see Philip H. Highfill Jr., "Performers and Performing," in *The London Theatre World,* ed. Robert D. Hume (Carbondale: Southern Illinois University Press, 1980), 143–80. No comprehensive sociology of the profession during this period has been compiled.

2. Joseph M. Levine, *The Battle of the Books: History and Literature in the Augustan Age* (Ithaca: Cornell University Press, 1991); Levine, *Between Ancients and Moderns.*

3. Sir William Temple, *Five Miscellaneous Essays by Sir William Temple,* ed. Samuel Holt Monk (Ann Arbor: University of Michigan Press, 1963), 62.

4. Curt A. Zimansky, introduction to *The Critical Works of Thomas Rymer,* ed. Curt Zimansky (Westport, Conn.: Greenwood, 1971), xxxii.

5. Levine, *Between Ancients and Moderns,* viii.

6. Levine, *Between Ancients and Moderns,* chaps. 3–5; Rymer, *Critical Works,* 19.

7. For the sake of convenience, I will refer to this character as written by Overbury even though the attribution is not definitive. For both texts and a discussion of attribution, see *A Cabinet of Characters,* ed. Gwendolen Murphy (London: Humphrey Milford, 1925), 127–8.

8. Murphy, *Cabinet of Characters,* 114–5.

9. Straub, *Sexual Suspects,* 25.

10. See Judith Milhous and Robert D. Hume's *A Register of Theatrical Documents,* 2 vols. (Carbondale: Southern Illinois University Press, 1991).

11. Jonas Barish has traced these debates in *The Antitheatrical Prejudice* (Berkeley: University of California Press, 1981).

12. Joseph Roach, *The Player's Passion* (Newark: University of Delaware Press, 1985).

13. *An Account of the Life, Conversation, Birth, Education, Pranks, Projects, and Exploits, and Merry Conceits, of the Famously Notorious Mat. Coppinger* (London: T. Hobs, 1695) (a notation in a seventeenth-century hand reads "5 March"). The copy of

this pamphlet in the Rosenbach collection in Philadelphia seems to be unique. A note on the flyleaf of the volume into which it is pasted states: "The *latter Tract* [*Coppinger*] I believe to be Unique. After a diligent inquiry among Booksellers & Collectors, I never heard of a second Copy. Mat: Coppinger wrote a volume of adulatory and indecent poems calculated for the [word illegible] of Charles y/e Second. . . . I possess a copy. It is a very uncommon, and worthless Book . . . George Daniel 1837."

The *Biographical Dictionary* (3:485) adds nothing to the biography's account; in *A Register of Theatrical Documents,* Milhous and Hume note a 1689 arrest order for unlicensed performance of drolls that includes Coppinger among seven actors named (#1348). They also list a 1694 manuscript version of Coppinger's "Sessions of the Poets" (#1484), which was published in 1705 by Thomas Atkinson.

14. Paul Salzman, *English Prose Fiction, 1558–1700* (Oxford: Oxford University Press, 1985); Peter Burke, *Popular Culture in Early Modern Europe* (New York: Harper and Row, 1978), 201–2; Lincoln B. Faller, *Turned to Account: The Forms and Functions of Criminal Biography in Late Seventeenth- and Early Eighteenth-Century England* (Cambridge: Cambridge University Press, 1987), 175. According to Salzman, rogue narratives recounted the lives of three types of social outcast, differing mainly in their level of seriousness. The dashing adventures of the picaro shade gradually into the more serious social transgressions of the rogue, and then into the violence of the criminal.

15. Peter Linebaugh, *The London Hanged: Crime and Civil Society in the Eighteenth Century* (Cambridge: Cambridge University Press, 1992), xix.

16. Matthew Coppinger, *Poems, Songs, and Love-Verses upon Several Subjects* (London: R. Bentley and M. Magnes, 1682); the manuscript version is in BL Add. MS 21,094, fols. 49r–51v, according to Milhous and Hume, *Register of Theatrical Documents* (#1484).

17. Of course, a real gentleman would not sully his hands with publication: see the following discussion of Betterton, as well as J. W. Saunders, "The Stigma of Print," *Essays in Criticism* 1 (1951): 139–64.

18. We cannot tell what Nutt's exact relationship with the printing of this text is simply from the imprint. He was involved in a broad spectrum of publications and probably stocked them all at his shop. He did not publish too many plays, though he was involved with the publication of some post-Collier stage controversy. A theatrical rogue biography fits well with other books upon whose titles pages his name appears: works by Ned Ward (*The Pleasures of a Single Life; or, The Miseries of Matrimony,* 1701) and Tom Brown (*Stage-Beaux Toss'd in a Blanket,* 1704).

19. Jest books quite often use popular comedians as their vehicles: for example, *Polly Peachum's Jests,* "In which are comprised most of the Witty Apothegms, diverting Tales, and smart Repartees that have been used for many Years last past, either at St. James's or St. Giles's: Suited aliked [*sic*] to the Capacities of the Peer, and to the Porter" (London: J. Roberts, 1728).

20. Tobyas Thomas, *The Life of the Late Famous Comedian, Jo. Hayns. Containing,*

His Comical Exploits and Adventures, Both at Home and Abroad (London: J. Nutt, 1701), A3v. I will include future page references parenthetically. Although "Haines" is the more common spelling of this actor's name—even Thomas uses several spellings throughout his *Life*—I have chosen to retain the spelling Thomas used in his title to avoid confusion.

21. In "Property, Authority, and the Criminal Law," in *Albion's Fatal Tree,* ed. Donald Hay et al. (New York: Pantheon, 1975), Hay tells us: "The most recent account suggests that the number of capital statutes grew from about 50 to over 200 between the years 1688 and 1820. Almost all of them concerned offenses against property" (18). Although Hay's Marxist interpretation of these laws and their enactments have been criticized, few historians argue that capital offenses did not increase. For one of many critical reviews of Hay's article, see John H. Langbein, "*Albion's* Fatal Flaws," *Past and Present* 98 (1983): 96–120.

22. Kenneth M. Cameron, "Jo. Haines, *Infamis,*" *Theatre Notebook* 24 (1969–70): 57; *Biographical Dictionary,* 7:7–8. This dilemma will not be uncommon for the modern reader of these players' *Lives,* since they are our primary source of information about a performer.

23. Tom Brown, *Letters from the Dead to the Living* (London: n.p., 1702), 40.

24. A facsimile of this elegy accompanies J. W. Robinson's "An Elegy on the Death of Mr Joseph Haines, 1701," *Theatre Notebook* 35 (1981): 99–100. It appears on page 121.

25. *Biographical Dictionary,* 7:8.

26. Hayns was indeed removed from Hart's company, perhaps more than once: see the *Biographical Dictionary,* 7:10–1.

27. Michael Quinn, "Celebrity and the Semiotics of Acting," *New Theatre Quarterly* 6 (1990): 156–7.

28. "The Petition of the Players" is printed in full in Judith Milhous, *Thomas Betterton and the Management of Lincoln's Inn Fields, 1695–1708* (Carbondale: Southern Illinois University Press, 1979), 225–9.

29. *A Comparison between the Two Stages,* ed. Staring B. Wells (Princeton: Princeton University Press, 1942), 11.

30. Oddly, though Collier stridently calls for changes in drama and better behavior from actors, he does not tell who should implement these changes and who should discipline the actors. Respondents in the "Collier controversy," as it has become known, understand Collier's arguments in terms of the ancients and moderns debate: for example, see the anonymous pamphlet (probably by James Drake), *The Antient and Modern Stages Survey'd* (London: Abel Roper, 1699).

31. The name of Tobyas Thomas does not appear on *Hayns's* title page, only at the end of the book's dedication. John Harold Wilson has corrected the misattribution of *Hayns* to Tom Brown in "Thomas's *Life of Jo. Hayns,*" *Notes and Queries* 206 (1961): 250–1. In "Jo. Haynes, *Infamis,*" Cameron alludes to attribution problems but does not explain how he comes to the conclusion, "I should suggest that the *Life* was compiled

by Tobyas Thomas from Haynes's papers, perhaps with Haynes's help" (57). The detail about Hayns's "papers" may derive from the verses appearing in *Hayns*, but I have found no other evidence to corroborate Cameron's assertion about sources.

32. *The London Stage*, part 1, ed. William Van Lennep (Carbondale: Southern Illinois University Press, 1963). The *Register of Theatrical Documents* notes that this warrant was canceled, apparently due to King William's death two weeks later.

33. Brown, *Letters*, 40.

34. Judith Milhous and others have remarked on the grim state of the theaters in the early years of the eighteenth century, so it is not surprising that an ambitious actor who wanted to eat would turn to composing popular literature for income. See *Thomas Betterton and the Management of Lincoln's Inn Fields*, chap. 5.

35. Gladfelder, *Criminality and Narrative*, 77.

36. Wilbur Samuel Howell, *Eighteenth-Century British Logic and Rhetoric* (Princeton: Princeton University Press, 1971), 182–9; Roach, *Player's Passion*, 31.

37. Charles Gildon, *The Life of Mr. Thomas Betterton, the Late Eminent Tragedian* (1710; reprint, New York: Augustus M. Kelley, 1970), vii. I will include future page references parenthetically.

38. *Biographical Dictionary*, 2:73–96.

39. Wells, *Comparison between the Two Stages*, 11.

40. *Roscius Anglicanus* concludes with a list of the plays in which Betterton took leading roles—a list that Gildon almost certainly cribs to include in the *Life*. See Milhous and Hume's edition of *Roscius Anglicanus* (London: Society for Theatre Research, 1987), 109.

41. Levine, *Between Ancients and Moderns*, 115–6.

42. Howell, *Eighteenth-Century British Logic*, 182–9. The English translation of this work was *An Essay upon the Action of an Orator* (London: Nicholas Cox, n.d.). Roach, *Player's Passion*, 31.

43. Gildon, *The Complete Art of Poetry*, 2 vols. (London: Charles Rivington, 1718), 1:118.

44. For some discussions of seventeenth- and eighteenth-century acting theory and practice, see Alan S. Downer, "Nature to Advantage Dressed: Eighteenth-Century Acting," *PMLA* 58 (1943): 1002–37; Dene Barnett, *The Art of Gesture: The Practices and Principles of Eighteenth-Century Acting* (Heidelburg: Carl Winter Universitätsverlag, 1987); Shearer West, *The Image of the Actor: Verbal and Visual Representation in the Age of Garrick and Kemble* (New York: St. Martin's, 1991); Roach, *Player's Passion*.

45. J. W. H. Atkins, *English Literary Criticism* (New York: Barnes and Noble, 1950), 146–9; J. C. Maxwell, "Charles Gildon and the Quarrel of the Ancients and Moderns," *RES*, n.s., 1 (1950): 55–7; Paulina Kewes, *Authorship and Appropriation: Writing for the Stage in England, 1660–1710* (Oxford: Clarendon, 1998), 221; G. L. Anderson, " 'A Little Civil Correction': Langbaine Revised," *Notes and Queries* 203 (1958): 269.

46. The book's imprint suggests that Gildon was working with a respectable

bookseller for *Life of Betterton*. The imprint cites only Robert Gosling, a bookseller whose name appears primarily on titles of a serious nature, such as sermons and legal texts. His range is much more limited, yet much more sober than that of *Life of Hayns*'s listed bookseller, John Nutt (though he was professionally involved with the Nutts for many years). However, Gosling also worked closely with Curll, and Curll's name appears in the imprint of the edition of Betterton's *Amorous Widow*, which is the play annexed to the *Life*. Gosling's and Curll's names also appear on a title page of the *Works* of St. Evremond in 1714. The biography of Betterton is still being offered at the shop of Henry Curll in 1727, according to his catalogue. Christopher Flint has shown how Gildon's *The Golden Spy*, printed a year before *Life of Betterton*, also shows Gildon's uneasy relationship to modern print culture: "Articulating the author's complex relation to print culture, these stories literalize the disjunction between writer and written matter that was intensified by eighteenth-century bookselling practices" (214). See "Speaking Objects: The Circulation of Stories in Eighteenth-Century Prose Fiction," *PMLA* 113 (1998): 212–26.

47. *Sketch of the Theatrical Life of the Late Mr. John Palmer* (London: H. D. Symonds et al., 1798), 39.

48. Ministers and attorneys would have had the requisite education to appreciate Gildon's profuse use of classical examples, but only the more fortunate of the actors (and none of the actresses) would have. For information on classical education in the early eighteenth century, see Nancy A. Mace, *Henry Fielding's Novels and the Classical Tradition* (Newark: University of Delaware Press, 1996). Mace's research shows that, except for Horace, Gildon's sources were not the most frequently studied classical authors. Thirty-four actors in the London theater companies during the season of 1709–10 have biographies available in the *Biographical Dictionary;* of these thirty-four, we have educational information for only seven. Educational backgrounds among these seven range from apprenticeship to a French upholsterer (Richard Elrington) to a Presbyterian academy (Theophilus Keene) to a Latin grammar school (Richard Estcourt). Excepting Elrington, the other six seem to have enjoyed some education that would have exposed them to classical languages. Generalizations from such a small sample seem impractical, and we must consider that these six may have had their educations recorded because they were such glaring exceptions.

49. As Angelica Goodden points out, this advice to players also had its classical roots: "Like the orator of antiquity, he [the actor] was to be morally good as well as skilled at declaiming or performing" (*"Actio" and Persuasion: Dramatic Performance in Eighteenth-Century France* [Oxford: Clarendon, 1986], 166).

50. Bourdieu, *Distinction*.

51. He suggests that men at the bar and pulpit could apply his lessons, too, thus linking acting to other traditional professions.

52. Rymer, *Critical Works*, 18. Even enthusiasts for modern theater such as French neoclassical critic Francois Hédélin, abbé d'Aubignac, decry the decline: "[W]e must

own that the Stage was fallen from so high a degree of Glory, into so much contempt and abjectness, that is was impossible to heal entirely those Wounds which it had received in its fall, nor to restore it, but after much Labour and Time. . . . 'tis to be feared that the Drammatick Art will never arrive to its perfection, and I doubt it will hardly maintain itself in the stage it is, any long time." From the English translation, *The Whole Art of the Stage* (1684; reprint, New York: Benjamin Blom, 1968), 12. Patrick Brantlinger traces the history of such issues in *Bread and Circuses: Theories of Mass Culture as Social Decay* (Ithaca: Cornell University Press, 1983).

53. *Biographical Dictionary*, 7:283; *Memoirs of the Life of Mr. Theophilus Keene, the Late Eminent Tragedian* (London: William Chetwood, 1718). This biography was probably penned by Richard Savage, himself a figure notable for struggles for legitimate authority amid an undisciplined private life. In the entry for Keene in his *General History of the Stage*, Chetwood remarks: "His Life was published by Mr. *Savage*, illegitimate Son to the Earl of *Rivers*" (London: W. Owen, 1749), 177. I assume that he refers to the 1718 biography. *Keene* has been subsequently attributed to both Richard Savage and Chetwood. The title page states, "*By several Hands*," although it does not clarify whether this refers to the whole work or to the verses. The *Dictionary of National Biography* and *Biographical Dictionary* (8:283) following Lowe, ascribe it to Savage; Arnott and Robinson enter the book as edited by William Chetwood (quoting Lowe: "We know little of Keene, except what is told by Chetwood") and note that the poem by Savage does not appear in his *Works* (1775); see *English Theatrical Literature*. In his *Life of Savage*, Johnson does not mention this biography as one of Savage's first productions.

54. *Memoirs of Mr. Theophilus Keene*, 3.

55. Benjamin Victor, *Memoirs of the Life of Barton Booth, Esq.* (London: John Watts, 1733), 31. I will include future page references parenthetically.

56. In *A General History of the Stage*, William Chetwood feels obligated to explain to his readers who Roscius really was—certainly a different assumption about the education of his audience than even Gildon makes. "Every Person may not know that *Marcus Tullius Cicero* and *Roscius* lived in the same Century . . . though the Orator was much the younger, and was taught all that Energy in his Orations he was so much famed for, by *Roscius*" (A2v). Later, when he translates Latin verses, Chetwood admits he does it "for fear some People may understand as little *Latin* as myself" (2).

57. Maxwell, "Gildon and Quarrel," 57.

58. Levine, *Between Ancients and Moderns*, ix–x.

59. This poem was printed in Gould's *Poems* (1689) and then revised and reprinted in *The Works of Mr. Robert Gould*, 2 vols. (London: W. Lewis, 1709). I quote from the 1709 edition, 255–7. Montague Summers reprints the later version in *The Restoration Theatre* (New York: Macmillan, 1934), 297–321.

60. "A film star's image is not just his or her films, but the promotion of those films and of the star through pin-ups, public appearances, studio hand-outs and so on,

as well as interviews, biographies and coverage in the press of the star's doings and 'private' life. Further, a star's image is also what people say or write about him or her, as critics or commentators, the way the image is used in other contexts such as advertisements, novels, pop songs, and finally the way the star can become part of the coinage of everyday speech" (Richard Dyer, *Heavenly Bodies: Film Stars and Society* [New York: St Martin's, 1986], 3).

61. For example, Henry Jenkins III notes that the desire of *Star Trek* viewers "to revise the program material is often counterbalanced by their desire to remain faithful to those aspects of the show that first captured their interests. See his "Star Trek Rerun, Reread, Rewritten: Fan Writing as Textual Poaching," *Critical Studies in Mass Communication* 5 (1988): 101. He expands his arguments in *Textual Poachers: Television Fans and Participatory Culture* (New York: Routledge, 1992).

2. THREE STORIES OF CELEBRITY

1. Examples are noted in Charles E. Pearce, *"Polly Peachum": Being the Story of Lavinia Fenton . . . and "The Beggar's Opera"* (New York: Brentano's, 1913).

2. *The Life of Lavinia Beswick, Alias Fenton, Alias Polly Peachum* (London: A. Moore, 1728); *Memoirs concerning the Life and Manners of Captain Mackheath* (London: A. Moore, 1728); George Akerby, *The Life of Mr. James Spiller, the Late Famous Comedian* (London: J. Purser, 1729). I will include future page references parenthetically.

3. Cited in Robert Folkenflik, ed., introduction to *The English Hero, 1660–1800* (Newark: University of Delaware Press, 1982), 11.

4. Schickel, *Intimate Strangers*, 31.

5. Braudy, *Frenzy*, 8.

6. James William Johnson, "England, 1660–1800: An Age without a Hero?" in Folkenflik, *English Hero*, 33.

7. Alexander Pope, *Pastoral Poetry and "Essay on Criticism,"* ed. E. Audra and Aubrey Williams (New Haven: Yale University Press, 1961), 293.

8. Braudy, *Frenzy*, 13.

9. George Anne Bellamy, *An Apology for the Life of George Anne Bellamy*, 6 vols. (London: for the author, 1785), 4:51.

10. Isaac Kramnick, *Bolingbroke and His Circle* (Cambridge: Harvard University Press, 1968); J. Douglas Canfield, "The Critique of Capitalism and the Retreat into Art in Gay's *The Beggar's Opera* and Fielding's *Author's Farce,*" *Tennessee Studies in Literature* 37 (1995): 320–34.

11. Cowen, *Fame*, 99–100.

12. Tracy C. Davis, "Private Women and the Public Realm," *Theatre Survey* 35 (1994): 71.

13. Claire Johnston, "Women's Cinema as Counter-Cinema," in *Notes on Women's*

Cinema (London: Society for Education in Film and Television, n.d.), 24–5; Laura J. Rosenthal, "'Counterfeit Scrubbado': Women Actors in the Restoration," *The Eighteenth Century: Theory and Interpretation* 34 (1993): 4.

14. Deborah C. Payne, "Reified Object or Emergent Professional? Retheorizing the Restoration Actress," in *Cultural Readings of Restoration and Eighteenth-Century Theater,* ed. Deborah C. Payne and J. Douglas Canfield (Athens: University of Georgia Press, 1995), 13–38.

15. Robert Gould, "The Play-house: A Satyr," in *Works,* 2:249.

16. For aspersions on Bracegirdle's reputation, see Wells, *Comparison between the Two Stages,* 12, and the anonymous "The Players Turn'd Academicks" (London: n.p., 1703), 4. Colley Cibber recounts the Santlow anecdote in *An Apology for the Life of Colley Cibber,* ed. B. R. S. Fone (Ann Arbor: University of Michigan Press, 1968), 47–8. I will include future page references parenthetically.

17. This anecdote comes from *History of the English Stage, from the Restauration to the Present Time* (London: E. Curll, 1741), supposedly penned by "Thomas Betterton," but actually compiled by Curll or one of his colleagues. It may or may not be true.

18. Straub, *Sexual Suspects,* 92–3.

19. Rosenthal, "Counterfeit Scrubbado," 4, passim.

20. "An Account of the Life and Writings of the Author," in *Plays Written by Mr. John Gay* (London: J. and R. Tonson, 1760), viii.

21. "Moore" printed *A Letter to Polly* (1728), *A New Ballad, Inscrib'd to Polly Peachum* (1728), *An Answer to Polly Peachum's Ballad* (1728), *Polly Peachum on Fire* (1728), and *Memoirs . . . of Captain Mackheath* (1728), discussed in the next section. In the *Dunciad,* Pope refers to this printer as "the phantom More" (*Poetical Works,* ed. Herbert Davis [Oxford: Oxford University Press, 1978], 498). M. R. A. Harris states that "'A. Moore' on an imprint seems to have been a generally accepted fiction of the period" in "Figures relating to the Printing and Distribution of the *Craftsman,* 1726–1730," *Bulletin of the Institute of Historical Research* 43 (1970): 234. Michael Treadwell convincingly establishes this in "Of False and Misleading Imprints," in *Fakes and Frauds,* ed. Robin Myers and Michael Harris (Winchester, England: St. Paul's Bibliographies, 1989), 41–3.

22. Toni-Lynn O'Shaughnessy, "A Single Capacity in *The Beggar's Opera,*" *Eighteenth-Century Studies* 21 (1987–8): 212–27.

23. *Polly Peachum on Fire* (London: A. Moore, 1728).

24. Rosenthal, "Counterfeit Scrubbado," 4.

25. The *Biographical Dictionary* calls *Polly* "a scurrilous and probably untrustworthy book which, unfortunately, is the only source" for information about Fenton (5:221).

26. Rosenthal, "Counterfeit Scrubbado," 20.

27. John J. Richetti, *Popular Fiction before Richardson* (Oxford: Clarendon, 1969), 35.

28. Braudy, *Frenzy;* Schickel, *Intimate Strangers;* Richard Dyer, *Stars* (London: BFI, 1979).

29. Braudy, *Frenzy*, 5.

30. Davis, "Private Women," 68.

31. Dyer, *Stars*, 30.

32. Thomas Herring, preface to *Seven Sermons on Public Occasions*, reprinted in J. V. Guerinot and Rodney D. Jilg, *Contexts I: "The Beggar's Opera"* (Hamden, Conn.: Archon, 1976), 122–3.

33. For Defoe's responses, see Paula Backscheider, *Daniel Defoe, His Life* (Baltimore: Johns Hopkins University Press, 1989), 518–9.

34. This is echoed in another pamphlet from the press of A. Moore, *An Epistle from Matt of the Mint, Lately Deceased, to Captain Macheath* (1729), in which Matt writes "to paint the wretched Place, / To warn Thee timely to Remorse and Grace [,] / To thy sad view those Punishments reveal, / Which *Here* the *ROBBERS* of the *PUBLIC* feel" (4). These verses were originally published in the *Craftsman* (1 March 1729).

35. On 1720s legislation, see Linebaugh, *The London Hanged*.

36. See Barish, *The Antitheatrical Prejudice*.

37. *Thievery a-la-mode; Or, The Fatal Encouragement* (London: J. Roberts, 1728), 15.

38. The *Biographical Dictionary* says he died after playing Clodpole in *The Rape of Proserpine* at Lincoln's Inn Fields on 7 February 1730. However, performance records in Stone, *The London Stage* imply that he died the year before (matching the date on Akerby's biography): Hippisley took over the role of Clodpole in February 1729, and the February 1730 calendar lists no performances of this play.

39. Sven M. Armens, *John Gay, Social Critic* (New York: Columbia University, King's Crown, 1954), 58.

40. John Gay, *The Beggar's Opera*, in *John Gay: Dramatic Works*, ed. John Fuller (Oxford: Clarendon, 1983), 2:48–9.

41. *Thievery*, 13.

42. Robert D. Hume, *Henry Fielding and the London Theatre, 1728–1737* (Oxford: Clarendon, 1988), 36–7.

43. Straub, *Sexual Suspects*, 30.

44. Fred Vermoral and Judy Vermoral, *Starlust: The Secret Life of Fans* (London: W. H. Allen, 1985), 249.

3. THE EIGHTEENTH-CENTURY ACTRESS AND THE CONSTRUCTION OF GENDER

1. Charlotte Charke, *A Narrative of the Life of Mrs. Charlotte Charke* (1755; reprint, Gainesville, Fla: Scholars' Facsimiles and Reprints, 1969). I will include future page references parenthetically.

2. Three other biographies appear in the years between *Fenton* and the *Narrative*: the anonymous *Authentick Memoirs of the Life of That Celebrated Actress Mrs. Ann Old-*

field (London: n.p., 1730), William Egerton [Edmund Curll], *Faithful Memoirs of the Life, Amours and Performances, of That Justly Celebrated, and Most Eminent Actress of Her Time, Mrs. Anne Oldfield* (London: [Curll, 1731]), and *Memoirs of the Life of Eleanor Gwinn, a Celebrated Courtezan, in the Reign of King Charles II and Mistress to That Monarch* (London: F. Stamper, 1752). We will look at these in chapter 6.

3. Straub, *Sexual Suspects,* 147.

4. I have previously presented this line of argument in an earlier version of this chapter in *Eighteenth-Century Life* 18 (1994): 75–90; since then, numerous scholars have followed my lead and augmented this idea considerably in the collection edited by Philip E. Baruth, *Introducing Charlotte Charke* (Urbana: University of Illinois Press, 1998).

5. Judith Keegan Gardiner, "On Female Identity and Writing by Women," in *Writing and Sexual Difference,* ed. Elizabeth Abel (Chicago: University of Chicago Press, 1982), 182–3.

6. Judith Butler, *Body Guards: Feminism and the Subversion of Identity* (New York: Routledge, 1990), 140.

7. Donald A. Stauffer, *The Art of Biography in Eighteenth-Century England* (Princeton: Princeton University Press, 1941), 109.

8. See Elizabeth Howe, *The First English Actresses: Women and Drama, 1660–1700* (Cambridge: Cambridge University Press, 1992); Katherine Eisaman Maus, "'Playhouse Flesh and Blood': Sexual Ideology and the Restoration Actress," *ELH* 46 (1979): 595–617.

9. *The Players: A Satire* (London: W. Mears, 1733), B7r. For earlier examples of such verse, see John Harold Wilson's collection, *Court Satires of the Restoration* (Columbus: Ohio State University Press, 1976).

10. Richetti has noted the increase of prostitutes' biographies in the early eighteenth century in his *Popular Fiction,* chap. 2.

11. Jacqueline Pearson helpfully reviews seventeenth-century interrogations of this male privilege to name in *The Prostituted Muse: Women Dramatists, 1642–1737* (New York: St. Martin's, 1988).

12. Much fruitless speculation has occurred over Charke's motivations for dressing as a man. Desire to escape her creditors, sexual proclivity, bids for masculine power— all of these theories have been offered, but unfortunately we will probably never know why she made this choice. Speculations appear in Charles D. Peavy, "The Chimerical Career of Charlotte Charke," *RECTR* 8 (1969): 1–12; Sallie Minter Strange, "Charlotte Charke: Transvestite or Conjuror?" *RECTR* 15 (1976): 54–9; Fidelis Morgan, *The Well-Known Trouble Maker: The Life of Charlotte Charke* (London: Faber, 1988). As well as Straub, *Sexual Suspects,* Terry Castle and Erin Mackie provide helpful analysis about the sexual implications of cross-dressing during this period. See Castle, "The Culture of Travesty: Sexuality and Masquerade in Eighteenth-Century England," in *Sexual*

Underworlds of the Enlightenment, ed. G. S. Rousseau and Roy Porter (Chapel Hill: University of North Carolina Press, 1988), 156–80; Mackie, "Desperate Measures: The Narratives of the Life of Mrs. Charlotte Charke," *ELH* 58 (1991): 841–65.

13. Butler, *Gender Trouble: Feminism and the Subversion of Identity* (New York: Routledge, 1990), 141.

14. Sidonie Smith, *A Poetics of Women's Autobiography* (Bloomington: Indiana University Press, 1987), chap. 6; Joseph Chaney, "Turning to Men: Genres of Cross-Dressing in Charke's *Narrative* and Shakespeare's *The Merchant of Venice,*" in *Introducing Charlotte Charke,* 200–26.

15. Straub, *Sexual Suspects,* 140–2.

16. Patricia Meyer Spacks, *Imagining a Self: Autobiography and Novel in Eighteenth-Century England* (Cambridge: Harvard University Press, 1976), 76.

17. Perhaps the third-person sections were designed to affect self-effacement or modesty: the later actress and singer Mary Wrighten will narrate her *Apology for the Life and Conduct* similarly.

18. Stauffer, *Art of Biography,* 109; Spacks, *Imagining a Self,* 76.

19. Straub discusses Cibber's role-playing in the *Apology* in *Sexual Suspects,* chaps. 2–4 and discusses the *Narrative*'s relations to it on pages 138–42.

20. Mackie, "Desperate Measures," especially 847–50.

21. Spacks, *Imagining a Self,* 73; Felicity Nussbaum, *The Autobiographical Subject* (Baltimore: Johns Hopkins University Press, 1989), 180.

22. Stone, *The London Stage* tells us that this benefit occurred on 4 September 1755. See vol. 1, part 4, 1747–76.

23. Samuel Whyte, "Anecdote of Mrs. Charke," in the *Monthly Mirror* (June 1794, from unpaginated scrapbook 939.b.1 in the British Library) describes her squalid living conditions at this time. He concludes: "Such is the story of the once-admired daughter of Colley Cibber, poet laureat and patentee of Drury-Lane, who was born in affluence, and educated with care and tenderness, her servants in livery, and a splendid equipage at her command, with swarms of time-serving sycophants officiously buzzing in her train; yet unmindful of her advantages and improvident in her pursuits, she finished the career of her miserable existence on a dunghill."

24. Works useful in understanding early women's autobiography are Pearson, *Prostituted Muse;* Nussbaum, *Autobiographical Subject;* Mary Beth Rose, "Gender, Genre, and History: Seventeenth-Century English Women and the Art of Autobiography," in *Women in the Middle Ages and the Renaissance,* ed. Mary Beth Rose (Syracuse: Syracuse University Press, 1986).

25. Lynda M. Thompson, *The "Scandalous Memoirists": Constantia Phillips, Laetitia Pilkington, and the Shame of "Publick Fame"* (Manchester: Manchester University Press, 2000), 14.

26. The exceptions are the two *Lives* of Ann Oldfield cited earlier (1730, 1731). But

even these devote more space to their subject's amours than do contemporaneous biographies of male performers.

27. Hans Turley, "'A Masculine Turn of Mind': Charlotte Charke and the Periodical Press," in *Introducing Charlotte Charke*, 180–99.

28. Smith states that Charke "ends up serving rather than challenging the pleasure of the patriarchs or the ordination of masculine autobiography" (*Poetics*, 122).

29. Butler, *Gender Trouble*, 141.

30. Straub shows how Charke's *Narrative* resists incorporation into the two mid-eighteenth-century categories of "female same-sex desire": "the commodifiable and recuperable ambiguity of the cross-dressed actress and the dangerous and marginalized transgressiveness of the female husband" (*Sexual Suspects*, 147).

31. Chaney, "Turning to Men," 207.

32. Nussbaum, *Autobiographical Subject*, xiv.

4. DISSECTING THE ACTOR'S AUTHORITY

1. See Peter Linebaugh, "The Tyburn Riot against the Surgeons," in Hay, *Albion's Fatal Tree*, 65–117; Ruth Richardson, *Death, Dissection, and the Destitute* (London: Routledge, 1987); Jonathan Sawday, *The Body Emblazoned: Dissection and the Human Body in Renaissance Culture* (London: Routledge, 1995); Thomas R. Forbes, "To Be Dissected and Anatomized," *Journal of the History of Medicine and Allied Sciences* 36 (1981): 490.

2. Straub, *Sexual Suspects*, 13.

3. *Biographical Dictionary*, 2:219.

4. Michel Foucault, *Discipline and Punish* (New York: Vintage, 1979), 43, 34.

5. Forbes, "To Be Dissected," 490; he cites W. Blackstone's *Commentaries on the Laws of England* (1769).

6. David Harley, "Political Post-mortems and Morbid Anatomy in Seventeenth-Century England," *Social History of Medicine* 7 (1994): 1–28.

7. See Isobel Grundy, *Lady Mary Wortley Montagu* (Oxford: Clarendon, 1999), 251.

8. *An Account of the Dissection of His Highness William Duke of Gloucester* (London: J. Nutt, 1700), 1–2.

9. William Oliver, *A Practical Essay on Fevers* (London: T. Goodwin, 1704), 83–4.

10. Sometimes these reports appeared in the periodical press, however. For example, the *Westminster Magazine* (February 1779) stated of David Garrick: "The disorder by which he was cut off, was what Mr. POTT, his surgeon, called the palsy in the kidnies, which mouldered away on being handled. On opening the body, it was found that the ducts leading from the kidnies to the bladder were so stopped, that a probe would not pass through them. One of the kidnies was entirely wasted, and resembled a lump of coagulated blood. In the bladder was a stone the size of a pigeon's egg, but with that

he might have lived many years" (58–9). Thomas Davies mentions an autopsy of Susannah Maria Cibber, who suffered from stomach worms (*Memoirs of the Life of David Garrick*, 3d. ed., 2 vols. [London: for the author, 1781], 2:109). I will include page references to Davies's biography of Garrick parenthetically, using the third, corrected edition (1781).

11. Booth also consulted Doctors Broxham, Friend, Colehatch, and Mead.

12. See Kenneth Dewhurst's *The Quicksilver Doctor* (Bristol: John Wright and Sons, 1957) or L. A. G. Strong's *Dr. Quicksilver* (London: Andrew Melrose, 1955).

13. The last edition of *The Ancient Physician's Legacy to His Country* in Dover's lifetime was the sixth (London: H. Kent et al., 1742), reprinted in Kenneth Dewhurst's *Thomas Dover's Life and Legacy* (Metuchen, N.J.: Scarecrow, 1974). Dewhurst reviews publication data in *Quicksilver Doctor*, 143.

14. While metallic mercury is not toxic taken orally, because the metal is not absorbed by the alimentary canal, mercuric compounds and mercury vapors are, as is absorption through the skin through frequent touching. Since Dover generally advised heating the metal before ingestion, both the vapors and the epidermal contact would have been more likely (Dewhurst, *Quicksilver Doctor*, 164).

15. Dewhurst, *Quicksilver Doctor*, 163–4.

16. Dover, *Ancient Physician's Legacy*, 138.

17. Dover, *Ancient Physician's Legacy*, 136, 138.

18. For information on Turner, see T. S. W., "Daniel Turner," *American Journal of Surgery* 23 (1934): 591, Philip K. Wilson, *Surgery, Skin, and Syphilis: Daniel Turner's London* (Amsterdam: Rodopi, 1999). Irvine Loudon, among others, has written about the slippery accusations of "quackery" over the centuries. He states, "Physicians, surgeons, apothecaries and others all held their own views on who was and who was not a quack. . . . At every level the individual shouted 'Quack!' at all below him." He concludes: "Social class . . . made a difference." See "The Vile Race of Quacks with Which This Country Is Infested," in *Medical Fringe and Medical Orthodoxy*, ed. W. F. Bynum and Roy Porter (London: Croom Helm, 1987), 106–7.

19. Wilson, *Surgery, Skin, and Syphilis*, 203.

20. Daniel Turner, *The Ancient Physician's Legacy Impartially Survey'd . . . to Which Is Added, in Way of Postscript, a Discourse on Quicksilver, As Now Commonly Taken* (London: John Clarke, 1733).

21. Turner, *Ancient Physician's Legacy Impartially Survey'd*, 133, 147.

22. Daniel Turner, *Syphilis: A Practical Dissertation on the Venereal Disease*, 3d ed. (London: J. Walthoe et al., 1727), A2r.

23. Turner, *Ancient Physician's Legacy Impartially Survey'd*, 268.

24. Wilson discusses Turner's use of case studies in *Surgery, Skin, and Syphilis*, 170–4.

25. Dewhurst, *Dover's Life and Legacy*, xxviii. In one of the publications, a handbook entitled *The Navy-Surgeon* (London: C. Ward and R. Chandler, 1734), John

Atkins considers the quicksilver debate in his section on venereal disease, considering impartially the advice of both Dover and Turner. He reprints the Booth case and concludes with his opinion: "Mercury should be never taken but *in Extremis*" (256).

26. Dewhurst, *Dover's Life and Legacy,* xxx.

27. *Biographical Dictionary,* 15:156.

28. Benjamin Victor, *The History of the Theatres of London and Dublin, from the Year 1730 to the Present Time,* 2 vols. (London: T. Davies et al., 1761); *History of the Theatres of London from the Year 1760 to the Present Time* (London: T. Becket, 1771). I will include future page references parenthetically for the former work.

29. *Life of That Excellent Tragedian Barton Booth Esq.* (London: John Cooper, 1733). I will call this biography "Cooper's biography," for ease of reference, and I will include future page references parenthetically.

30. Anthony Highmore, *A Treatise on the Law of Idiocy and Lunacy* (1807; reprint, New York: Garland, 1979), 134.

31. Andrew Scull, *The Most Solitary of Afflictions: Madness and Society in Britain, 1700–1900* (New Haven: Yale University Press, 1993).

32. *A Treatise on Mercury* (London: J. Roberts, 1733), 6, 5.

33. Roach, *Player's Passion,* 47. Surprisingly, Roach does not mention this account of Booth.

34. Barbara Maria Stafford, *Body Criticism: Imaging the Unseen in Enlightenment Art and Medicine* (Cambridge: MIT Press, 1991), 5.

35. Helen Deutsch, "Doctor Johnson's Autopsy, or Anecdotal Immortality," *The Eighteenth Century: Theory and Interpretation* 40 (1999): 120.

36. Deutsch ("Doctor Johnson's Autopsy") quotes the anonymous *The Life of Samuel Johnson, LL.D.* (1786), 121.

37. Dover, *Ancient Physician's Legacy,* 150.

38. Hayns also adopts a mountebank persona, "Seignior Giusippe Hanesio," a "High German Doctor," in Tom Brown's *Letters of the Dead to the Living* (in *The Works of Mr. Thomas Brown,* 4 vols. [London: Samuel Briscoe, 1715], 1:157–83).

39. Roy Porter, *Health for Sale: Quackery in England, 1660–1850* (Manchester: Manchester University Press, 1989), 4.

40. A London Physician, *The Modern Quacks Detected* (London: M. Cooper, 1752), A2v, A3v, C1r.

41. Tom Brown, *Amusements, Serious and Comical,* in *Works,* 3:97.

42. Stafford, *Body Criticism,* 47.

43. See the prefatory *Life* to *The Dramatic Works of David Garrick,* 3 vols. (London: A. Millar, 1798), 1:ii.

5. ACTOR v. AUTHOR

1. Griffin, *Literary Patronage in England.*

2. Elizabeth L. Eisenstein, *The Printing Press as an Agent of Change,* 2 vols. (Cambridge: Cambridge University Press, 1979), 1:103.

3. Gerard Langbaine, *An Account of the English Dramatic Poets* (Oxford: West and Clements, 1691), 378, 265.

4. Wells, *Comparison between the Two Stages,* 58, 16.

5. Anthony Aston, also known as "Mat. Medley," prefixed a short autobiographical sketch to his play *The Fool's Opera* (London: T. Payne, 1731), which could claim precedence as the "first" English thespian autobiography. This piece recounts his travels and includes even less information on the actor's private life than most of the biographies we have so far examined. See the reprint in *Church Music and Musical Life in Pennsylvania in the Eighteenth Century,* 3 vols. (Philadelphia: Pennsylvania Society of the Colonial Dames of America, 1938), 3:129–37. Cibber may have known Aston's publications, though since Aston was primarily a stroller, Laureate Cibber may not have wanted to acknowledge him or his work. (Aston will also write a continuation of the *Apology.*) In *Life of Hayns,* Tobyas Thomas claims that Hayns himself would have published his own memoirs had he lived.

6. Jean-Christophe Agnew, *Worlds Apart: The Market and the Theater in Anglo-American Thought, 1550–1750* (Cambridge: Cambridge University Press, 1986), 168.

7. Lois Potter, "Colley Cibber: The Fop as Hero," *Augustan Worlds,* ed. J. C. Hilson, M. M. B. Jones, and J. R. Watson (New York: Barnes and Noble, 1978), 156.

8. Straub, *Sexual Suspects,* 151–73.

9. Schickel, *Intimate Strangers,* 327. The theme of popular economic control of art and culture leading to the downfall of civilization is well documented in Brantlinger's *Bread and Circuses.*

10. Richard Hindry Barker, *Mr. Cibber of Drury Lane* (New York: Columbia University Press, 1939), 113.

11. Leonard R. N. Ashley, *Colley Cibber* (New York: Twayne, 1965); Barker, *Mr. Cibber;* Fone, introduction to *Apology for the Life of Colley Cibber,* xxii.

12. Barker, *Mr. Cibber,* 201.

13. Stauffer, *Art of Biography,* 38; Ashley, *Colley Cibber,* 131; Spacks, *Imagining a Self,* 195, 205, 223, 221; J. Paul Hunter, *Before Novels: The Cultural Contexts of Eighteenth Century English Fiction* (New York: Norton, 1990), 331, 330.

14. Straub, *Sexual Suspects;* Potter, "Colley Cibber"; Jean Marsden, "Charlotte Charke and the Cibbers: Private Life as Public Spectacle" in Baruth, *Introducing Charlotte Charke,* 70.

15. Hunter, *Before Novels,* 325; Barker, *Mr. Cibber,* 194.

16. Jonathan Swift, *The Battle of the Books,* ed. Herbert Davis (Oxford: Blackwell, 1965), 144.

17. Robert D. Spector, *Political Controversy: A Study in Eighteenth-Century Propaganda* (New York: Greenwood, 1992), vii.

18. Barker, *Mr. Cibber,* 112.

19. This play was a fairly free adaptation of Molière's *Tartuffe* with political implications. Following at a safe distance the Jacobite Rebellion of 1715, *The Non-Juror* satirizes Roman Catholics as well as clergymen who refused to swear allegiance to the Hanoverians. It generated quite a response from the presses. Some chastise Cibber for ridiculing the clergy onstage, others express their disgust at Cibber's political opportunism, still others mock his literary pretenses. Some do all three. These attacks often answer other attacks: Barker claims that *A Clue to the Comedy of the Non-Juror* (1718), often attributed to Pope, is a response to Cibber's humorous allusions onstage to the Scriblerians' failed comedy, *Three Hours after Marriage* (1717)—which itself included satirical pokes at Cibber. See Barker, *Mr. Cibber,* 204–6. Charles D. Peavy documents the Pope-Cibber print war in his "The Pope-Cibber Controversy: A Bibliography," *RECTR* 3 (1964): 51–5. Indeed, Pope was one of the few writers who could surpass Cibber on number of times attacked in print: see W. L. Macdonald, *Pope and His Critics* (London: Dent, 1951); J. V. Guerinot, *Pamphlet Attacks on Alexander Pope, 1711–1744* (New York: New York University Press, 1969).

20. Swift, *Battle,* 149. Macdonald's study of Pope's involvement in print controversy describes but does not catalogue these qualities. For instance, he recognizes the circularity of pamphlet warfare, how one publication fuels a multitude of responses (*Pope and His Critics,* 41–42). He also notes the customary tone: "Pamphleteering literature in the Augustan age is notorious for the malignancy of personal invective" (39). His main argument is that such controversy focuses on the *personalities* of the figures involved.

21. See Edward L. Ruhe's discussion of John Baker and Edmund Curll's associations in the Sacheverell trial, "Curll and His Early Associates," in *English Writers of the Eighteenth Century,* ed. John H. Middendorf (New York: Columbia University Press, 1971), 77.

22. Pope, *Poetical Works,* 480–1.

23. *The Laureat* (London: J. Roberts, 1740), 1, 57–8. I will include future page references parenthetically.

24. Barker, *Mr. Cibber,* 200.

25. Straub, *Sexual Suspects,* 43, 41, 40.

26. Maynard Mack, *Alexander Pope: A Life* (New York: Norton, 1988), 781.

27. A Strolling Player [John Roberts], *An Answer to Mr. Pope's Preface to Shakespear* (London: n.p., 1729).

28. Matthew Coppinger, *Session of the Poets* (London: Tho. Atkinson, 1705), B1v.

29. *The Memoirs of Perdita* (London: G. Lister, 1784), 40–1.

30. Martin Battestin and Ruth Battestin, *Henry Fielding: A Life* (New York: Routledge, 1989). Helene Koon argues that Fielding wrote both, though they came out

within six months of the *Apology* and are very different in content, style, and tone; I do not find her arguments convincing. See her *Colley Cibber* (Lexington: University Press of Kentucky, 1986), 151–3.

31. Colley Cibber, *The Egotist* (London: W. Lewis, 1743), 49.

32. *An Apology for the Life of T . . . C . . .* (London: Mechell, 1740), 28–9. I will include future page references parenthetically.

33. Richard G. Schwarz, "Patrimony and the Figuration of Authorship in the Eighteenth-Century Literary Property Debates," *Works and Days* 7 (1989): 29–54. Feminist scholars have recognized this metaphor for some time: see, for example, Sandra M. Gilbert and Susan Gubar, *The Madwoman in the Attic* (New Haven: Yale University Press, 1979).

34. Boswell, *Life of Johnson*, 416, 770.

35. Drama-oriented histories include those by Langbaine and Gildon, Giles Jacob's *The Poetical Register; or, The Lives and Characters of the English Dramatic Poets* (two volumes, 1719 and 1720), the anonymous *The British Theatre. Containing the Lives of the English Dramatic Poets; with an Account of All Their Plays. Together with the Lives of Most of the Principal Actors, as Well as Poets. To Which Is prefixed, a Short View of the Rise and Progress of the English Stage* (1750), and David Erskine Baker's *The Companion to the Play-House* (first appearing in 1764, it was continued and corrected by Isaac Reed in 1782 and then by Stephen Jones in 1812). More stage-based approaches are Richard Flecknoe's nine-page "Short Discourse of the English Stage" appended to his play *Love's Kingdom* (1664), James Wright, in *Historia Histrionica* (1699), Downes's *Roscius Anglicanus* (1708), William Rufus Chetwood's *General History of the Stage* (1749), Lewis [Luigi] Riccoboni's *Historical and Critical Account of the Theatres in Europe* (1738; English translation, 1741), "Thomas Betterton's" [Curll's] *History of the English Stage* (1741), Thomas Wilkes's *A General View of the Stage* (1759), and Edmond Malone's *An Historical Account of the Rise and Progress of the English Stage* (1790). In a Curllean manner, many of the theater histories that follow Cibber lift large chunks of text from his *Apology*.

36. Thomas Davies, *Dramatic Micellanies: Consisting of Critical Observations on Several Plays of Shakespeare*, 3 vols. (London: for the author, 1783), 2:319–20

37. David Charles Douglas, *English Scholars, 1660–1730* (London: Eyre and Spottiswoode, 1951), 36.

6. INHERITED AUTHORITY?

1. I assume that these authors use "apology" because of Cibber, though they may be referring to the tradition of religious apology. The chances are small, I believe, that they are trying to echo the title of Thomas Heywood's *Apology for Actors* (1612).

2. Bellamy's book has been attributed to Alexander Bicknell; some say that it was edited by him. Cyril Hughes Hartmann makes the most convincing case for editorship in *Enchanting Bellamy* (London: Heinemann, 1956), 306–12. See also *Biographical Dic-*

tionary, 2:18. Both sources note the numerous inconsistencies and inaccuracies in Bellamy's *Apology*.

3. North, *General Preface*, 59–60.

4. Lawrence Stone, *The Family, Sex, and Marriage in England, 1500–1800* (New York: Harper and Row, 1977).

5. See the entry for Theophilus in *Biographical Dictionary*, 3:242–60. Hume chronicles this transaction and the ensuing actor rebellion in *Henry Fielding and the London Theatre*, 155–60.

6. *A Letter from Theophilus Cibber, Comedian, to John Highmore, Esq.* (n.p., [1733]), 2.

7. *Biographical Dictionary*, 3: 247, 244.

8. In *English Theatrical Literature*, Arnott and Robinson list the anonymous pamphlets surrounding this scandal as items 2595–608. The "Advertisement" was printed with no reference to publisher, place, or date; it appears neither in Arnott and Robinson nor in the *Register of Theatrical Documents*. Theophilus had published an earlier letter, stating: "*This is to forewarn all Persons* whatsoever (*at their Peril*) to harbour, countenance, or trust the said *Susanna Maria*—her Husband being resolv'd not to pay any Debts she shall contract."

9. In *Mr. Cibber*, Barker notes Theophilus's ads and claims that he did not publish his *Apology* because of *T . . . C . . .* 's appearance (201–2); the *Biographical Dictionary* agrees (3:255). As far as I am aware, no notes or drafts of his attempt are extant.

10. Theophilus Cibber, *Romeo and Juliet . . . to Which Is Added, A Serio-Comic Apology, for Part of the Life of Mr. Theophilus Cibber, Comedian* (London: C. Corbett, [1750]), 71.The *Apology* was originally published separately in Dublin in 1748. I will include future page references parenthetically.

11. Theophilus's approach to his marital problems throws into relief his father's public position: Colley ignored his son's improprieties (as well as his own). Even though Theophilus's affairs were popular grist for the print mill throughout the late thirties, when Cibber was composing the *Apology*, not the slightest whiff of admission or embarrassment tinges that book.

12. Theophilus Cibber, *The Lives and Characters of the Most Eminent Actors and Actresses of Great Britain*, part 1 (London: R. Griffiths, 1753), xiv. Part 1 seems to be the only part Cibber published, and most of the volume is "The Life and Character of that Excellent Actor Barton Booth."

13. Marsden, "Charlotte Charke and the Cibbers," 71, 73. However, Marsden fails to comment on the incestuous overtones of Theophilus's father role: he presents himself as a good father to his daughter, Jenny, through his partnership with her in playing Romeo against her Juliet onstage. Since we know how bad a husband Theophilus was, we can interpret this either as his finding his true, virtuous role in being a father, or as his twisting of that role, too, to salacious ends—especially since, as his daughter, Jenny was dependent on him in ways that his wives were not.

14. For information on the Curll/Pope feud, see Ralph Straus's biography, *The Unspeakable Curll* (London: Chapman and Hall, 1927).

15. Frank Arthur Mumby, *Publishing and Bookselling: A History from the Earliest Times to the Present Day*, rev. ed. (London: Jonathan Cape, 1949), 158. Most criticism of Curll and his works derives from scholarly interest in literary qualities and from disgust at Curll's underhanded commercial practices. Robert Halsband, for instance, sees Curll's contribution to literary biography as negligible and labels him "the most conspicuous of Grub Street's biographical scavengers" ("The 'Penury' of English Biography before Samuel Johnson," in *Biography in the Eighteenth Century*, ed. J. D. Browning [New York: Garland, 1980], 112–27). Stauffer admits Curll's commercial practices to be "sordid," but he also emphasizes Curll's importance in the history of biography (*Art of Biography*, 535, 234–5).

16. The contemporary comment comes from *Remarks on Squire Ayre's Memoirs of the Life and Writings of Mr. Pope. In a Letter to Mr. Edmund Curl* (London: M. Cooper, 1745), 44.

Curll's interest in biography is apparent when we compare his to other printers' lists: from 1729 to 1764 the press of Robert Dodsley issued twenty-four biographies out of over 1,100 books (approximately 2 percent); in its long history from 1675 to 1767, the Tonson press printed only fourteen (approximately 1 percent). See Straus's *Curll*, 201–314; Ralph Straus, *Robert Dodsley: Poet, Publisher, and Playwright* (London: John Kane, 1910), 311–83; G. F. Papali, *Jacob Tonson, Publisher* (Auckland: Tonson, 1968), 144–213. These calculations include all works except novels cited as memoirs, characters, *Lives,* and histories of times. These counts are complicated by the inaccuracy of the lists from which they were taken. Straus's lists often record the existence of preface *Lives;* Papali's does so inconsistently. All three sources find some of their information in newspaper ads and thus may not reflect what was actually published. In addition, Ruhe explains the complicated relations among printers, which led to "many confusions in Straus's Handlist" ("Curll and His Early Associates," 81)—but he does not tell us what those confusions are or who has identified them (77). Nevertheless, I believe the comparison to be valid, though the numbers may not be unerringly precise: Curll published many more biographies than his more prestigious publishing colleagues.

17. Thomas Amory, *The Life of John Buncle, Esq.*, 2 vols. (1756; reprint, New York: Garland, 1975), 2:382.

18. Jonathan Swift, *The Poems of Jonathan Swift*, ed. Harold Williams, 3 vols. (Oxford: Clarendon, 1958), 2:560–1.

19. The *Grub-street Journal* was continually hostile to Curll because of its connections with Pope. For a discussion of these connections, see James T. Hillhouse's *The Grub-Street Journal* (Durham: Duke University Press, 1928), 78–83.

20. Stauffer discusses Curll's popularization of the "last will and testament" pamphlet in *Art of Biography*, 206–7.

21. Hunter, *Before Novels*, 315.

22. Boswell, *Life of Johnson,* 770.

23. Arthur Murphy, *The Life of David Garrick,* 2 vols. (1801; reprint, New York: Benjamin Blom, 1969), 1:3. I will include future page references parenthetically.

24. Curll's documentary method helped him use up old stock and reduce time and effort in investigating his subjects. As the *Grub-Street Journal* noted, Curll's *Wilks* includes sections from his *Oldfield,* and his later *History of the English Stage* (which he published in 1741 as having been written by Thomas Betterton) also reprints an abridged version of his *Oldfield.* Curll's recycling program proves that generic development sometimes occurs for very nonliterary reasons.

25. John Nichols, in his advertisement for his four-volume edition of Francis Atterbury's *Letters* (1783), quoted in Stauffer, *Art of Biography,* 235. Nichols apparently assumed that Curll's information was accurate.

26. Including all kinds of anecdotal and digressive information also prepares for the depth of detail in Boswell's *Johnson* and for the later eighteenth-century interest in collections of "-ana," such as Hester Thrale Piozzi's *Thraliana.* Stauffer notes that Curll's *Atterburyana* and *Whartoniana* (both 1727) are "pointless jumbles beneath contempt" (*Art of Biography,* 491), yet Curll was one of the earliest to recognize readers' interest in volumes of trivia and digression—an interest upon which Lawrence Sterne was to capitalize in *Tristram Shandy,* itself an influence on thespian biography, as we see in the next section.

27. However, Cibber's bookseller John Watts seems to have had a fairly respectable business, publishing discourses on moral and religious subjects, a study of Palladio, and Cibber's own later *On the Character and Conduct of Cicero* (1747).

28. Straub, *Sexual Suspects,* 112.

29. *Rosalind; or, An Apology for the History of a Theatrical Lady* (Dublin: Booksellers, 1759). I will include future page references parenthetically. I will refer to this actress as Ann Dancer, her name at the time *Rosalind* was published. The *Biographical Dictionary*'s main entry for her is under "Ann Barry"—the name of her most famous spouse and the name under which she was known in London.

30. I use a male pronoun for the narrator because he refers to himself as "a great Man."

31. *Theatrical Biography; or, Memoirs of the Principal Performers of the Three Theatres Royal* (London: S. Bladon, 1772) informs us that Coupée was a M. Poicteur, probably the dancer and violinist Charles Poitier who, the *Biographical Dictionary,* notes was active in Dublin's Crow Street theater during the same season the Dancers were engaged there.

32. For discussion of the charges against Sterne's work, see Alan B. Howes, *Yorick and the Critics* (New Haven: Yale University Press, 1958).

33. *Memoirs of the Celebrated Mrs. Woffington,* 2d ed. (London: J. Swan 1760), 13, 14–5, 46.

34. Not only actress biographers, but an enormous number of other writers copied

Sterne. J. M. S. Tompkins discusses many of the imitators of Sterne in *The Popular Novel in England, 1770–1800* (1932; reprint, Lincoln: University of Nebraska Press, 1961), 50–3. Even *Rosalind,* published in Dublin in 1759, the year that the first volume of *Tristram Shandy* appeared, already hints at Sterne's influence in its use of dashes and some of its references. For example, Rosalind's father resembles Walter Shandy in some ways: "of all the species of wit, that of punning was his mortal hate" (26).

35. Straub, *Sexual Suspects,* 125.

36. "Tristram Shandy," *Miss C——y's Cabinet of Curiosities; or, The Green-Room Broke Open.* The imprint reads, "Utopia: Printed for William Whirligig, at the Maiden's Head, in Wind-mill-street. 1765." Internal evidence suggests it was printed in Dublin. In addition to its use of Sterne, this narrator also invokes Cleland briefly (20). I will include future page references parenthetically.

37. This book was advertised as published in two volumes duodecimo, for 5 shillings, by Roson, in the *Town and Country Magazine* 5 (1773): 669. However, I have not yet located a copy; neither had Arnott and Robinson in *English Theatrical Literature.*

38. The figure of the actress is not part of Trumbach's work at present. See Randolph Trumbach, *Sex and the Gender Revolution,* vol. 1 (Chicago: University of Chicago Press, 1998).

39. Rosenthal, "'Counterfeit Scrubbado,'" 20.

40. A good reading of Bellamy's *Apology* can be found in Straub, *Sexual Suspects,* chap. 6.

41. The end of Wrighten's *Apology* tells how she is continuing her stage career in America. In *The History of the American Theatre,* 3 vols. (1888–91; reprint, New York: Benjamin Blom, 1968), George O. Seilhamer chronicles Wrighten's "great career" in the New World, where she assumed the name of Mrs. Pownall. His account, however, is clouded by the rumors of her unhappy marriage that she had tried to discount: "According to the 'Thespian Dictionary,'" Seilhamer reports, "Mrs. Wrighten eloped from her husband, and deserted her daughters, in consequence of which poor Wrighten died of a broken heart" (3:45). This is vastly different from the version she presents.

42. George Stayley was an Irish actor-author who published *The Life and Opinions of an Actor: A Real History, in Two Real Volumes* (Dublin: for the author and G. Faulkner; London: J. Hinton, 1762). I will include future page references parenthetically. Very little information exists on Stayley. Besides listings in performance calendars, the only information is based on his *Life and Opinions.* See, for example, Esther K. Sheldon's *Thomas Sheridan of Smock-Alley* (Princeton: Princeton University Press, 1967), 183–4. Many other books used the "Life and Opinions" title popularized by Sterne: for example, *The Life and Opinions of Miss Sukey Shandy* (1760) and *The Life and Opinions of Bertram Montifichet* (1761).

43. George Alexander Stevens, *The Dramatic History of Master Edward, Miss Ann, and Others,* 2d ed. (London: J. Murray, 1785). The first edition was printed in 1763,

although its title page reads 1743. I will include future page references parenthetically.

44. Like *The Beggar's Opera* and *Tristram Shandy,* Stevens's *Lecture* was enormously popular, encouraging editions, imitations, and piracies (of which he complained). Similarities may exist between the *Lecture* and *The Dramatic History,* but I have not pursued them because Stevens invented the *Lecture* (first performed 1764) after the *History* (1763), and because texts of the *Lecture* are of dubious relation to what Stevens actually performed on stage.

45. Gerald Kahan, *George Alexander Stevens and the Lecture on Heads* (Athens: University of Georgia Press, 1984).

46. *British Magazine and Monthly Repository* 7 (1767): 564–6.

7. PARABLE OF THE TALENT(S)

1. For a discussion of this incident, see Judith Milhous and Robert D. Hume, "The Drury Lane Actors' Rebellion of 1743," *Theatre Journal* 42 (1990): 57–80.

2. Quoted in James Thompson, *Models of Value: Eighteenth-Century Political Economy and the Novel* (Durham: Duke University Press, 1996), 36.

3. Sir Richard Steele, *The Conscious Lovers* (London: J. Tonson, 1723), 62–3.

4. Colin Nicholson, *Writing and Rise of Finance: Capital Satires of the Early Eighteenth Century* (Cambridge: Cambridge University Press, 1994), 7.

5. P. G. M. Dickson, *The Financial Revolution in England: A Study in the Development of Public Credit, 1688–1756* (London: Macmillan, 1967), 35. See also Julian Hoppitt, "Attitudes to Credit in Britain, 1680–1790," *Historical Journal* 2 (1990): 305–22.

6. Jonathan Swift, *The Examiner,* ed. Herbert Davis (Oxford: Clarendon, 1957), 5, from 2 November 1710. Swift links the calamitous change in the social order with the continuing prosecution of the Continental war: "Let any Man observe the Equipages in this Town; he shall find the greater Number of those who make a Figure, to be a Species of Men quite different from that were ever known before the Revolution; consisting either of Generals and Colonels, or of such whose whole Fortunes lie in Funds and Stocks" (5).

7. Thompson, *Models of Value,* 2.

8. Thompson, *Models of Value,* 19, 37.

9. Information on stars' salaries is more plentiful than that for players on the other end of the spectrum. I review some of the lower-end payments in two articles: "Mary Morein (fl. 1707): Drury Lane Actress and Fair Performer," *Theatre Survey* 32 (1991): 22–30; "Contracts for Two Drury Lane Actresses in 1822," *Harvard Library Bulletin* 5 (1994): 53–67.

10. See Edward Copeland, *Women Writing about Money: Women's Fiction in England, 1790–1820* (Cambridge: Cambridge University Press, 1995). Ian Watt's figures for annual income are: paupers (£6–20), farmers (£42–55), shopkeepers/tradesmen (£45), artisans (£38). See *Rise of the Novel* (Princeton: Princeton University Press, 1957), 40.

11. See *Biographical Dictionary,* 11:109, 12:232, 12:284.

12. This figure is from 1799–1800, *Biographical Dictionary,* 14:22–3.

13. Since I will focus here on amounts reported in the biographies, my survey of actors' salaries and benefit amount is necessarily incomplete. For more exact figures, see *Biographical Dictionary.*

14. See *Biographical Dictionary,* 11:107–9, 12:230, 14:23.

15. *Biographical Dictionary,* 12:286.

16. *Authentick Memoirs of Oldfield,* 21; Bellamy, *Apology,* 3:82.

17. Bourdieu, *Distinction,* 2.

18. Useful information on the origins, timing, and profits of actor benefits can be found in Robert D. Hume's "The Origins of the Actor Benefit in London," *Theatre Research International* 9 (1984); 99–111; Matthew J. Kinservik, "Benefit Play Selection at Drury Lane in 1729–1769: The Cases of Mrs. Cibber, Mrs. Clive, and Mrs. Pritchard," *Theatre Notebook* 50 (1996): 15–28.

19. *The Life of James Quin, Comedian* (London: S. Bladon, 1766), 48.

20. *The Players,* A6v, B3r, B8v.

21. Churchill, *The Apology,* 44.

22. Aaron Hill and William Popple, *The Prompter,* ed. William W. Appleton and Kalman A. Burnim (New York: Benjamin Blom, 1966), 42, 32.

23. *Sketch of the Theatrical Life of John Palmer,* 43.

24. Hill and Popple, *Prompter,* 14.

25. *Memoirs of That Celebrated Comedian and Very Singular Genius, Thomas Weston* (London: S. Bladon, 1776), 12. I will include future page references parenthetically.

26. Daniel O'Bryan, *Authentic Memoirs; or, The Life and Character of That Most Celebrated Comedian, Mr. Robert Wilks* (London: S. Slow, 1732), 23.

27. *Memoirs of Gwinn,* 34.

28. *Memoirs of Gwinn,* 44.

29. Bellamy, *Apology,* 4:78, 2:87–8, 3:193.

30. *Authentick Memoirs of Oldfield,* 27.

31. Old Comedian, *The Life and Death of David Garrick, Esq.* (London: J. Pridden, 1779); Stone and Kahrl, *David Garrick;* Boswell, *Life of Johnson,* 770.

32. Deidre S. Lynch, *The Economy of Character: Novels, Market Culture, and the Business of Meaning* (Chicago: University of Chicago Press, 1998), 100.

33. Egerton [Curll], *Faithful Memoirs of Oldfield,* 4.

34. Wilson, *Court Satires,* 219–20.

35. "Tunbridge Satire," Stowe MS 969, 45.

36. John Dunton, *Night Walker* (October 1696): 101.

37. Erin Mackie, *Market a la Mode* (Baltimore: Johns Hopkins University Press, 1997), 39.

38. Hill and Popple, *Prompter,* 38. For thorough coverage of payment to opera singers, see Judith Milhous and Robert D. Hume, "Opera Salaries in Eighteenth-

Century London," *Journal of the American Musicological Society* 46 (1993): 26–83. Interestingly, no biographies of foreign opera singers seem to exist in English—surprising when one considers their incredible popularity.

39. Hill and Popple, *Prompter,* 39.

40. Hill and Popple, *Prompter,* 39.

41. Brown, *Works,* 4:A5r, 127.

42. Bellamy, *Apology,* 1:151.

43. Bellamy, *Apology,* 4:100.

8. THE AUTHORITY OF THE CELEBRITY

1. George Winchester Stone Jr., "David Garrick and the Eighteenth-Century Stage: Notes toward a New Biography," in *In Search of Restoration and Eighteenth-Century Theatrical Biography,* ed. Stone and Philip H. Highfill Jr. (Los Angeles: University of California Press, 1976), 9. This count does not include "day-by-day account of his every day appearance on the London stage from 1741 through 1776," his verse (mainly prologues and epilogues) and plays, published letters by and to him, and biographies. In his *David Garrick: A Reference Guide* (Boston: G. K. Hall, 1980), Gerald M. Berkowitz lists 767 items from 1741 to 1779; however, this total includes multiple editions of Garrick's numerous plays and adaptations, including those in series such as John Bell's British Theatre series. Whatever the exact total, the number of items printed by or about Garrick is phenomenal. In addition, the *Biographical Dictionary* lists over 280 portraits, prints, statues, busts, and other memorabilia.

2. *D——ry-L——ne P——yh——se Broke Open. In a Letter to Mr. G——-* (London: M. Cooper, 1748), 1–2.

3. Roach, *Player's Passion,* 12, 57.

4. Old Comedian, *Life and Death of Garrick,* 64.

5. Some of that journalism had been reprinted in the "Old Comedian" biography.

6. For Boswell's reference to the biography, see the *Life of Johnson,* 1058. In *Life of Garrick,* Arthur Murphy reports that Johnson himself was hoping to write a biography of the actor and to collect and edit his works (2:191). He was waiting for Mrs. Garrick to ask him; however, she never did.

7. Stone and Kahrl, *David Garrick,* 155–6.

8. See *Biographical Dictionary,* 4:203–9. For Boswell's first encounter with Johnson, see *Life of Johnson,* 276.

9. Stauffer seems not to have been familiar with the Davies-Garrick relations and is surprised that Davies's *Life* includes "many little weaknesses and secrets which Roscius alive might not have enjoyed" (*Art of Biography,* 40). Since most accounts testify to Garrick's sensitivity to criticism, Stauffer may be correct, but as we have seen, Davies says nothing that Garrick had not heard during his lifetime. I find Davies's account remarkably admiring of Garrick for their circumstances. Indeed, if the anti-Garrick

Genuine Narrative of the Life . . . of Mr. John Henderson (1777) is by Davies (as certain sources, notably the *Biographical Dictionary,* maintain), this work seems more in tune with what we know about the Davies-Garrick relationship. Davies thus would have had it published anonymously—and sold through another bookseller—to avoid censure. See also "Thomas Davies and the Authorship of *A Genuine Narrative . . .* , The Life of John Henderson," *RECTR* 9 (1970): 24–34.

10. *Life of James Quin,* 3.

11. Boswell, *Life of Johnson,* 1020. Goldsmith's lines come from "The Retaliation," in *Collected Works of Oliver Goldsmith,* ed. Arthur Friedman, 5 vols. (Oxford: Clarendon, 1966), 4:357.

12. Sir Joshua Reynolds, *Portraits by Sir Joshua Reynolds,* ed. Frederick W. Hilles (London: William Heinemann, 1952). 86–7.

13. Robert R. Bataille suggests that Garrick may have manipulated presses via patronage in "The Kelly-Garrick Connection and the Politics of Theatre Journalism," *RECTR,* 2d ser., 4 (1989): 39–48.

14. Davies relies on the reader's prior knowledge in other places, as well: for instance, on John Rich's famous pantomimes: "It would be idle to dwell long upon a subject which almost every body is as familiar with as the writer" (*Memoirs of Garrick,* 1:130).

15. Two sources hint at Garrick's premarital affairs: the *Town and Country Magazine* tells its readers that Garrick "had almost as many Cleopatras off as on the stage, and the world has made pretty free with some living names, which we shall suppress" (February 1779: 79), and Edward Kimber's novel *David Ranger* (1755) tells of several early amours, though Ranger is always noble-minded: he is no sexual adventurer, like Tom Jones. These are our only sources for rumors about Garrick's mistresses, besides Peg Woffington—and not very reliable sources at that.

16. Janice Farrar Thaddeus provides a good account of Mrs. Garrick's public and private lives in "A Spirit Free and Female: Eva Maria Garrick," *Eighteenth-Century Life* 10 (1986): 86–103.

17. Straub, *Sexual Suspects,* 61.

18. Howard Hunter Dunbar, *The Dramatic Career of Arthur Murphy* (New York: Modern Language Association, 1946), 294.

19. Jesse Foot, *The Life of Arthur Murphy* (London: J. Faulder, 1811), 333.

20. This may be authorial posturing to hide other, more practical motives: the *Biographical Dictionary* suggests that Murphy spent his last years in a somewhat strained financial situation (10:398).

21. Michael Dobson, *The Making of the National Poet: Shakespeare, Adaptation, and Authorship, 1660–1769* (Oxford: Clarendon, 1992), 172–6.

22. Garrickiana grows even more luxurious later in the nineteenth century: Boaden's *Private Correspondence of David Garrick* (1831–2) is a large-format two-volume quarto collection of letters, with frontispiece, index, and expansive page layout.

23. *Life of Quin,* 63.

24. *Theatrical Biography,* 84–5.

25. "A Memoir of David Garrick Esq.," *Universal Magazine* (October 1776): 187.

26. John Hill, *The Actor: A Treatise on the Art of Playing* (London: R. Griffiths, 1750), 16, 22. For discussion of the relation between the "passions," or states of emotional or psychological agitation, see George Taylor, "'The Just Delineation of the Passions': Theories of Acting in the Age of Garrick," in *The Eighteenth-Century English Stage,* ed. Kenneth Richards and Peter Thomson (London: Methuen, 1972).

27. *Monthly Review* (August 1780): 116.

28. Dobson, *Making of Poet,* 176–84.

29. Judith Pascoe, *Romantic Theatricality: Gender, Poetry, and Spectatorship* (Ithaca: Cornell University Press, 1997).

30. *Memoirs of Perdita,* 2.

31. Old Comedian, *Life and Death of Garrick,* 26.

32. Bellamy, *Apology,* 2:157.

33. Reynolds, *Portraits,* 99.

34. Dobson, *Making of Poet,* 176.

CONCLUSION

1. See Joseph Donohue, *Theatre in the Age of Kean* (Oxford: Basil Blackwood, 1975), 12–14; *Biographical Dictionary* for Palmer (12:87–9).

2. Cowen, *Fame,* 112.

3. Cowen, *Fame,* 70.

4. Marc Baer, *Theatre and Disorder in Late Georgian London* (Oxford: Clarendon, 1992); Elaine Hadley, *Melodramatic Tactics: Theatricalized Dissent in the English Marketplace, 1800–1885* (Stanford: Stanford University Press, 1995).

5. *Theatrical Biography,* 1:vi.

6. *Theatrical Biography,* 1:107.

7. *British Magazine and Monthly Repository* 7 (1767): 564–6.

INDEX

✧

✧

D0072443